The DRUG of the New Millennium

The Science of How Internet Pornography Radically Alters the Human Brain and Body

Mark B. Kastleman

Another quality title from The BestSellers Media Group, Inc.

Distributed by:

Granite Publishing and Distribution, LLC
868 North 1430 West
Orem, Utah 84057
(801) 229-9023 • Toll Free (800) 574-5779
Fax (801) 229-1924

Second Edition, December 2001
Third Printing

Cover Design by: Steve Gray
Page Layout and Design: Myrna Varga • The Office Connection – Orem, Utah

Library of Congress Catalog Card Number: 2001094019
ISBN: 1-930980-63-9

For information about Mark Kastleman's availability for speaking engagements or to purchase his audio tapes, visit
www.kastleman.net
or
call 801-944-4612

To register for Mark Kastleman's free monthly newsletter, visit his website at
www.kastleman.net

Contents

The Latest Internet Pornography Statistics

At the last moment, when this book was ready to go to print, Chris Johnson, CEO of SurfPartner Corporation, e-mailed me some of the latest Internet Pornography statistics. They were so startling that I felt compelled to make them available to everyone who would read this book. Because there was no time to incorporate these statistics into the appropriate chapters, they have been inserted here.

40 million adults in the U.S. visit **Internet porn sites**—and the numbers are growing rapidly. **70%** indicated that they keep their online porn usage a **secret**,[1] [a sure sign that they could be headed for, or are already addicted].

72 million people worldwide will visit **Internet porn sites** this year.[2]

Internet surfers spent approximately **one billion dollars** on access to **Internet porn** sites and this number is expected to rise to more than **$3 billion** by the year 2003.[3]

Pornography is now **number one** in terms of all categories of Internet sales. It is accessed more than games, travel, jokes, cars, health, weather and jobs **combined**.[4]

---

[1]New York-based poling firm of *Zogby International* and studies by *Stanford and Duquesne Universities* as quoted in a question and answer format at http://www.thecrossworksnet/answers.htm

[2]According to *Flying Crocodile, Inc.*, a Seattle-based company tracking on-line porn traffic, as quoted by Heather Stringer in her article *CyberXXX*, as featured at www.TechWeek.com, 9/19/2000

[3]*U.S. News & World Report*, 3/27/2000, as quoted in *Recent Statistics on Internet Dangers*, at www.YourRevolution.com

[4]*Alexa Research*, as quoted in a question and answer format at http://www.thecrossworks.net/Answers.htm

Up to **1,000 brand new Internet porn sites** are created every single day.[5]

In the United States, if given the opportunity, **86% of men** are likely to click on Internet sex sites.[6]

At a recent *Promise Keepers* event, **53% of men** admitted to dabbling in pornography during the last week.[7]

1 out of 5 men and **1 out of 8 women**, admitted to accessing **sexually explicit material** on the Internet while at **work.**[8]

The average age of **first exposure** to Internet Pornography is **age 11.**[9]

The **12–17 age group** is the largest consumer of Internet Pornography.[10]

In the last year, **1 out of 5** young Internet users received an **unwanted sexual solicitation.**[11]

In a new survey, one in 10 respondents indicated that they are addicted to sex on the Internet. And one in four respondents acknowledged that, on at least one occasion, their online sexual activities have felt out of control or caused problems in their lives.[12]

---

[5]According to *4decency.org* as quoted in a question and answer format at http://www.thecrossworks.net/Answers.htm

[6]Recent survey in the *Journal of the American Psychological Association.*

[7]According to poll taken by *711.net* as quoted in a question and answer format at http://www.thecrossworks.net/Answers.htm

[8]According to *MSNBC* as quoted in a question and answer format at http://www.thecrossworks.net/Answers.htm

[9]*The American Family Association* as quoted in a question and answer format at http://www.thecrossworks.net/Answers.htm

[10]According to *4decency.org* as quoted in a question and answer format at http://www.thecrossworks.net/Answers.htm

[11]According to a study at the *US Department of Justice* by David Finklehor, Kimberly Mitchel and Janus Wolak, as quoted in a question and answer format at http://www.thecrossworks.net/Answers.htm

[12]According to a study Alvin Cooper, director of the San Jose Marital Services and Sexuality Centre, and a staff psychologist at Stanford University, as quoted in an article by Charlene Laino, *Cybersex Addiction Widespread*, www.NSNBC.com, 7-18-01

Acknowledgments

My ability to write this book is the result of a lifetime of love, friendship, lessons, contributions, insights, sharing and support from a host of wonderful individuals. I would like to express my deepest appreciation and gratitude to the following:

My beloved friend and companion, Ladawn, for her unconditional love, endless patience, constant support and much-needed encouragement. Also, for unselfishly absorbing many of my parental responsibilities during the many hours of research and writing. This book would've remained only a dream without her.

Our six incredible children, Jared, Joshua, Krystal, Jordan, Jacob and Jason. They have demonstrated tremendous patience and support in "sharing their father" with this project for what must seem like an eternity.

My mother Elaine, her husband Don, and my sisters Karma, Lynette, Janice and Gail for "believing in me" and offering constant moral support and encouragement.

My wife's family, for their support, encouragement and patience.

My dear friend, mentor and "brother," Bruce Wright. His tremendous love, loyalty and long-suffering have been a priceless gift in my life. From the time we were teenagers, Bruce recognized and helped bring out abilities and talents in me that may have remained dormant forever.

James Michael Pratt, for daring to dream and paving the way for me to follow. He paid a tremendous price to become a *New York Times* Best Selling author and then graciously took me under his wing and shared his wealth of experience and knowledge without thought of profit or praise. He is a man of integrity, vision and charity, a friend and brother with whom I hope to pursue many more worthy projects in the future.

My personal coach and dear friend, Leo Weidner. Through his wise teachings and guidance, I learned to establish new mental models and mindbody programming. Leo lead me from a world of fear, limits and despair, to a whole new world of self-discovery with limitless possibilities. Leo continues to help me discover "who I really am" and how I can use my gifts and talents to love, lift and serve others. To me, Leo is a wise sage whose teachings and influence I hope to help carry to the peoples of the world.

My father, Harry Kastleman, for teaching me the value of "hard work."

Chris and Lawana Johnson of the SurfPartner Corporation, for their inspiration, support and encouragement from the very moment this book was conceived. I also want to thank them for their incredible personal sacrifice in developing and maintaining an Internet protection service so critical to families throughout the world. They are literally "saving" families, marriages and individual lives every day.

Dr. Victor Cline, Dr. Judith Reisman and John Harmer for their keen insights and valuable suggestions in the review of my manuscript. Each has dedicated their lives to the battle against pornography and the protection of children and families. I salute them and thank them with all my heart for sharing their precious time and tremendous expertise.

My editor, Steven Anderson, for working miracles with the manuscript. He took the often awkward ramblings of a would-be author, and transformed them into an effective tool of communication. I thank Steven for really "making me better than I am."

Dr. Page Bailey, for introducing me to the world of mindbody science. His bright intellect, revolutionary teachings and deep insights were the catalyst that unlocked my understanding and launched the genesis of this book.

My dear friend, John Hewlett, for inspiring me with his charisma and "can-do" attitude. He offered me a "safe harbor" in a dark and desperate time and gave me the opportunity to recuperate and heal. His generosity and compassion will never be forgotten.

My friend and inspiration for more than 20 years, Brent Yorgason. From my time in his classroom as a freshman in college, through the years of reading his books and listening to his dynamic orations, he has set the standard for me to strive for. Then, graciously, he opened the doors of opportunity for me and stepped aside as I walked through and moved on. His inspiration and example are with me still.

Dan Gray, Todd Olson, Scott Peterson, Mark Chamberlain and Steve Johnson of the S.T.A.R. group for introducing me to the world of pornography/sex addiction treatment and recovery. They have generously shared with me knowledge and techniques that have required years of dedication, study and hands-on experience to obtain. The recovery chapter in the book would not have been possible without them. I also want to express my admiration and awe at the magnificent contribution they are making to humanity. They are truly rescuing individuals, couples and families from the pit of despair and a life of disaster. To me, they are true heroes.

So many relatives, friends and associates that are too numerous to mention—you know who you are—thank you for being a part of the tapestry of my life and helping to make me who I am and able to undertake and complete this project.

The recovering addicts who so humbly and graciously granted me interviews and trusted me enough to "bare their souls." Your words will be a lifeline to others who are where you have been. Your success will help them find the courage to reach out for help and begin to make their way back. May God continue to watch over the strengthen you in your sobriety.

And last, but certainly not least, all the counselors, therapists, clergy, spouses, parents, activists and volunteers who fight in the trenches every day in the war of pornography addiction. May peace, strength and courage be yours and may you find your victories one rescued soul at a time.

Foreword

Mark Kastleman, author of *The Drug of the New Millennium—Internet Pornography* is in my view a Mr. "Everyman." As he saw not only the tremendous contribution of the Internet, but also its dark side with its many victims, he became increasingly concerned about how parents would better protect their children from its potential for harm.

With a strong moral sense and a foundation of his own core values, he commenced an intense journey of discovery. And this book is a record of that journey. In the beginning he was an innocent investigator, but in time that innocence turned to outrage as he came to understand that the Internet could not be tamed. Filters that were supposed to protect children were badly flawed—they gave pretense of protecting the young but abysmally failed in this regard.

He discovered that the Web was truly world-wide where anyone could put anything up for everyone to see, even materials that represented extremes in evil or antisocial content: How to make bombs, how to kill people, how to cheat on exams at school, and the most perverse sexual imagery imaginable—all of this available to anyone of any age within seconds while surfing the Web.

This is a good read. What works with regard to healing Internet porn addicts? How do you best protect your children? Are adults vulnerable to its addicting potential? Is it just a male problem? Read this book and find out.

–Victor B. Cline, Ph.D.,
Psychotherapist-sexual addictions,
Professor Emeritus of Psychology,
University of Utah

Foreword

On March 3, 1865, concerned that small, grainy, black and white pornographic pictures were exploiting the loneliness of Union soldiers far away from home, Honest Abe Lincoln signed the legislation banning further importation of materials "of a vulgar and indecent character" into the U.S.A.

Mark Kastleman's work on mind/body responses to pornography brings cutting-edge, scientific validation to President Lincoln's discernment regarding the toxic physiological effects of sexually explicit media on his military forces. Kastleman's fresh and intriguing book *The Drug of the New Millennium—Internet Pornography*, confirms Lincoln's sense and sensibility with *verifiable,* hard, scientific data. The author makes an articulate case for *all* sexually explicit material as metamorphosing into an endogenously produced, drug-high, inherently subversive of cognition and first amendment speech protections. A thought-provoking book indeed!

Kastleman's study reveals pornography not only as a self-medicating drug which creates "a vulgar and indecent character," but also as a drug which, on the evidence, causes vulnerable viewers to act out sex crimes on innocent children and women.

Mark Kastleman's research substantiates what we in the child-protection arena have long observed. Pornography has long been aiding and abetting in a discriminatory sexual holocaust against a specific class of Americans—our children. Data from the Department of Justice (DoJ) and the American Humane Association show a 5,171% increase in confirmed child sex abuse reports from 1976 to 1999. Recent DoJ data find 67% of sex abuse victims are children under age 18, with 34% of victims under age 12 and 64% of forcible sodomy victims boys under age 12! And, these data are missing from the FBI Uniform Crime Report, which excludes statutory (child rape) as "rape."

Kastleman's lucid book may just help redress the righteous grievances of America's children against an adult society which indulges in erotic excess at the cost of children's right to life in a safe and sane society in which they may find liberty and pursue happiness.

–Judith A. Reisman, Ph.D., Author:
Kinsey, Sex & Fraud; "Soft Porn Plays Hardball; Images of Children, Crime & Violence" in Playboy, Penthouse and Hustler; and *Kinsey, Crimes & Consequences.*

Author's Note

We live in a society filled with more pressure, stress, anxiety and fast-pace than at any other time in history. Many seek escape and relief from the tremendous strain of life by *self-medicating* through the use of alcohol, drugs (both illegal and prescription), cigarettes, food and other substances. Now, millions are turning to the most powerful drugs ever created—**Internet Pornography and Cybersex Chat Rooms.** These instant *plug-in, push-of-a-button drug*s are capturing new addicts—both male and female—by the thousands every day.

Using scientific research, this book explains why this **drug** called pornography is so powerful once it enters the human brain and body. You will learn how to protect yourself, your family, friends, congregation, patients, etc. You will also learn what to do if you or someone you care about is already trapped in the shackles of this addiction. This book is about the *mindbody science* of porn addiction, practical solutions for prevention and treatment, and **HOPE** for those trapped in the prison of addiction

I invite you to thoroughly investigate the science herein, carefully contemplate the variety of ideas and viewpoints, and embrace truth as you find it.

Introduction: What Makes Men and Women Do Such Stupid Things?

Over the past five years or so, I have witnessed a shocking and bewildering trend. We see it spattered across the headlines, featured on the evening news and unfolding right in our own families, neighborhoods, schools and towns.

- "Prominent politician caught in sex scandal."
- "Respected minister charged with soliciting prostitute."
- "Teacher arrested for sexual abuse of student."
- "Child pornography found in CEO's home."
- "Teen boys sexually assault and murder young girl."
- "Pro athlete accused of date rape."
- "Mother of 5 leaves family for cybersex charmer."

Such behavior has been around throughout history. But over the last few years, I have noticed three major differences:

- News articles reporting sex crimes and perversions have increased at an alarming rate. Dr. Judith Reisman, one of the world's leading researchers on the effects of pornography warns about a "chilling increase in sexual violence so brutal it compares only to the marauding male hordes of primitive folklore."[1]

- Hard-core sexual depravities once considered rare are becoming commonplace.
- Sexual misdeeds once confined to perverts, felons and the uneducated are now committed by world leaders, religious icons, business executives, educators, devoted fathers, professionals, and even women, teens and children.

The front pages and television newscasts tell the sad tale: Respected, highly-educated, successful men risking everything for a sexual escapade, turn-on or fantasy. In the process they sacrifice not only their personal integrity, but, indeed, their very reputations, careers, marriages and families! Men thought to be kind, caring and compassionate are unmasked as molesters, abusers and rapists.

Several years ago as this trend became more and more apparent, I asked myself, "How could intelligent, logical men do such things?" It is as if they had completely lost their minds to some bizarre drug or irresistible, evil power.

Then I discovered a link, a common thread in the lives of nearly all of those involved in sexual crimes and perversions: **Pornography**.

As I read the accounts, spoke with law enforcement officials, and even interviewed perpetrators, I found that in virtually *every* case, the perpetrator admitted to having viewed pornography on a regular basis. And not surprisingly, most did not start out committing sexual perversions and crimes. They initially discovered pornography out of curiosity and/or were exposed to it by family, friends, on store shelves, and in growing numbers, on the Internet. **But for these individuals, what began as mere curiosity quickly transformed into a "drug of choice"—a way to *self-medicate* and escape the stress, pressure, pain and trials of life.** But like any "drug" addiction, they needed harder and more perverse images to achieve the same "high." And when images were no longer enough, many turned to acting out what they had seen in pornography.

Most perpetrators reported viewing what the sex industry falsely entitles the "adult" and "hard-core" variety—the kind one finds primarily in pornography stores or through mail-order. But where did these otherwise ordinary people obtain this kind of pornography? Surely most of them, especially the more prominent individuals, would not risk being seen frequenting a sleazy pornography store in a seedy part of town. And how in the world did the teens and children who were committing sexual perversions and crimes get a hold of these kinds of materials?

Then it hit me like a bolt of lightning—***the Internet****! Of course, the Internet.* (Remember, this was in 1996. Never having even been "online," I was naive regarding the Internet.) "But is there really that much pornography on the Internet?" I wondered. "And aren't there laws against the more explicit, degrading pornography? Surely children can't view this stuff without giving a credit card number or passing some kind of age verification . . ."

Boy, was I wrong. There are laws governing pornography on the Internet, but shockingly, with the exception of child pornography, these laws are rarely enforced! Anything and everything from all over the world can be accessed instantly: explicit sex, rape, bestiality, incest, live sex—the list is almost endless.

And incredibly, there are *no* age restrictions on the Internet! It's true that some Internet porn sites require a credit card to subscribe, but so many private or free sites offer everything at no cost. And most of the pay sites offer enough "teaser" photos, videos and so forth to keep viewers occupied for hundreds of hours.

So there it was: Unlimited explicit, dehumanizing and degrading pornography of every kind imaginable (and much that most people *can't* imagine) available at the push of a button, much of it free, for any man, woman or child to view in the privacy of his or her home or office, 24 hours a day!

But how many families actually have the Internet in their homes and how many would actually view pornography? Currently there are over 429 million Internet users worldwide.[2] U.S. citizens make up over 168 million of this total, or nearly 40% of the world's Internet users.[3]

According to Cyveillance, a Washington, D.C., artificial-intelligence search-and-analysis development company, we can now surf our way through **2.1 billion** unique, publicly available Web pages. Its study, "Sizing the Internet" says that the Web is growing by more than **7 million pages each day**—which means it will double in size to **4 billion pages in 2001**.[4]

(You can see a "real-time web page count"
ticker on the Cyveillance home page at
http://www.cyveillance.com/newsroom/pressr/000710.asp)

Based on surfing logs, some industry leaders believe that 10 to 30% of all websites on the Internet contain some form of pornographic material.[5] Internet pornographers generated in the neighborhood of 1.5 billion dollars in 1999 alone.[6] And this dollar amount is expected to multiply at a furious pace in the coming years.

After reviewing these numbers, I understood why sexual crime, perversion and deviance is soaring. Ever-increasing numbers of men, teens, women and even children make it their practice to view pornography on the Internet. Many are making it their "drug of choice" to escape the often harsh realities of life.

So why does pornography act as a catalyst, trigger or fuel for sexual perversion and crime? Why, in the process of and after viewing pornography, do otherwise normal, intelligent individuals do things that are perverted, cruel, foolish, embarrassing and even depraved? Under the influence of pornography, why will they sacrifice everything—their personal values, self-esteem, reputations, careers, marriages, families and freedoms—for a series of meaningless but destructive flings?

These questions I could not readily answer. However, after four long years of exhaustive research the answers have become more clear.

The findings will astound you. In the pages that follow, you will learn how pornography *actually changes the physical and chemical structure of the brain and body of every man, woman and child who views it.* Pornography literally changes who you are, how you think, and how you behave. You will learn why pornography is the **most addictive drug on earth**. You will learn *how pornography literally makes men and women stupid* and why every sector of our society suffers as a result. You will also understand what you can do to protect yourself and those you care about from this destructive tidal wave of Internet Pornography.

If you are (or someone you know is) already involved with pornography, you will learn how to break the awful chains of addiction and restore peace and hope to your life, and help others do the same.

Can anyone accurately predict the consequences of this wave? Yes, we can examine history and analyze the complete ruin of civilizations who chose a path of unbridled sexual permissiveness. But no past civilization has ever experienced the free and open distribution of every type of porn at this level; no other social paradigm comes even close.

Those who claim viewing pornography is all harmless fun are nothing short of foolish, ignorant and arrogant and/or addicts themselves. Those who claim that it is a First Amendment issue will soon witness the loss of the very freedoms and basic human rights they seek to defend. (I will address this First Amendment argument in a later chapter.)

Already we see victims falling by the thousands all around us. As I pondered the above-mentioned facts and so many others, I knew the time had come for me to take a stand, to speak out. I knew I had to make the findings of my investigation available to the world. I had to write this book.

A Special Note About Women and Pornography

As I conducted research over the years, consulted therapists, and interviewed those hooked on pornography, it became clear that pornography is mostly a "male problem." This book was originally titled *How Internet Pornography Makes Men Stupid.* Its focus was on the severe problem of male Internet porn addiction and how it radically alters the brain and nervous system of every man who views it.

As a result of these physiological changes in men, women suffer as secondary victims to Internet pornography. Internet pornography addiction in women—or so I thought—was a rare condition. The entire book followed this line of reasoning.

Then as I approached the final stages of editing, I was introduced to a man who would forever change my way of thinking: Willie Draughon, Assistant Chief of Criminal Investigations with the State Attorney General's Office.

.For eighteen years Willie focused on crimes against children. In the early '90s he began investigating Internet crimes against children, including child abduction, child pornography and adults using the Internet to arrange sexual encounters with children.

Willie read my manuscript and told me that I was dead on with my conclusions about men and Internet porn. "But," he added, "your book is missing the other half of the story. You've completely overlooked the severe problem of women and Internet pornography addiction."

I stared at him incredulously. "You're joking, right?"

What happened next left me with my mouth hanging open and my mind racing with confusion. Willie recounted for me his experiences with investigations connected to the Attorney General's office. In his investigations he encountered increasing numbers of women addicted to Internet porn, particularly sexually-oriented Internet chat-rooms. Internet cybersex, he claimed, is a major problem for women.

Immediately I began researching this claim, but could find very little with regards to women and pornography addiction. So, I went right to the source and sought out women to interview, some over the telephone, others in person. Some of the women I interviewed had never been exposed to pornography to any degree. A startling number, though, had sunk deep into Internet pornography and "cybersex" addiction.

I was stunned. I'd spent so much time and energy researching and writing about Internet pornography addiction as a "male-only" problem that I had unwittingly left out half the equation.

I now recognize that Internet porn addiction can be a serious problem for women—in some ways a more damaging problem than it is for men. I don't claim to have all the answers regarding this issue. At this point in time, there just is simply not enough prior information and research available.

I will, however, share what I discovered through my interviews, my discussions with therapists who have treated these women, and insights into how all this relates to the structure of the female brain and nervous system.

Suffice it to say, Internet pornography addiction is no longer directed to men and teenage boys alone. Internet pornographers have discovered—and are aggressively exploiting—a new and profitable market.

Thus, not only are women and girls targets for abuse at the hands of men and teenage boys who view Internet porn, now they are primary targets for Internet pornography addiction itself! Internet porn knows no gender boundaries. Everyone is at risk.

1

INTERNET PORN AND CYBERSEX CHAT ARE "DRUGS," AND PORNOGRAPHERS ARE "DRUG DEALERS"

Today, we live with more stress, pain and anxiety than perhaps any other society in the world's history. Viewing Internet porn and/or engaging in cybersex chat, coupled with masturbation, cause the brain and body to release drugs back into its own nervous system. No wonder so many are turning to the Internet. Based on its ability to produce self-medication, mask pain, escape reality and provide the means to achieve orgasm (one of the body's most powerful peak experiences), *Internet pornography has been placed in direct competition with illicit drugs!*[1]

If you think about it, in many ways Internet pornography is preferable to traditional drugs. For one thing, it can more easily be hidden from view. If you achieve your high through Internet porn or cybersex, do you stagger around, slur your words or pass out? After an Internet porn or cybersex fix, might you be pulled over and cited for DUI? What other drug can you sample for free as long as you like? (There are enough "free" and "sampler" porn sites and thousands of cybersex chat rooms available through standard Internet services to keep an addict occupied for years.) And if the free or sample drugs aren't strong enough, what other drug could you purchase in large enough quantities—not to mention a constantly changing variety to satisfy your changing mood, craving or preference—for just the cost of your Internet connection?

Do you see the point? Can you understand why addicts of Internet porn eventually will outnumber cocaine, crack or meth addicts? Consider the myriad ways the Internet porn/cybersex "drug" eclipses and outperforms common street drugs:

- The drug is free or relatively cheap.
- It can be used as often as desired.
- Regular users of the drug don't manifest any embarrassing outward physical signs.
- The drug, with rare exceptions (i.e., child pornography), is completely legal.
- No prescription is required.
- The drug producers (Internet pornographers) are shrouded in an anonymous Internet mantle of secrecy.
- Producers are able to pump the drug right into the private home or office.
- The drug supply is endless and instantly available at the push of a button, 24 hours a day.
- Unlike other drugs, porn leaves behind no trace of physical evidence—no smell, no residue, no paraphernalia. Any physical hint of its use vanishes when the computer is turned off.
- The addict has access to a constantly changing variety of drugs. With thousands of choices, he can switch to a new, different or harder drug at the push of a button or the click of a mouse.

With traditional forms of pornography, wives or parents could chance upon a magazine stashed under the mattress, a video hidden in the closet. Not any more. Internet pornography is the new *"Stealth Drug."*

What can compete with this? And think about it from the perspective of the drug-pushing pornographer: every single male on the planet is a potential customer because each is "pre-wired" to be so. And now pornographers are increasingly concentrating their efforts on marketing gimmicks to lure in and addict the female consumer. Internet pornographers have a virtually unlimited market!

- Rich or poor, educated or unschooled, executive or laborer—all are potential customers.
- Regardless of age, gender, religion, race or ethnic background, all are susceptible to addiction.
- The only limitation is the potential customer's access to the Internet.

With the dramatic drop in the cost of computers and Internet access, and with millions joining the "online" ranks every year, in time this latter limitation will all but disappear. It's a porn-drug lord's fantasy come true.

THE PORN ADDICTION PROCESS IS LIKE THAT OF ANY OTHER DRUG ADDICTION

Internet porn/cybersex addiction follows a similar pathway as traditional drug addiction. In order to mask or deaden the pain of life, the porn addict seeks a quick mood change, some sort of stimulation, an escape.

Eventually he becomes powerless. He further spins out of control as the compulsion takes over his life. Even severe threats to job, family or health cannot slow down the obsession. He is caught in a cycle of the need for mood change, stimulation, escape and temporary relief, a vicious gripping cycle that both repels and draws him, repulses and arouses.

Often the addict *wants* to change, in fact knows he *must* change or succumb to disaster. Virtually every porn/cybersex addict reaches the point where he realizes the craving is simply too powerful; he cannot stop without help. At this point, most porn or cybersex addicts enter into what Dr. Page Bailey calls the *Hopeless Dialogue.*[2]

THE "PRIVATE HELL" THAT THE PORNOGRAPHERS NEVER TELL YOU ABOUT

Men, women and teens engulfed in pornography/cybersex addiction experience a wide range of emotions. Some become so desensitized that they don't feel anything at all. Some feel a variety of negative emotions but choose to ignore them. But many feel intensely guilt-ridden, shameful, angry, lonely, and a host of other negative emotions, living in their own "private hell" whenever they are not directly engaged in a porn/cybersex session. What I am referring to is what Dr. Page Bailey calls the "Hopeless Dialogue," a painful, personal conflict porn addicts (and other addicts) wage within themselves.

Anything that takes place on the road to sexual arousal and orgasm is habituation at its most powerful level. An addict's belief system may include a conviction that he should not view porn or engage in sexually-oriented conversations in chat rooms. Still, the addict, according to form, succumbs to the habit.

After orgasm, the man or woman may feel embarrassed and ashamed. But the turmoil felt remains a mystery. "Why did I abandon everything I believe and hold dear?" he may ask. "Why has my heart grown cold and lifeless?" she sighs.

The porn/cybersex addict enters into an inner ***hopeless*** *dialogue* in that it is hopeless to pit lofty values and an ethical belief system against the addictive power of sexual excitement, arousal and orgasm coupled with the host of drugs released into the brain and body by porn and cybersex. *Hopeless* because the mind/body left to itself inevitably will choose the sexual pleasure and drug-high generated by the porn/ cybersex process. It's virtually a sure bet.

Though this conflict elicits feelings of guilt and shame, since these emotions are forms of mind/body stimulation, they serve to generate the release of neuro-chemicals into the brain and body, thus adding to the power of the pornography/cybersex habituation.[3]

Why does the porn viewer or cybersex participant experience shame? Because his thoughts and actions are not in harmony with his internal values, dignity, integrity and spoken beliefs. These feelings of shame and repugnance leave behind a sense of emptiness, despair and self-loathing, which only drive the addict to self-medicate by way of more pornography viewing or cybersex chat. This downward spiral often leads to other addictions such as smoking, drugs and alcohol use.

PORN ADDICTION, LIKE OTHER ADDICTIONS, BUILDS UP A TOLERANCE

Alcoholics are notorious for their ability to consume enormous amounts of liquor; chain smokers can burn through several packs of cigarettes a day.

It is the same with pornography and cybersex chat—greater and greater stimulation is needed to produce an ever-diminishing gratification.[4] Porn and cybersex addicts have acquired a tolerance to perverse and obscene material, material that would leave most sick to their stomachs. And the desire for harder and more explicit material and conversations grows stronger—not weaker—with each attempt to satisfy it.[5]

PORN ADDICTS SUFFER WITHDRAWAL

Porn or cybersex addicts suffer withdrawal symptoms when they try—or are compelled—to relinquish their vice for any length of time. An alcoholic gets the shakes without alcohol; the porn and cybersex addict's world starts to shake when the overwhelming urge to view pornography or start up a cybersex conversation hits and he can't get online.

It's as if he might go crazy without another session. The withdrawal pains may drive an addict to find porn or sexual arousal any way and anywhere he can[6]—often causing him to act out his needs in inappropriate ways.

With the Internet, however, it's usually all too easy to satisfy the craving (at least in the early stages of addiction) by heading for the computer screen. With such ease of access and frequency of use, how quickly do you think a porn or cybersex addiction will accelerate until it is out of control? How quickly will an addict become bored with soft-porn or tame sex conversations and proceed to the hard stuff?

When compared to the rate of addiction with traditional pornography mediums of the past, Internet porn and cybersex have accelerated porn addiction to the speed of light.

INTERNET PORN BECOMES "OBSESSIVE-COMPULSIVE"

Any addiction will eventually take over the addict's life. Thoughts of alcohol, a cigarette, cocaine, food or gambling begin to crowd everything else out of his or her mind. It is no different with porn and cybersex addiction.

Viewing porn or talking in a chat room often starts out as a simple curiosity, which usually turns into repeated exposures. Soon the daily habit becomes an obsession; then it evolves into a compulsion. Addicts find themselves performing acts and wallowing in places they wouldn't ever do or frequent under normal circumstances—though they keep promising themselves they'll never do that or go there again. It's as if they're undergoing an out-of-body experience where they stand pleading with their real self to "Stop!." But there are few strong enough to rein in their newfound obsession. Staring blankly at the images on the computer screen, their real self is deaf to their cries. Without seeking outside help, it is truly a "hopeless dialogue."

Key Points

A reference tool for
spouses, parents, clergy,
counselors and others

- Internet pornography is in direct competition with illicit drugs.
- Like any other drug or substance addiction, pornography addiction escalates until the individual's life is out of control and he or she becomes powerless to stop.
- The addict enters into a *hopeless dialogue* phase which accelerates the downward spiral of the addiction.
- As with drugs, the porn addict builds up a tolerance to pornography and must have harder and more explicit material to achieve the same release, relief or "high."

2

THE "UNDERNET"—A PORNOGRAPHER'S MARKETING DREAM COME TRUE

During the 20th century the telephone, radio and television made this world of ours "a smaller place." And now in the 21st century computers and the Internet will shrink it even further, simultaneously taking us to soaring heights of communication and learning, dizzying journeys that only a few short decades ago were considered fantasy.

Millions of homes and schools across America and across the world are connecting their computers to the "Information Super Highway" via telephone, cable and satellite. This is what is referred to as "going online."

Logging on from their own home computers, online adults and children alike can communicate with individuals, businesses and organizations across the world. We now have instant access to massive volumes of information that previously would have taken years to gather.

Many "online" services are maintained by commercial, self-regulated businesses that may or may not screen or provide controls for the material on their systems. The "Internet," however, as a *global* network, is not governed by any such entity. This means that there are no limits or controls on the kinds of material accessible to Internet users, including teenagers and children. In essence, the Internet is a pornography vendor's heaven.

Those who distribute information via the Internet are mostly good, decent people who are driven by positive or, at worst, commercial motives. Then there are those who use the Internet to degrade, exploit and enslave. Internet pornographers have forged a dark, destructive side of the Internet aptly labeled by many as the "Undernet."

THE "UNDERNET"—A PORNOGRAPHER'S MARKETING DREAM COME TRUE

The Internet has spawned a pornography marketing and distribution vehicle that up until a few short years ago didn't exist, not even in pornographers' wildest imaginations. Think of it—

- No more city ordinances or other governmental restrictions on selling explicit, degrading porn of every type.
- No more hassles with city zoning laws to build "adult" bookstores and video arcades.
- Elimination of all magazine printing costs, postage, expensive advertising, video duplication, etc.

Now at a fraction of the cost, with little overhead, pornographers can pipe their wares directly into the home and office of anyone who has a personal computer! It's pure profit! It's a marketer's dream-come-true utopia! And its effect is the spread of pornography at a rate that already is off the charts.

MILLIONS OF FREE PORN IMAGES AT THE PUSH OF A BUTTON

Some industry leaders have estimated that somewhere between 10 and 30% of all sites on the Internet have a pornographic orientation and that the number is growing rapidly.[1] If these figures hold true, that means that of the over seven million new webpages appearing on the Internet every day, some 700,000 to 2.1 million can be considered pornographic.[2]

In addition, tens of thousands of *website* addresses are out there that are designed to automatically lead users back to these pornographic webpages. Multiple addresses means that any number of different web addresses will link back to the same site, making estimating the number of actual porn sites virtually impossible.

Multiple addresses also means that the likelihood of child, teen and adult Internet surfers being exposed to hard-core pornography is extremely high.

Virtually all of these sites post "teaser" photos that anyone can access without adult age verification. Just click on the box that says: *"I'm over 18, let me in."*

Once in, a user can sample, at no cost, everything explicit imaginable—even beyond imagination. And there are a growing number of sites that allow users to view everything in the site at no charge at all, the costs subsidized by the affiliated pay sites.

Another problem revolves around the explosion of amateur pornographic sites created by people who do not charge an access fee but simply post the images for the thrill of it. For example, in reviewing sites to determine their safety for family use, SurfPartner Corporation, an Internet protection service, came across an amateur porn site with thousands of photographs all completely accessible free of charge. The site, dreamed up by the owner of a bar, featured explicit photos of regular people from his community.

This amateur porn site trend is ballooning. The disturbing part is that if by some miracle the commercial Internet pornographers do become subject to laws that protect children, these laws largely will be ineffective against the amateur sites!

Of course the end goal of the pornographer is to get the viewer *addicted.* If a free site starts a viewer down the path to addiction where he's constantly got to get his fix of more and harder pornography, then the pornographers don't mind in the least allowing him some complimentary surfing.

The point is, we're not talking about some girly magazines and other so-called "harmless" stuff. Today's pornography is a far cry from the X-rated movies and magazines it was in the '50s, '60s and '70s. (And believe me, those were bad enough!) It has evolved into much more than that. And if we are to make sound, informed decisions for ourselves and our children regarding this issue, we too must evolve, bring our thinking up to date.

MOST PORNOGRAPHY ON THE INTERNET IS "HARD-CORE"

The vast majority of pornography distributed in America and in the world today can be termed "hard-core," in that its content is abusive and predatory. It eroticizes violence and degradation. It preys upon the dignity of women and children, humiliating them in its images and intent. Examples of hard-core pornography found on the Internet include:

- Sadism—depicts pain as being pleasurable
- Body-piercing, torture and mutilation
- Rape—emphasizes the "rape myth"
- Incest—females or males reportedly initiating and enjoying sexual abuse inflicted by family members
- Snuff films—low-budget films in which the actor is sexually abused and then murdered
- Combining human excrement with sexual activity
- Orgies/group sex
- Necrophilia—sex with a corpse
- Bestiality—sex with animals
- Ritualistic sexual abuse
- Degradation of pregnant women
- Crossover Videos—depicts serial progression from heterosexual acts to bisexual acts to homosexual acts, the latest fad in the pornography market[3]

I hope you, the reader can realize that I do not take describing these hard-core images lightly. I hesitate even to mention them, knowing that I may be exposing you to shocking, vulgar, and blatantly loathsome concepts, but the truth must be rendered accurately. These inherently detestable acts are being played out on the Internet. Unfortunately, there is no way to "sanitize" or describe them without stating exactly what they are.

Then there is "*cybersex*," which involves Internet users having sexually explicit conversations with each other, often in online "chat rooms." These conversations often lead to more pornography viewing, fantasizing, and even personal meetings for illicit sex with strangers. Extremely habit-forming, cybersex has been a contributing factor in broken marriages, has forged new addictions, and generally has provided a venue of self-indulgence with disastrous consequences to individuals, families and society. Ironically, people usually start out by "chatting" in a social way that is generally acceptable and seems harmless.

The latest Internet trend just now being employed thanks to recent technological breakthroughs is "Virtual" or "Interactive Sex." With new high-speed DSL and other broadband Internet connections, users not only are chatting through a keyboard but are using video cameras so that they can see and hear each other "live," taking cybersex to a whole new level.

And last but not least, pornographers, as part of this virtual sex, are now selling the first generation of "interactive stimulation" devices. These devices can be attached to parts of the body, then stimulated remotely by the virtual sex partner on the other end of the Internet line.

ARE THERE REALLY THAT MANY PEOPLE INVOLVED WITH INTERNET PORN AND CYBERSEX?

By now you may be asking yourself, *Are there really that many people who enjoy looking at Internet porn or engaging in such illicit sexual activities?*

The number of people visiting sex sites on the Web doubled over the last year, outpacing the number of new Internet users. Some of the more popular sex Web sites attract in excess of 50 million hits, or visits, a month, according to the ratings services Nielsen/Net and Media Matrix.[4]

On the Internet, sex is one of the few things that prompts large numbers of people to disclose their credit card information. According to two Web ratings services, about one in four regular Internet users, or 21 million Americans visits one of the more than 60,000 sex sites on the Web at least once a month—more people than go to sports or government sites.[5] It's not unusual for a single, very moderate-sized porn site to pull in over $1 million in net annual profits.[6] Though estimates have been greatly inflated by some e-commerce sex merchants, analysts from Forrester Research say that sex sites on the Web generate at least $1 billion a year in revenue. These are expected to increase dramatically over the next several years.[7]

Is it any wonder that estimates range from tens of thousands to hundreds of thousands of pornographic webpages being added to the Internet every day? I have heard the argument, "Yeah, there's pornography on the Internet, but the amount is small and it's just not that easy to get to. Besides, it's really not all that bad."

I invite you to consider all the facts, then decide for yourself.

Key Points

A reference tool for
spouses, parents, clergy,
counselors and others

- Beware of the antiquated perception that "there isn't that much pornography on the Internet" and "it's not that easy to get to." Pornography is the Internet's largest sector and its biggest money-maker. And it's all available at the push of a mouse button—whether you're looking for it or not.
- An adult or minor **does not** need a credit card to get to the "hard stuff." Pornographers want to recruit as many new addicts as possible. They place enough free "teaser sites" on the Internet to last a curious viewer many hundreds of hours. There is no proof of age required to get into these explicit sites.
- The perception that most of the pornography on the Internet "isn't that bad" is an ignorant and dangerous mind-set. Most Internet porn is incredibly graphic and degrading.
- Some naively claim, "There aren't that many people looking at it." Pornography attracts more visitors on the Internet than any other single sector, and the numbers are growing daily.
- The Internet is a powerful influence that is here to stay. Internet pornography must not be ignored, underestimated or taken lightly.

3

What's the Big Deal? Internet Pornography Doesn't Really Hurt Anyone . . .

Ted Bundy Speaks Out

Over a 20-year period, Ted Bundy went on a rampage of rape and murder. Across the U.S. the bodies of young women "missing" for years finally turned up as Ted Bundy confessed to the sex-torture murders of his innocent victims.

The night before his execution, Bundy spoke to psychologist Dr. James Dobson. Bundy insisted that "drug store pornography" helped transform a baby-faced boy into a brutal mass murderer. In Bundy's own words:

This is the message that I want to get across, that as a young boy, and I mean a boy of twelve and thirteen certainly, that I encountered . . . in the local grocery store the pornography that people call "soft-core" . . . [W]hat I am talking about happened twenty, thirty years ago in my formative stages.[1]

I take full responsibility for whatever I've done. The question and issue is how this kind of literature contributed and helped mold and shape these kind of violent behaviors.[2]

The pornographic images, Bundy continued, eventually broke down his "*last vestiges of restraint—the barriers to actually doing something.*"[3]

In a more chilling statement made moments before he was electrocuted, Bundy warned America about the sado-sexual material (material combining sex and violence) children consume today:

What scares and appalls me, Dr. Dobson, is when I see what's on cable TV, and some of the movies and some of the violence in the movies that comes into homes today, with stuff that they wouldn't show in X-rated adult theaters thirty years ago . . . as it gets into the home to children who may be unattended or unaware that they may be a Ted Bundy.[4]

Bundy went on to point out how odd it is that society still strongly condemns his behavior *"while they're walking past magazine racks full of the very kinds of things that send young kids down the road to be Ted Bundys. That's the irony."*[5]

What did Ted Bundy have to gain by his confession? He was about to die. Yet even on the threshold of death, he predicted a future that most of the "experts" (academicians, sociologists, psychologists, sexologists) still ignore. In a final testimony to the harm pornography can wreak on its victims, Bundy told Dr. Dobson:

There are lots of other kids playing in streets around this country today who are going to be dead tomorrow, and the next day and the next day and next month, because other young people are reading the kinds of things and seeing the kinds of things that are available in the media today.[6]

Studies confirm Bundy's candidly frightening observations. Sexual and violent media flood America today. But adults are not its only audience. In fact, a recent Canadian study found more adolescents than adults using pornography.[7]

Younger and younger children are exposed to sex and violence by way of television, comic books, music videos, film, and books (all now instantly available on the Internet). Children by the millions see far more sexual and violent material than anything Ted Bundy saw as a boy in the 1950s.

If Bundy represents the worst-outcome scenario "drug store" pornography could have back then on a young boy, what is the worst we ought to expect from children influenced by today's excess of explicit images displayed at the push of a button on the Internet?

PORN IS CAUSING AN AVALANCHE OF SEXUAL VIOLENCE

An avalanche of sexual violence, unsurpassed in our Nation's history, is assaulting us. News headlines are smothered by its weight. Just one example in thousands: On October 26, 1990, the Associated Press reported a nine-year-old in Norman, Oklahoma, whose genitals were mutilated and an eye gouged out. Police subsequently called for *Hustler* magazine to be taken off local store shelves after the discovery that a recent issue featured a scene where a child underwent similar torture.[8]

The "fantasies" displayed in porn magazines too often serve as blueprints for brutal crime. The Pollyannas who argue that sado-sexual pictures do not encourage and stimulate anger, aggression and crime in some children and adults should, as they say, wake up and smell the coffee. Or start reading the reports—like the FBI study which found that nearly all serial rapist-murderers admit pornography as their primary interest.[9]

Is this fact merely coincidence? The media claim that Bundy was a rare case. But virtually all rapist-murderers in prisons today readily confess a consuming passion for pornography.[10]

Perhaps the most tragic element of Bundy's story is that it is no longer news. His testimony concerning the critical—and tragic—role pornography played in his life now typifies the confessions of most serial rapist-murderers.[11]

PORN ADDICTION YIELDS SHAME AND BLAME

When a man or teenage boy begins viewing pornography, he rationalizes it as "simple curiosity," "no big deal," or "simply temporary"—"I will quit after this one session." Soon, however, it becomes obvious that he cannot quit.

For that matter, the obsession grows. The addict finds that the material must become progressively harder and more depraved in order to satisfy his craving. Soon his behavior is such that even he himself abhors it. This, of course, brings feelings of shame. To escape being crushed by the full burden of his guilt, the addict will often shift the blame for his addiction to parents, wife, financial difficulties, an abusive childhood, work stress, etc.

STRESS ADDS TO THE POWER OF THE PORN ADDICTION

When a man or boy is engaged in the "neural narrowing" process of pornography viewing, the right side of his brain and his entire body become super-charged with an acceleration of emotion-producing chemicals.[12] And so it is up to logic and reason, found largely in the *left* hemisphere of the brain, to figure out why the brain and body are responding sexually to the nude images on the computer screen, movie screen or magazine page.

As a man or boy tries to logically sort out the "whys" for his behavior, feelings such as guilt, shame and anger often rise up and produce "stress" in the viewer. This stress releases chemicals into the brain and body and actually intensifies the pornography addiction.

The viewer may also harbor in the back of his mind a feeling of "fear of getting caught." In some cases, this adds to the stress and/or "excitement" of the experience. The viewer may feel greater shame; he knows that what he is doing is not in harmony with his morals or beliefs, or he might feel that he is betraying the trust of his wife or parents. All these feelings combined create "stress" in both the brain and body.

When caught in any stressful situation, humans secrete hormones that attempt to provoke the brain/body to excitement, a variation of the fight/flight response that generates an "adaptive-natural" neuro-chemical high.[13]

But when it is pornography that generates this "stress cue," the brain is tricked into to a fight or flight *arousal* state. The body is ready to deal with an emergency or an intense event (like sex), but there is none. It's all a fake. Still, the brain and body respond to the pornography as if the viewer is about to have a real sexual encounter.[14]

An increase in heart rate, blood pressure, respiration, etc.,occur. But because these responses are brought on by pornography, feelings such as fear, anger, shame and guilt are thrown into the mix. All this generates an extreme amount of stress, which in turn produces an equally powerful release of emotions and chemicals in the porn viewer's brain and body. In effect, the intensity of the arousal experienced through pornography is normally very high because the stress level is very high.

WHEN THE "STRESS" OF "SOFT-PORN" IS NOT ENOUGH

(Note: The following citations and discussion on pornography's impact on stress draws extensively from Dr. Judith Reisman's pioneering research reported in both *"Soft" Porn Plays Hardball* and from her monograph *Sexually Explicit Media: Changes In the Structure of the Human Brain & American Law & Public Policy*.

What about men or boys who view pictures of nude women yet are no longer "aroused" or sufficiently stimulated by them? Their heart rate does not increase as much, their pupils no longer dilate, nor does their breathing deepen. This is known as "desensitization" or "habituation," the natural decrease in response to a continued or repeated stimulus.

With repeated exposure to the same stimulus, the brain and body eventually cease to respond to the stimulus; they become desensitized or habituated. In the human brain, this ability to cease responding to a monotonous stimulus is adaptive: It allows us to pay attention to new or more important stimuli. In other words, it wards off boredom by moving us toward freshly stimulating material.

Unfortunately, when this adaptive ability is applied to pornography and violence (which, as we have seen, often go together), the results often turn tragic.

Let's look at an example: Nathan is raised in a typical American home. He watches the typical sitcoms with their endless sexual jokes, sex scenes, and focus on women's bodies. During his teen years he witnesses a variety of Hollywood movies that mix extreme violence with nudity, vulgarity and profanity.

One day while surfing the Internet, Nathan happens upon a porn site that features calendar girls or centerfold-type images of nude women. At first these images are exciting and easily produce the stress/sexual response that lead to masturbation. But soon he becomes desensitized, inured to or "bored" with these images. Since they no longer give him the "high" they once did, he searches out other porn sites.

Soon he descends a step lower and begins viewing pornographic images of couples having sex, lesbian images, group sex. These images add to Nathan's feelings of shame and guilt because they are in direct violation of his inner—or religious—beliefs. (Even though he has watched sitcoms, R-rated movies and other programming in clear violation of his moral beliefs, he never gave it much thought or just ignored it. After all, everyone was doing it.)

But now he is alone in front of the computer screen overdosing on pornography and masturbating. This seems "different" somehow—even more wrong, as the shame and guilt he suffers only adds to the "intensity" of his chemical/sexual arousal. But over time, he becomes desensitized to these more explicit and degrading images as well.

Then he discovers the "taboo sites" that depict scenes of rape, incest, bestiality, sadism, etc. Again, the increased sense of shock, shame and guilt at viewing these images, mixed with an overabundance of sexual emotions and the "fear" of being caught, add to the intensity of his arousal.

Nathan, step by step, has become progressively hooked to his vice, like a drug addict or an alcoholic who's got to have harder and harder stuff to obtain the same high.

Nathan may even progress to Internet porn sites that blend torture, mutilation and other atrocities with sexual images. He is striving to reach the next "high," or at least maintain past levels. All the while he is becoming more and more desensitized, deadened to his feelings.

Before long, this young man is scarcely moved even by the most perverted sexual and violent scenes imaginable. Somehow he has managed to stash his morals and beliefs in a separate compartment when he views pornography.

How long do you think it will be before Nathan no longer can find the arousal he craves by gazing at a computer screen? How long before he seeks the "thrill" of live victims?

Think of the myriad images stored in this man's memory and all of the links to physiological, chemical and biological responses coursing throughout his brain and body. Little by little, every fibre of his being has been trained in the black art of sexual debauchery and perversion.

His conscience is completely seared, leaving him no choice but to become totally immersed in "self"—self-centered, self-serving, self-gratification. (Months or years of viewing porn while masturbating forges an astonishingly high level of selfishness.) He now views virtually all women as objects with but one purpose: to satisfy his craving, his appetite, his addiction.

I know that this scenario may seem overly dramatic or exaggerated to some. But I caution the reader to review the headlines and study the statistics and then ask and answer honestly: "Is the process of addiction I have described so outlandish or unusual?"

Not at all. It's happening all across America. This is the path of "desensitization" that men like Ted Bundy and Gary Bishop followed. And there are thousands just like them in our prisons today who followed a similar process of desensitization. How many men and boys like them are not locked up in prison but loose on our streets? How many men and boys are somewhere in the desensitization process described? They aren't yet a Ted Bundy, but they're well on their way.

Key Points

A reference tool for
spouses, parents, clergy,
counselors and others

- Pornography is a catalyst for negative male emotions and acts of anger, aggression and violence, especially against women and children.
- Pornography produces shame, guilt and stress in the human brain and body. These emotions release chemicals into the brain and body that add to the intensity of the arousal experience.
- Over time, desensitization and habituation drive the viewer to harder, more depraved and violent pornography and in many cases, to actually "act out" against another human being. With instant access on the Internet to the most violent and hard-core images, this total addiction can happen very quickly.

4

It's *Not* About the First Amendment—It's About Money

It never ceases to amaze me the lengths pornographers will go to distract us from the true issues of pornography by invoking the argument that "It's all about *your* First Amendment rights!"

In their smoke-and-mirrors efforts to draw us away from the truth, they would have us believe that they are "champions of the First Amendment" sent to guard this freedom for all of us. This, they assert, is their high and noble right or purpose in making pornography available to the masses.

I find this impossible to believe and I am insulted that they would consider the public so ignorant and gullible as to buy into this "smoke screen."

It has been said: "Your actions speak so loudly that I cannot hear what you are saying." Such is the case with pornographers. They flourish on the oxygen of freedom, then turn around and pollute the very air that made their existence possible. Pornographers prosper financially by stealing personal freedom from others. The more "addicts" they can create, the more money they make.

A pornographer claiming to champion the cause of freedom is like a slave trader who says he is leading his captives to freedom, only to have them discover the real truth when it is too late—when they are in chains below deck! How many men, teenagers and even women, who considered viewing pornography a freedom issue, are now hopelessly shackled in the irons of sexual addiction?

WHAT'S IN IT FOR THE INTERNET PORNOGRAPHERS?

Over the years I have spent hundreds of hours conducting educational workshops covering a variety of subjects. One of the principles I teach deals with "motive." I teach participants that whenever someone is trying to sell you something or convince you to do something, you should always ask, "What's in it for you? What is your *motive*?"

In a June 14, 1999 *Forbes* article titled *Porn Goes Public*, Richard C. Morais offered the following profit figures provided by Private Media Group, Inc:

***Legal* Pornography Sales World-Wide For the 1999 Year:**

1. **Porn video retail sales – $20 billion**: In the U.S. alone, Americans rented 686 million porn videos in 1998 compared to 7.7 million in 1985. Also in 1998, 8,948 new porn videos were produced and released to the U.S. retail market, up from 1,275 new porn videos released in 1990.
2. **Sex clubs – $5 billion:** The major part of this figure was garnered by approximately 2,500 U.S. strip clubs located in the U.S.
3. **Porn magazines – $7.5 billion:** Includes *Playboy*, *Penthouse*, *Hustler* and numerous other even more explicit titles.
4. **Phone sex – $4.5 billion**
5. **Escort services – $11 billion**
6. **Porn on cable/satellite/pay-per-view–$2.5 billion:** Includes *The Playboy Channel*, *Spice*, *Adam & Eve* and hotel pay-per-view services.
7. **Porn on CD-ROM/DVD-ROM–$1.5 billion**

8. **Internet porn sales and memberships–$1.5 billion**
9. **Adult novelties–$1 billion**
10. **Other porn sales–$1.5 billion**

Total pornography-related sales for the 1999 year = $56 billion

(Of course, these figures fail to take into account any of the numerous "illicit" markets around the world.)[1]

FBI statistics reveal that pornography is the third largest revenue producer for organized crime, trailing only drugs and gambling. Many Internet pornographers make millions of dollars in net profits every year by sending their material directly to the computer screens of people all over the world. In fact, more and more Internet porn companies are entering into the stock market as highly profitable publicly traded companies.

One U.S. Internet porn company with '98 revenues of $20.5 million and another with revenues of $34 million are now traded on the Nasdaq stock exchange. Another U.S. Internet porn peddler boasting $50 million in annual profits is preparing for its first stock offering. A German porn company with $98 million in annual revenues hopes to become Europe's biggest sex store chain, and presently has a $65 million stock offering on the Frankfurt stock exchange.[2]

Isn't the pornographer's true motive obvious? How many of these pornographers would be touting themselves as "champions of the First Amendment" if there was no money in the distribution of pornography?

Just as Hollywood discovered long ago, pornographers are well aware of the fact that "sex sells"—period. But you have to admit, the First Amendment decoy is a wickedly brilliant strategy, as it sidetracks the public from examining the *real issues* and makes it difficult for those who have insight into the pornographer's true motive to be understood as they speak out.

Anyone who challenges the pornographers is labeled "pro-censorship," or a "right wing religious fanatic," or is said to favor a "police state."

Isn't it interesting—and not a little disturbing—how easily "good can be twisted to appear evil" and "evil can be disguised as good?" With greed as their driving force, pornographers will stop at nothing to increase and protect their profits. They will use every trick in the book to attract and addict as many people as possible.

And anyone seriously addicted to anything will tell you that the most precious gift they have forfeited is their freedom. How can a group of individuals dedicated to the promotion of addiction for the sake of profits dare claim they are defenders of the constitution?

PORNOGRAPHERS REVEAL THEIR TRUE MOTIVES— INDEX WORDS ON THE INTERNET

If you want further evidence that pornographers only care about profits and couldn't care less about freedom and the First Amendment, consider how they intentionally expose the innocent to pornography on the Internet.

STEALTH INTERNET SITES

Thousands of pornography sites appear on the Internet specifically designed to take advantage of innocent mistakes in order to expose adults, teens and children to graphic sexual images:

- **Mirror Sites:** By simply altering the ending of a website address, pornographers are able to expose adults and children to their wares. For example, if someone searching for the official website for the White House types ***www.whitehouse.com*** instead of ***www.whitehouse.gov,*** he or she will be exposed to a hard-core porn site.
- **Spelling Errors:** Pornographers have intentionally given their porn sites addresses that match up to commonly misspelled Internet addresses. For instance, if an Internet user types in ***www.betscape.com*** rather than ***www.netscape.com,*** or ***www.-sharware.com*** instead of ***www.shareware.com,*** he will be confronted with live sex shows and other X-rated offerings.
- **Misuse of Brand Name:** An innocent search on *"Disney Cartoons"* will of course bring up Internet links to wholesome

cartoons—as well as a host of links to sites showing popular cartoon characters engaged in sex acts.

INTERNET PORNOGRAPHERS SEEK TO EXPOSE AND ADDICT THE INNOCENT AND THE YOUNG THROUGH "INDEX WORDS"

When someone is trying to find information on a particular subject on the Internet, he will often enter a word or phrase and request a search be done to find the sites that match up to those words.

As part of programming, websites contain a list of index words supposedly pertaining to the material contained on them. Internet search engines use these index words to provide surfers with a list of websites related to these index words. Many children's Internet sites include index words in their programming ("toys," "dollhouse," "girls," "pets," "Beanie Babies," etc.) Teen sites might include index words such as "NBA," "sports," "boys," "cars," etc. Searching the Internet using these words can take the Internet surfer to sites appropriate to children and teen sites, but also to porn sites.

You would expect that pornography websites would only include index words like "sex," "nudity," and other words too explicit to list here. The idea being that if someone really wants to view pornography, he can enter specific search words and the pornographic websites will pop up. Not so.

A few years ago a friend shared his dismay at having porn sites appear when he did a search on the word "basketball." As he investigated the internal programming code of one of the porn sites, he was shocked to discover that the site had included the word "basketball" in its index word list. This meant that any person typing in the word "basketball" would have any number of porn sites thrown into the mix of legitimate sites dealing with basketball. But what was even more disturbing to my friend was that the porn sites had also included in their index word list the names of popular video games and television programs oriented to young children and teenagers. Internet pornographers were clearly attempting to lure innocent children and unsuspecting teens to their sites! This clearly illustrated that Internet pornographers are not a strictly adult-to-adult business. Rather, they are "trolling" our youth to see how many they can snare in their addictive net, knowing that an addicted youth becomes a profitable adult buyer.

Some words on Internet porn index lists appear to be nothing more than gibberish until you realize that they are words that people often misspell or in which letters are easily transposed: IMB instead of IBM. Yes, pornographers have even studied what common words tend to be typed incorrectly when a person is working on a keyboard, and have purposely included those words in their index word lists.

Why would they spend the time and money to put these completely unrelated terms and nonsense words into their programming? In fact, when you first pull up a pornography website's massive index word list, you ask yourself, "Why on earth are all these words listed? They have nothing to do with pornography." Then it hits you! *Pornographers are predators who are baiting and stalking anyone and everyone.*

MOUSE-TRAPPING

If anyone is yet unconvinced of pornographers' true motives, then this should be the final self-incriminating evidence against them: Every day innocent adult and child viewers are exposed to Internet pornography by one or more of the dastardly techniques discussed above. But then when the viewer attempts to close the unwanted porn site, he is thwarted by a technique called "mouse-trapping," "auto-spawning" or "looping," which automatically begins opening additional sites on the surfer's computer screen. Many adults and children have described the shock of seeing one porn site after another bursting open on their screen faster than they can close them. Finally, the only way to halt the onslaught is to turn the computer's power switch off. But by that time what assortment of explicit images has the innocent viewer been exposed to?

A Special Note About E-Mail

Pornographers commonly engage in plucking e-mail addresses off the Internet. Then they may send out e-mail to 20 million addresses at once and "spoof" an innocent Internet user by showing the e-mail coming from a source such as "Christian Church." When a user opens her e-mail, she is instantly exposed to pornography. On one occasion a friend of mine received an e-mail message from "Karen," along with a note that read, "Haven't heard from you in a while." In that he has a sister named Karen, he opened the e-mail and was instantly blasted with pornographic language text inviting him to click on the link and gain instant access to Internet porn sites.

Make no mistake: Internet pornographers are ruthless and they will literally stop at nothing to make a profit and ensure the long-term continuation of that profit by hooking as many viewers as possible.

An Additional Note On the First Amendment

I believe it is a tremendous insult to our Founding Fathers to suggest that they intended to include pornography in their efforts to ensure freedom of expression to the citizens of this nation. Rather, the purpose of the First Amendment is to protect our *right to express ourselves freely*. Pornographers have distorted and twisted this noble intention to satisfy their own greed by exploiting the sexual appetites of men, women and teens.

Consider the fact that the First Amendment ***does not*** protect slander, false advertising, or perjury. It is a serious offense to yell "Fire!" in a theater or even to joke about having planted a bomb in an airport. Why, then, do pornographers argue that the First Amendment should protect something so obviously harmful, degrading and destructive to our society as hard-core and child pornography?

It is interesting to note that Internet pornographers don't even *try* to disguise what it is they are selling. On their own websites they use phrases like, "The best filth on the web" or "The raunchiest site on the Internet," two of the more tame references used.

Pornographers arrogantly flaunt the fact that their material is utter trash; their defiance is legendary. They constantly make reference to and encourage the men and teens who view their material to masturbate. In addition, they refer to and even graphically display masturbation in their Internet advertisements.

Is this what our Founding Fathers fought so hard to protect?

Key Points

A reference tool for
spouses, parents, clergy,
counselors and others

- In the minds of Internet pornographers, the Internet is not about the First Amendment, it's about creating an addiction that leads to greater profits.
- Pornographers use various sinister and disguised techniques to expose and entrap the innocent, the underage, the unsuspecting and the curious. This is why adults must be vigilant in protecting themselves and their children when using the Internet.

5

The Internet—A Law Unto Itself

An Internet Tidal Wave

The introduction and subsequent massive growth of the Internet has generated a serious problem with regard to the distribution of illegal pornography. Laws that do exist, designed to prevent pornographers from distributing illegal materials "over the counter," do not apply to the Internet. Through the Internet, obscenity, material harmful to minors, and indecent material—all under the heading of "illegal pornography"—can easily and instantly be distributed by pornographers from anywhere around the world to anyone with a computer. There currently are no statutes in the U.S. regarding the display of any and all forms of illegal pornography on the Internet, with the exception of child pornography.

And even with child pornography, there is so much of it on the Internet that law enforcement can only keep tabs on a fraction of the violators.[1] Unfortunately, when an arrest is made for child pornography violations, there is no guarantee that the charges will hold up in court.

Recently a high-profile business executive was arrested and charged for the possession of child pornography and soliciting sex with a 13-year-old over the Internet. It appears, though, that the courts will dismiss the child porn possession charges due to a technicality in the law.[2]

Even though laws do exist against children being displayed in pornography, no laws are on the books to protect children from being exposed to Internet pornography. Amazingly, anyone can freely and deliberately show explicit, degrading and violent pornographic images to children via the Internet without fear of legal recourse!

INTERNET PORNOGRAPHERS CAN LEGALLY PROVIDE PORNOGRAPHY TO CHILDREN

If a pornographer sells his wares to a child over the counter, he or she can be prosecuted and punished under the law. But that same pornographer can provide the very same pornographic images to a child on the Internet using "teaser photos" and face no legal consequences of any kind.

What sort of images can be displayed on the computers of children, teens and adults? The simple answer is, "Anything goes!"

The Internet was first developed as a fast and inexpensive way for scientists and other researchers at one location to communicate via the computer with colleagues at another location. No one could accurately predict what far-reaching effects this technology would have.

For years it was assumed that the Internet was merely a toy for computer whizzes and would never really catch on with the general public. No one really paid much attention to it. But, as the features and benefits of the Internet grew, it became very clear that it had enormous potential and that its use and appeal were not limited to a small group of computer technicians.

Almost over night use of the Internet exploded. A wide range of organizations "logged on." Powerful entrepreneurs and prestigious corporations began to recognize the Internet's tremendous value as a source of new sales and revenue. Simply put, everyone was taken by surprise. Suddenly, there it was—Cyberspace. No controls, no laws, no guidelines. All brand new! And still the Internet is a law unto itself in essence—it has no laws.

ATTEMPTING TO REGULATE THE INTERNET

Once people realized the true power of the Internet, including the ability of pornographers to use it without rules or restrictions, a movement began to try and bring law and order to the Internet environment.

On February 8, 1996 the Communications Decency Act (CDA) was signed into law. The provisions of the Act were designed to punish those who distributed pornographic materials to minors over the Internet. Violators would face fines and imprisonment.

Immediately there arose an uproar from pornographers and other groups: "This is a violation of the First Amendment!" On June 12, 1996 a three-judge panel in Philadelphia federal district court agreed and declared the CDA unconstitutional.[3]

On June 26, 1997 the Supreme Court of the United States subsequently affirmed the lower court's ruling that the CDA was unconstitutional.[4]

It's interesting to note that *Penthouse* magazine posted the following statement on its Internet site shortly after the Court struck down the CDA legislation intended to protect children on the Internet: *The Supreme Court has cleared the way for Penthouse to build the Ultimate Empire of Sex on the Internet. . . . You will see a new, hotter, harder Penthouse.*[5]

In striking down the CDA, the Supreme Court ruled that the language in the Act was "too broad." So, taking into account the Court's opinion, a few members of the Senate and Congress tailored a new act with a much "narrower" approach. Called the "Child Online Protection Act" or COPA, it was passed in October of 1998 as part of the Omnibus Spending Bill.[6]

COPA contains major revisions that attempt to comply with the U.S. Supreme Court's ruling regarding CDA. These revisions include:

- Specifically exempting material with serious literary, artistic, political or scientific merit;
- Addressing only commercial pornographers, not amateur postings;
- Addressing only the World Wide Web, not News groups, e-mail or chat rooms; and

- Defining minors as those 16 or under.

This Act nearly died on a number of occasions, but a flood of calls from citizens prompted Congress to pass it. However, the American Civil Liberties Union (ACLU) and the Electronic Frontier Foundation, crying "censorship," immediately filed a lawsuit against the measure. In February of 1999, U.S. District Judge Lowell Reed imposed an injunction against the law, thus preventing its enactment and tying it up in the infamous appeals process.[7]

On June 23, 2000, CNET News reported the following: *In a unanimous decision yesterday, a three-judge panel of the 3rd U.S. Circuit Court of Appeals reluctantly upheld an earlier ruling by a lower court judge, who found that the Child Online Protection Act (COPA) violated the First Amendment right to free speech. Appeals court Judge Leonard Garth stated: "Sometimes we must make decisions that we do not like. We make them because they are right, right in the sense that the law and the Constitution, as we see them, compel the result."*

Once again, pornography on the Internet is without rules, regulations or restrictions and the pornographers, together with those who support their cause, will do everything in their power to keep it that way. It should be clear by now that you cannot rely on laws to protect you and your family when it comes to pornography on the Internet. Once you enter the unbridled prairie of cyberspace, be prepared to ride a wild pony. Mavericks are the rule. "Anything goes."

DON'T GIVE UP—YOU CAN MAKE A DIFFERENCE

Observing the unconscionable actions of the ACLU, the courts, pornographers and others in relation to the protection of children and families, it's easy to throw your hands in the air and simply give up. Take courage—you're not alone in this fight. There are a number of national organizations providing tremendous support and resources for the protection of children and families from the devastation of pornography. I urge you to contact these organizations and obtain their information and materials. They will show you, step-by-step, how to make a powerful difference in your own family and community.

National Coalition for the Protection of Children & Families
800 Compton Road, Suite 9224
Cincinnati, OH 45231-9964
513-521-6337
www.nationalcoalition.org
(Internet safety, faith outreach, victim assistance, education & awareness, Model Cities of America)

American Family Association
P.O. Drawer 2440
Tupelo, Mississippi 38803
601-844-5128
www.afa.net
(Helpful Resources: What one person can do . . . Fight Back Book, etc.)

Enough is Enough
P.O. Box 30117
Santa Ana, CA 92705
703-278-8343
www.enough.org
(A variety of wonderful resources, pamphlets and newsletter)

Morality In Media
475 Riverside Drive, Suite 239
New York, NY 10115
212-870-3222
www.moralityinmedia.org
(Excellent newsletter and resources)

Washington Watch
(Family Research Council)
801 G Street NW
Washington D.C., 20001
202-393-2100
www.frc.org
(Information on current national issues)

Focus on the Family
Colorado Springs, CO 80995
800-232-6459
www.fotf.org
(Citizen Magazine and newsletter)

Key Points

A reference tool for
spouses, parents, clergy,
counselors and others

- We cannot count on the "law" to protect our children while on the Internet. Pornographic materials that cannot legally be distributed to children over the counter are made available to them on the Internet without any legal constraints.
- Numerous attempts to pass legislation to protect children from pornography on the Internet have been defeated by the ACLU and the courts.
- Just because proposed laws have been defeated in the past, doesn't mean you should give up. Contact the organizations listed in this chapter and learn how you can protect children and families in your community.

6

Pornography Is <u>Not</u> Protected By the First Amendment

What Is Pornography? You May Be Surprised

An intense debate rages on in America about what is and what is not "pornographic," and whether pornography is really all that harmful. One side claims that pornography is mainly a form of entertainment, potentially educational, at times sexually arousing, but for the most part, harmless. Or they say that at the very least there is no conclusive scientific evidence that pornography in and of itself causes harm.

The other side insists that porn addiction exacts serious consequences and cites examples of rapists, sex-murderers, molesters and others who use the excuse that "pornography made me do it." Opposing sides each espouse their unique perception of the pornography issue. But what is the "reality" of the issue or the "truth"?

The word *pornography* itself comes from the Greek words "porno" and "graphia," which mean literally *"depictions of the activities of whores."* In today's language, pornography is generally defined as: "Writings, photographs, movies, etc., intended to arouse sexual excitement."[1]

THE SUPREME COURT ALLOWS THE COMMUNITY TO DECIDE WHAT IS "OBSCENE"

In the *Deseret News, Salt Lake City, Utah, April 30, 2001*, an editorial by John L. Harmer titled *Amendment Doesn't Protect Porn* was published. The editorial read as follows:

The Deseret News article of April 21, titled "Even pornography under protection," was filled with misstatements regarding the status of pornography under the U.S. Constitution. Contrary to the assertions in your report of the meeting at Utah State University, pornography is not now nor has it ever been protected by the First Amendment to the Constitution. The U.S. Supreme Court has consistently held that many forms of speech, including pornography, are outside the protection of the First Amendment and are quite lawfully subject to suppression or censorship under the First Amendment. The statement attributed to the representative of the American Civil Liberties Union (as is typical of that organization's total disregard for fact) that "the only instances in which pornography would not be permissible under the First Amendment would be if it could be scientifically and factually proven to cause harm or if it constituted an actual or imminent harm to others—a clear and present danger" is a ludicrous fabrication of fantasy that has never appeared in any Supreme Court decision regarding pornography.

The law in the United States today with regard to the prosecution of pornography was established by the U.S. Supreme Court in its landmark case of Miller v. California (413 U.S. 15)(1973) in which the Court reaffirmed that pornography is never protected by the First Amendment, and in which the Court then addressed the cardinal issue that apparently was never mentioned in the forum reported in your paper. That issue is not whether or not pornography is protected by the First Amendment but what forms of communication are in fact pornographic or obscene.

In that decision the court said: "To equate the free and robust exchange of ideas and political debate with commercial exploitation of obscene materials demeans the grand conception of the First Amendment and its high purposes in the historic struggle for freedom. The protection given speech and press was fashioned to assure unfettered interchange of ideas for bringing about of political and social changes desired by people. But the public portrayal of hard core sexual conduct for its own sake and for ensuing commercial gain is a different matter." The court then went on to establish a three-part criterion regarding what constitutes pornography. That three-part criterion is the reason pornography is so rampant in our society today. The Supreme Court held that for a public prosecutor to establish that an item was obscene or pornographic, the prosecutor must prove that "the average person, applying contemporary community standards, would find that the work, taken as a whole, appeals to the prurient interest" and that "the work depicts or describes in a patently offensive way, sexual conduct."

The reason pornography has now become so rampant in our society is because a prosecutor cannot prove that according to "contemporary community standards" the work or item involved is "patently offensive." In other words, our society has become so desensitized to obscenity and perversion that it has become nearly impossible to meet the Supreme Court's criteria that before an item can be suppressed or censored as pornography it must be proven to be "offensive to contemporary community standards."

Pornography exists in our society because we as a civilization have become so accustomed to the presentation of obscenity throughout the mass media that even the most graphic and vulgar depictions of sexual perversion no longer offend us.

To assert that the First Amendment was ever intended to protect or allow such obscene and despicable materials as are now commonly presented through our mass media and the Internet is not only an outrageous misrepresentation of the law and fact, but it is also an insulting aspersion upon the intent and the values of those who drafted the First Amendment to our Constitution.

John L. Harmer of Bountiful is a member of the bar of the Supreme Court of the United States and author of several books and articles on pornography.

In addition to the general definition of pornography, the U.S. Supreme Court has originated the legal term "Obscenity." For something to be found "obscene," and therefore not protected by the First Amendment, a judge or jury representing a cross-section of the community must determine that the material:

1. Taken as a whole, appeals to a prurient (sick, morbid, shameful or lustful) interest in sex;
2. Depicts sexual conduct in a patently offensive manner (i.e., goes beyond contemporary community standards with regard to depictions of sexual content or activity); and
3. Taken as a whole, lacks serious literary, artistic, political, and scientific value.[2]

This appears to be a clear enough definition of what *should* be considered pornographic or obscene. Why then is there so much controversy?

You will note that in the Supreme Court's definition they instruct that the three standards above should be applied and interpreted by a "cross section" of our society. I submit that this is the source of the dispute. There is a wide range of opinions in society today as to what should be considered obscene. As is discussed in a later chapter, the "dumbing down" or desensitizing of America through the media over the last thirty-plus years has fueled this controversy.

SUPERIOR COURT JUDGE RULES THAT HARD-CORE PORN IS "NOT" OBSCENITY

In May of 1989 a Los Angeles Superior Court judge dismissed complaints against four pornographic films because "he could not conclude that the films were patently offensive in an area as diverse as Los Angeles" (*Los Angeles Times,* Thursday, May 4,1989). The four films included graphic depictions of group sex, oral sex, beatings, sadism, gang rape, and of a woman committing suicide after she had been sexually attacked. "I cannot say beyond a reasonable doubt that community standards were violated," the judge declared.[3]

In our parents' and grandparents' day, the vast majority of people held a clear view of what was pornographic and obscene and what could be considered "meritorious art" or had "serious literary, political or scientific value." With so much controversy today, how can we judge what is and what is not appropriate? Let me offer one approach:

Little children have not yet been "dumbed down" or "desensitized." As the father of six, I have always been amazed at how perceptive children are. Generally they are far more intelligent and discerning than we give them credit. This is especially true in the years before they are bombarded with the violent and sexually oriented images and expressions that saturate the media.

If you want to judge whether or not something is pornographic, vile, vulgar or obscene, *try to imagine the way a child might react to the material.* You will discover as you use this gauge that the so-called "gray areas" quickly disappear.

I am certainly not suggesting that this simple test is the answer to the entire controversy or that we should start using a panel of children as our "pornography review board." I am merely trying to make the point that as adults we are exposed to so much obscenity in all its subtle and various forms, that we've become somewhat callous and conditioned to its effects.

So perhaps we need to take a step back and look at the pornography issue with a fresh perspective—through the eyes of a child.

Key Points

A reference tool for spouses, parents, clergy, counselors and others

- Internet pornography is **not** protected by the First Amendment.
- What is deemed to be "obscene" or "pornographic" is determined by a local "community standard." Thus the excuse "there's nothing we can do about it" is inaccurate when a moral community joins together to keep pornography out.
- As adults we must realize that we can become desensitized, numb and "dumbed down" as a result the glut of sexual images that surround us on TV, in movie theaters and in magazines. We must reassess our attitudes and perceptions about what is and what is not appropriate and uplifting. Otherwise, we and our families become susceptible to the allure of Internet pornography.

7

Pornography and Cybersex Chat Are Drugs As Real As Cocaine

Cigarettes Aren't Addictive and They Don't Cause Cancer—At Least According To the Tobacco Companies

Up until a few years ago, the tobacco companies insisted that cigarettes were not addictive and didn't cause cancer. Finally after more than 40 years of investigative research, testing and tracking, the evidence is so completely overwhelming that the tobacco companies could no longer credibly deny it.

Of course, most reasonably intelligent people have recognized the dangers of smoking for decades. The signs and evidence were decisive. We didn't need a panel of scientists and doctors to verify the facts we saw all around us. And now that the tobacco companies have finally admitted (or at least stopped denying) that their product is a silent killer, how does that help those already afflicted with lung cancer or emphysema? It doesn't. For them it's too late. But hopefully future generations won't be so foolish.

Do you see any correlations between the tobacco and the pornography industries? What do pornographers and those who support them say? "Internet pornography is just a harmless hobby." "It's a harmless way to blow off sexual tension." "What's wrong with a woman having an affair over the Internet?" "Women should be able to fantasize with porn just like men do." "Porn doesn't hurt anyone; if you don't like it, then don't look at it."

But just as with cigarette smoking, the signs and evidence are all around us. Rape, incest, child sexual abuse, teen pregnancy, venereal disease, crime rates, glazed-over fathers and husbands, aloof wives and mothers. And like second-hand smoke, ingesting pornography doesn't harm just the viewer, it damages all those within the viewer's sphere of influence.

There are now hundreds of credible medical, psychological and neurological studies which clearly show that pornography is harmful and dangerous to all involved, directly and indirectly. There is no need to wait for additional research or more millions of victims—the results are in.

THE CHEMICAL ADDICTION TO PORN

In her book *Soft Porn Plays Hardball*, Dr. Judith Reisman underscores the forceful writings of David Mura:

The Japanese-American poet David Mura writes in his award-winning essay A Male Grief: Notes on Pornography and Addiction (1987), that "flesh" can provide the same stimulating and addicting effects as a chemical drug.

Scientists are beginning to understand Mura's poetic references to the relationship between seeing pornography ("flesh") and the brain's release of its own intoxicating chemicals ("drugs").

"Start with the premise that a person—generally a male—may be addicted to pornography," Mura writes. "This addiction may be part of a larger addiction to any number of other sexual highs."

"Some of these include adultery, promiscuity, visits to prostitutes, homosexual or bisexual activities, anonymous sex, exhibitionism, voyeurism, and so on."

Says Mura, "At the essence of pornography is the image of flesh used as a drug, a way of numbing psychic pain. But this drug only lasts as long as the man stares at the image."

"Both the highs and the lows of the pornography fantasy affect the minds and imaginations of adult and adolescent consumers." According to Mura, winner of the Milkweed Creative Non-Fiction Award, " . . . the pornographic fantasy first attracts, then like tranquilizers and stimulants, the fantasy becomes an addiction."

"Those who stand back from the world of pornography cannot experience this falling, this rush. . . . But for the addict the rush is more than an attraction. He is helpless before it. Completely out of control."

"However, as is the case with all drugs, the promised happiness and relief lasts only momentarily:"

"[H]e has sex with his wife while fantasizing of another . . . and a rush of excitement does occur. But afterwards the unhappiness returns, the drug has worn off. And the addict becomes angry. . . ."

"The 'eye' of the fantasy," writes Mura, "leads to darkness, despair, and desperation. To get the pornographic high, one must also feel other emotions such as shame, fear, and anxiety. Fun sex it is not."[1]

PORNOGRAPHY IS A DRUG AND PORN PRODUCERS ARE DRUG DEALERS

As will be detailed in future chapters, the structure of the male brain predisposes virtually all men and teenage boys to some level of porn attraction and/or addiction. To a lesser degree, women also are at risk. Many today agree that the greater danger for women and teenage girls is cybersex through Internet chat rooms.

For some, as we have discussed, pornography and cybersex are simply part of the process of becoming sexually aroused and excited to the peak experience of orgasm. Pornography and cybersex are a means to satisfy a sexual urge. Many pro-pornography activists at this point would cry out and say, *"Exactly right! That's what we've been saying all along. Porn and cybersex are harmless outlets for men, women and teens to satisfy their normal, healthy urges."*

If only it were that simple. To the contrary, the hard facts prove otherwise. With rare exception, once a person sets off down the path of regular pornography use and/or cybersex chat, it becomes much more than a "harmless outlet for normal, healthy urges." For millions of men, women and teenagers, sexual stimulation is but a piece of the puzzle. Pornography and cybersex become a habit-forming drug used as an escape—escape from the pressures of life, from stress and pain, from fear, loneliness, emptiness, regret, rejection, childhood abuse and a host of other human emotions and memories. Pornography and cybersex temporarily mask the pain. They fill the "void," the "hole in the soul," and provide momentary "self-medication."

Viewing pornography and engaging in sexual chat are ways to "feel good" by passing time in an all-consuming activity that blocks out the trying realities of life, the difficulties at hand.

But for pornography and cybersex addicts, exacting, time-consuming rituals leading up to the "main event" become a major part of the process. Thus a man may invent elaborate excuses for his wife as to why he is spending so many late nights at the office. He may put stacks of files in his briefcase and bring them home, going on and on about how "swamped" he is. The longer and more elaborate the ritual, the more time he can spend away from the pressing realities of his life.

A woman may neglect her home and family because she is obsessed with Internet chat rooms. She, too, will employ a litany of excuses and go to great lengths to cover up her addiction.

Whether the motive for consuming pornography and cybersex is sexual appetite, escape/self-medication, or a combination of the two, engaging in these addictions causes the brain and body to "endogenously" produce and release chemical drugs into its own system, just as if they had been injected with a hypodermic needle. These chemicals include: epinephrine (an adrenal gland hormone that "locks-in" memories of experiences occurring at times of high arousal), adrenaline, adrenocorticotropic hormone (ACTH), noradrenaline, norepinephrine and testosterone, among others. This at-the-push-of-a-button drug injection is dragging millions of troubled victims along in its destructive wake.[2]

Thus, persistent accessing of porn and cybersex not only provide the addict with sexual arousal, but offers a way to "self-medicate" in order to escape the realities of life and, if only temporarily, "make the pain go away."[3]

THE FOUR STAGES OF PORNOGRAPHY ADDICTION

In order to understand pornography addiction and the severe consequences it yields in the lives of addicts and the people around them, first you must understand the stages of addiction. Over the course of many years as a clinical psychologist, Dr. Victor Cline, one of America's leading authorities on pornography addiction, has treated some 300 sex addicts, sex offenders, and other sufferers of sexual illness. With very few exceptions, Dr. Cline says pornography was a contributor or facilitator in the acquisition of the sexual deviation or addiction.

In the myriad cases where pornography was a contributor or facilitator, Dr. Cline found a four-stage process common to nearly all his clients, especially in their early involvement with pornography. His authoritative work *Pornography's Effects on Adults & Children*[4] outlines these four stages:

1. **Addiction:** The first change that took place was an *addiction effect*; the porn-consumers got hooked. Once involved in pornographic

materials, they kept coming back for more and still more.[5] The material seemed to provide a powerful sexual stimulant or aphrodisiac effect, followed by sexual release, most often through masturbation. The pornography provided an exciting and powerful imagery which they frequently recalled to mind and elaborated on in their fantasies.[6] (As we will soon discuss, cellular-memory groups in the brain where porn images are stored can be activated and accessed at any time merely through imagination.)

Dr. Cline found that, once addicted, men, teenage boys, and in limited cases, women, "could not throw off their dependencies on the pornography by themselves, despite many negative consequences such as divorce, loss of family, and problems with the law."[7]

A most intriguing discovery was that his most intelligent male patients appeared to be the most vulnerable. "Perhaps [this is] because they had a greater capacity to fantasize," he theorizes, "which heightened the intensity of the experience and made them more susceptible to being conditioned into an addiction."[8] (This dispels the misconception that only the homeless, poor or uneducated are addicted to pornography.)

Sgt. Bob Navarro, a longtime investigator of the porn industry with the Los Angeles Police Department, has commented:

Believe it or not, the higher their education, the more prone these people are to becoming addicted to this material, and, of course, the more money they have to spend on it. . . . Many people have testified to their extreme addiction to the material in terms of having their whole lives consumed by it; sitting for hours masturbating to adult material and needing progressively stronger, harder material to give them a bigger kick. Like an alcoholic or a drug addict, they are looking for that big kick and they need more just to keep them at the level of feeling 'OK.'[9]

2. **Escalation:** "The second phase was an escalation effect," writes Dr. Cline. "With the passage of time, the porn addict required rougher, more explicit, more deviant, and 'kinky' kinds of sexual material to get their 'highs' and 'sexual turn-ons.' It was reminiscent of individuals afflicted with drug addictions. Over time there is nearly always an increasing need for more of the stimulant to get the same initial effect."[10] (The human brain and body are always seeking for a "higher peak experience"—and we decide what that "peak experience" is and how to achieve it.)

   "If their wives or girlfriends were involved with them, they eventually pushed their partners into doing increasingly bizarre and deviant sexual activities." (Men who consistently view porn often try to "copycat" what they have seen.) "In many cases, this resulted in a rupture in the relationship when the woman refused to go further—often leading to much conflict, separation or divorce."[11]

   "Being married or being in a relationship with a willing sexual partner did not solve their problem. Their addiction and escalation were mainly due to the powerful sexual imagery in their minds, implanted there by exposure to pornography. They often preferred this sexual imagery, accompanied by masturbation, to sexual intercourse itself. This nearly always diminished their capacity to love and express affection to their partner in their intimate relations."[12]

   "The fantasy was all powerful, much to the chagrin and disappointment of their partner. Their sex drive had been diverted to a degree away from their spouse. And the spouse could easily sense this, and often felt very lonely and rejected. I have a number of couple-clients where the wife tearfully reported that her husband preferred to masturbate to pornography than to make love to her."[13]

   In a similar manner, more and more women caught up in cybersex chat rooms find intimate interaction with their husband boring when compared with their erotic, stimulating online conversations. Via the Internet, they may feel they are receiving the intense sexual, emotional and chemical stimulation that their mind/body craves in its addicted state.

3. **Desensitization:** "The third phase that happened was desensitization," Dr. Cline continues. "Material which was originally perceived as shocking, taboo-breaking, illegal, repulsive or immoral, though still sexually arousing, in time came to be seen as acceptable and commonplace. The sexual activity depicted in the pornography (no matter how antisocial or deviant) became legitimized. There was increasingly a sense that 'everybody does it' and this gave them permission to also do it, even though the activity was possibly illegal and contrary to their previous moral beliefs and personal standards."[14]

   Mild Dr. Jekyll gradually transformed into the brutal Mr. Hyde through a process of desensitization.

4. **Acting Out Sexually: "**The fourth phase that occurred was an increasing tendency to act out sexually the behaviors viewed in the pornography that the porn-consumers had been repeatedly exposed to, including compulsive promiscuity, exhibitionism, group sex, voyeurism, frequenting massage parlors, having sex with minor children, rape, and inflicting pain on themselves or a partner during sex.

   This behavior frequently grew into a sexual addiction which they found themselves locked into and unable to change or reverse—no matter the negative consequences in their life."[15]

Key Points

A reference tool for
spouses, parents, clergy,
counselors and others

- Pornography addiction is a **drug addiction**. In order to escape from the pain, pressures and stress of life, some self-medicate with alcohol, drugs, food, cigarettes and other substances, and some turn to the medication of pornography and its accompanying sexual addictions.
- For a more detailed overview of pornography/sex addiction and treatment see **Chapters 30-36**.

ATTENTION!

THE FOLLOWING CHAPTERS

CONTAIN MATERIAL

THAT INTERNET PORNOGRAPHERS HOPE

YOU WON'T READ!

THE FOLLOWING CHAPTERS CONTAIN DETAILED
INSTRUCTION AS TO HOW THE BRAIN
AND BODY LEARN ADDICTION!

THEY WILL EXAMINE HOW WHAT WE LOOK
AT AND LISTEN TO LITERALLY ALTER
THE PHYSICAL AND CHEMICAL
STRUCTURE OF THE BRAIN AND BODY!

8

How Internet Pornographers Use Mind/Body Science To Attract and Addict Their Customers

To more fully understand the effects of pornography on men, women, teens and children, one must first understand how the human brain and body process and store information.

Those who promote or defend pornography frequently make statements like these:

- "Porn is a harmless outlet for men, women and teens to let off the steam of natural impulses."
- "What people view in the privacy of their own homes or offices doesn't hurt anyone and is none of our business."
- "Boys will be boys."
- "Pornography is a choice. If you don't like it, then don't buy it."

And the list goes on. Those who produce Internet pornography and those who indulge themselves in it would have us believe that it's a harmless pastime that the "prudes," "religious wackos," and "anti-constitution proponents" are blowing all out of proportion.

But pornography claims its victims without regard to age, gender, race or religion. No one is immune; all are at risk. In its insidious wake lie the tractable innocent and the eager participant, side by side. With the unlimited distribution potential and capability of the Internet, pornography's casualty list grows longer with each passing day.

Now, as author of this book, if I simply cited these facts, made these accusations and left it at that, this book would be grossly incomplete and you, the reader, then could simply view the words I have written as just another opinion. But what I am about to share with you has nothing to do with my opinions, rather, with hard fact. Namely, the fact that pornographers don't want you to comprehend exactly how the mind and body work together to create an addiction.

The following is a compilation of hundreds of hours of research by recognized, credible organizations and scientists on the damaging effects pornographic images can have on the human brain and body.

HOW YOUR BRAIN AND BODY RECEIVE, PROCESS AND STORE INFORMATION

An infant sees shapes, recognizes images and hears sounds long before it can speak words. Just as a video camera records and stores sounds and images, our ears and eyes take in millions of bits of data, which then are stored in our memories. Neurologists report that we store pictures and sounds faster and with more permanence than words stored in the pages of a book.[1] Our minds literally fasten onto images and don't let go.

The more provocative, dazzling, threatening, horrifying or stimulating an image is, the more likely it will be stored in the brain and body as *reality*.[2] Take for instance how you react when in a theater, watching a movie in 3–D. Even though your logic tells you it is only a movie, you still instinctively flinch when a ball of fire hurls toward you from the screen. In other words, your brain is "hard-wired" to believe what your eyes see and your ears hear. In 3/10ths of a second your brain has convinced you that what you are experiencing is real and your body has recoiled in response. Thus, the many images that we allow our eyes (video camera lenses) to view and the range of sounds we allow our ears (audio recorders) to hear, are tucked away in our brains as "realities from the outside world."

Because of the nature of pornography and our natural neuro-physiological (brain and body) response to it, it too is stored in our brain/body as another of the many *realities from the outside world.*[3]

WHAT WE SEE AND HEAR CHANGE US—LITERALLY!

An image or sound that is perceived, recorded, and then stored in memory, chemically and structurally alters the human brain and nervous system. In fact, Neuroscientist, Dr. Gary Lynch of the University of California at Irvine, in discussing the brain's processing of images and sounds, states:

What we are saying here is that an event which lasts half a second, within five to ten minutes has produced a structural change that is in some ways as profound as the structural change one sees in [brain] damage.[4]

Commenting further on how a single word or image can immediately alter the brain structure, Dr. Lynch writes;

. . . In a matter of seconds, taking an incredibly modest signal, a word, which is in your head as an electrical signal for no more than a few seconds, can leave a trace that will last for years.[5]

What an awesome storage capacity our brains possess! Is it any wonder, then, that pornography wields such a powerfully destructive force? Imagine the deep trench-like scars left on our brains after hours or even a few minutes of viewing pornographic images on the Internet.

THE "AIR TRAFFIC CONTROLLER" OF THE HUMAN BRAIN

Many of our bodily functions take place automatically. You don't have to remember to breathe or will your heart to beat; you needn't tell your skin to sweat when you're hot. In like manner, messages pass back and forth between your brain stem and your heart, chest muscles and other organs, keeping your body functioning "automatically." These messages, however, only reach the base of the brain or the brain stem, and do not pass to the higher regions of the brain where you become consciously aware of them.

In the center of the brain is a region of densely-packed nerve cells known as the *reticular formation*. This comprises the "air traffic controller" of the brain. Every second, millions of messages fly into the brain along "nerve strings" leading from the eyes, ears, nose, mouth, and other sensory body parts.

The *reticular formation*, acting out its role as an air traffic controller, decides which of these messages to let through to the brain. Certain images, ideas and feelings it allows to land and become part of our being; others it keeps in "holding patterns," leaving the sensory images circling outside our conscious reality. In this way we are only aware of a few things at any one time, guarding against "sensory overload." As one scientist explains, "With so much of interest happening around us, we can't afford to notice the way our socks feel on our feet."[6]

HOW DOES THE RETICULAR FORMATION DECIDE WHICH MESSAGES TO LET THROUGH?

Neurologists largely agree that the brain can only process a few of the roughly 100 million messages it receives each second. How, then, does our "air traffic controller" decide which messages to admit into the brain?

Pioneering neuropsychologist A.R. Luria reports that the brain obeys a "law of strength." **The more interesting, exciting, threatening, horrifying, arousing or in some other way stimulating an image is, the**

more quickly it will be let through by the reticular formation and stored in the brain, and the more "storage space" it will be allotted.[7]

And remember, it is not only the image itself that is being let through and stored. ***Every emotion and belief associated with the image is also stored!*** And so to carry Luria's law of strength to its conclusion, a "strong outside stimulus evokes a strong and diverse response in the brain and body."[8]

For example, the "never-to-be-forgotten" image of a bizarre or threatening person, a Nazi Swastika, an American flag . . . each stands for and can evoke a wide range of memories, feelings and even physiological responses in the brain and body. And as you will see, Internet pornography can evoke one of the most powerful neurological and physiological responses known to humankind.

WHAT HAPPENS WHEN THE RETICULAR FORMATION LETS A MESSAGE THROUGH?

This "message assessment" process is going on many times each and every second. The message itself is sent in the form of tiny bursts of electricity from some part of the body along the nerves (like electric wires) through the spinal cord to the Reticular Formation. And according to Dr. Candace Pert in her book *Molecules of Emotion*, in addition to the body's electrical message system, there is also an extensive and even more vast *chemical* message system.[9]

As our air traffic controller, the reticular formation acts as a filter to allow only certain chosen tiny bursts of electricity or chemical messages to pass through to the brain. And where is this message stored in the brain? Where it's most comfortable, of course. It quickly searches for the *Cellular-Memory-Group* that houses messages or stimuli that are most similar to itself. Each *Cellular-Memory-Group*, like a library catalogue system, contains messages, information, images, emotions, etc.,that are all related or "like-kind."

(**Author's Note:** There are scores of theories surrounding exactly how it is that the human brain and nervous system receive, process and store visual, auditory and tactile information from the outside world. In all my reading and research of these theories, I have discovered that no one scientist claims to have all the answers. In fact they all agree that there are countless things about the human brain and nervous system that we simply don't understand.)

With this in mind, I was faced with a difficult challenge: Which theories and bodies of knowledge do I use to explain what pornography does once it enters the brain and body? In the end, I chose to combine the study and conclusions of many of the world's leading scientists, to allow for what I feel is a more cohesive, comprehensive approach.

The following is in no way intended to be a complete treatise, but rather a brief and practical application of what science and medicine have discovered about the human brain and nervous system, and pornography's affect on them.

In her book *Mind & Brain—Principles of Neuropsychology,* Dr. Alberta Gilinsky discusses how the human brain and body receive and process information from the outside world.[10] Candace Pert in her profound book *Molecules of Emotion* also describes this process in great detail. I want to thank Dr. Page Bailey and his revolutionary work known as *Educotherapy*. Dr. Bailey introduced me to a fascinating and exhilarating universe of mind/body science that was the catalyst and scientific foundation for the creation of this book.[11] I would also like to give special recognition to the remarkable and courageous research and writings of Dr. Judith Reisman and her works *"Soft Porn" Plays Hardball* and *Sexually Explicit Media: Changes In the Structure of the Human Brain & American Law & Public Policy.* Much of the material that follows would not have been possible without the tremendous efforts and dedication of these esteemed and dedicated professionals, as well as those of other leading scientists.

IMAGES, FACTS, EXPERIENCES AND FEELINGS ARE ALL STORED IN THE CELLS OF OUR BRAINS AND BODIES

Receiving and processing information begins from the very moment you enter this world; indeed, it takes place in your mother's womb. The process begins with attention—you notice something. Pavlov called this natural response the "orientation reflex," the "what-is-it?" reaction to stimulus from the outside world.

Let's review the steps which take place after you "notice something":

Step #1

As a newborn, your body is made up of trillions of cells. Certain of these cells, according to Dr. Gilinsky, have the capacity to receive and store information. She refers to these cells as *cognons*, meaning *neurons that are cognitive or intelligent.*[12]

Dr. Candace Pert, in *Molecules of Emotion*, indicates that there are cells throughout your entire brain and body with the capacity to store information and memories.[13] Rather than attempt to describe each and every type of cell, and every theory regarding the process by which information is stored in these cells, I have chosen to refer to the mind/body's information storage mechanism as ***cellular-memories***, or memories stored in our cells.

When you see, hear, smell, taste or feel something for the very first time, that critical, fresh information is stored in your cells, which act like little video cameras, anxiously waiting to record images, sounds, feelings and perceptions. This new bit of information is stored away as a *cellular-memory*. (Keep in mind that the cells in your brain and body are far from being "blank video tapes" at birth. Your cells already contain information placed there through genetic coding.)

Note: Many people think of "memories" as only being stored in the brain. Actually, memories seep into every part of your brain and body! In her remarkable book *Molecules of Emotion*, Candace Pert states, *"It's true, we do store some memory in the brain, but by far, the deeper, older messages are stored in the body . . ."*[14]

Again, remember that for simplicity's sake I am using the term *cellular-memories* to describe the mind/body's information storage mechanism. The science of receiving, processing and storing information in the human brain and body is obviously very complex. If you would like an in-depth and marvelous overview of this process, I highly recommend that you read Dr. Pert's book *Molecules of Emotion*.

Step #2

According to Dr. Gilinsky, when a cell receives a certain type of information for the first time, it immediately clones itself into a group of cells, all storing the same information. The more exciting, frightening, traumatic or arousing the information, the larger this cellular-memory group will be and the easier it will be to access this stored information in the future.[15]

If the information received from the outside world is more on the neutral side, void of feeling or less interesting to the receiver, then the cellular-memory group will remain small and the information forgotten rather quickly. This is why it is often difficult for people to remember phone numbers, bits of trivia, odd facts and figures: they have little meaning or emotion attached to them.[16] Teenage boys may be able to recite by memory statistical numbers regarding their favorite athlete's achievements but for the life of them be unable to recall the year the Declaration of Independence was signed.

Step #3

On the other hand, if the image, sound or feeling received has a great deal of meaning or excitement attached to it, the cellular-memory group formed to store this information will expand. The cellular-memory group will then seek throughout the brain and body to find other cellular-memory groups that are related to it. When it locates these related groups, it will form a pathway linking itself to them. All of this can happen within a matter of seconds, or over time, depending on the circumstances.[17]

For example, as an infant you learned that you were hungry when you felt a certain kind of discomfort in your stomach. This in turn caused you to cry out. Soon you would hear your mother's voice and food would follow, relieving the discomfort.

Can you trace the various related cellular-memory groups linked together in this example? Cellular-memories in your stomach linked up to cellular-memories in your vocal cords, which in turn linked up to your hearing, then to your taste buds and so forth. An entire network of cellular-memory groups worked in unison—all spawned by hunger pangs!

As mentioned, with cellular-memory groups, *"birds of a feather flock together."* In fact, some scientists believe that individual memories are stored in each of the related cellular-memory groups that range throughout the entire brain and body.[18]

Step #4

When the same sort of image, feeling or information "catches your attention" again in the future, it is directly routed to the same cellular-memory group that contains the original image, feeling or information. Each time this happens, the original cellular-memory group and all the groups it is linked to grow larger and more dominant. The more that pathways linking one cellular-memory group with another are traveled, the wider and deeper these linking pathways become—like the wheel ruts in a well-traveled dirt road.[19]

Can you see why hunger, with all of its links to so many parts of the brain and body, is so powerful? It is the basic reason you feed yourself every day: because of the network of pathways that have been traveled numerous times each day over an entire lifetime. Thus, the feeling of hunger carries with it some incredibly deep-seated urges and emotions in that the cellular-memory groups associated with hunger are themselves deep-seated and dominant.

Step #5

The interacting cells throughout your brain and body are intelligent, always learning, and constantly seeking to become more efficient. As an image, feeling or event from the past is received repeatedly, each time with additional emotions or information attached to it, the cellular-memory groups will establish even more pathways to additional related cellular-memory groups throughout the brain and body.[20]

THIS IS HOW WE LEARN

This five-step process, employed automatically by our brain and body, day by day, year by year, is how we "learn." Learning relies on "new pathways" being established among the vast network of cellular-memories in the brain and body. And learning, of course, can lead to positive or negative results.

Suppose you are learning to play the guitar. Your brain sends out messages to the muscles in your arms and hands, telling them to work together to place your fingers in a particular position on the strings, then to pluck the strings with the fingers of your other hand. At first, as the messages travel back and forth along existing pathways, the movements are slow and uncoordinated. With more practice, though, the same messages are passed more quickly.

Little by little, you increase in skill because the neural pathways begin to expand, bringing together groups of "matched" or "like-kind" cellular-memories. Short-cuts are established through the maze of neural pathways. As new, faster, more coordinated pathways develop, you find that you can move your fingers more quickly and precisely. Eventually, you can play accurately and with feeling, without looking at your hands. The positive result of your learning and persistent practice is that you become a more accomplished guitarist.

As human beings, we possess an ability to learn at many different levels and with many different outcomes. This all depends on the desired cellular-memory groups being formed and the appropriate pathways linking them together. By this method, we can learn to develop wonderful talents and abilities. We can learn to love, lift, serve and give, all positive results. On the contrary, by this same method we can also learn to be hateful, lustful, selfish, jealous, prejudice and dishonest, clearly all negative results.

As you will see, what we learn depends almost entirely on the information, images, sounds, etc.,that enter our brain and body. What we allow to pass though our eyes and ears into our minds has everything to do with who we are and how we behave.

THIS DETERMINES "WHO WE ARE"

Who are you? Whether you know it or not, you are the cumulative product of your memories—your unique network of neural pathways and groups of "like-kind" cellular-memories. These have literally "changed" the physical make-up and structure of your brain and body. This structured network, more than anything else, determines your personality, what you say, think and feel, how you interact and react to the situations and people around you. This structure further determines your habits, fears, joys and tears.

So how does this "change" in the structure of your brain and body have such a powerful effect on "who you are"? When the same messages or stimuli are directed to follow the same neural pathways over and over again, each time accessing the same network of cellular-memory groups, this is what we call a "habit." Your habits become the dominant pair of glasses through which you tend to view and interpret your world.

So how does all of this apply to Internet pornography and its devastating effects on society? Read on . . .

CELLULAR-MEMORY GROUPS, NEURAL PATHWAYS, AND PORNOGRAPHY

Let's take the example of a man (it could just as easily be a woman, teen or child) being introduced to Internet pornography. What happens to his brain and body? The answer will come as we review and trace the process using the five steps just introduced:

Step #1

Let's call our subject "Stan." Stan is surfing the Internet and stumbles across a site. Obscene images of a woman appear on the computer screen. Remember, the *Reticular Formation*, or "air traffic controller" in Stan's brain obeys the "law of strength"—the more exciting, frightening, interesting, shocking or arousing an image is, the more priority the air traffic controller will give it.

As Stan has intuitively known since he was a teen, the emotional and physical arousal capacity of pornography on him (and most human beings) is powerful. Well, Stan's air traffic controller quickly scoots this arousing image through the checkpoint and into the higher regions of his brain. He is alternately shocked, dazzled and hypnotized by what he is seeing.

Under normal circumstances, Stan would never sneak into a porn shop to satisfy his urges. However, because of the privacy, anonymity and instant, easy access to porn on the Internet, he is drawn to the images portrayed, lured in by normal curiosity. Soon this curiosity turns to sexual arousal and addiction. Stan may initially be shocked by the images. Nonetheless, as a result of this shock, the *air traffic controller* instinctively allows them to pass into the higher regions of his brain. Little does he realize that this element of shock is one of the pornographer's primary tools to initially get the image locked onto its target.

Once inside the brain, the pornographic images seek for a place to be stored. Since this is Stan's first exposure to pornography, the images will travel neural pathways to cellular-memory groups that most closely match the "meaning" that Stan attaches to the images.

Step #2

The cells where Stan's images are ultimately stored immediately begin cloning themselves so that before long there are many cells now storing the images.[22] The size of this cellular-memory group depends on how exciting, arousing or shocking Stan found the experience. Given the explicit and often shocking nature of pornography, it is very likely that the cellular-memory group formed in Stan's brain and body will be quite large. The images will have left a deep impression on him, so that they will be easily remembered and retrieved.

Step #3

Now the question is: "Where will these new pornographic images be stored and what other cellular-memory groups in the brain and body will they be linked to?" This all depends on the **meaning** that the image has for Stan. Remember, for the brain and body, "meaning is everything."[23]

For instance, Stan is driving down the road one spring day, listening to music, very relaxed. Suddenly his body stiffens. His heart begins to race. His face flushes and his blood pressure soars off the charts. What starts out as total surprise and shock, quickly turns to anger and disgust as a string of cuss words escape his lips.

What force could possibly have transformed him from totally calm one moment to being washed over by a tidal wave of negative emotions the next? Simple: the flashing red lights of a highway patrol car in his rear-view mirror! How could simple red lights have such an overpowering effect? To Stan, the flashing red lights signify a traffic fine, higher insurance rates, a visit to traffic school, and a confrontation with a patrolman. As the image entered his brain and body, the meaning attached to the image accessed and activated a whole network of cellular-memories. This network contains links to various parts of Stan's body, and triggers physiological responses like increased heart rate and blood pressure, perspiration, shaking, etc.

Take the same situation and assume that Stan's two-year-old son is in the car with him. His son has a toy police car at home and loves the flashing red lights. What network of cellular-memories would be activated in the child, based on this opposite "meaning?" How could the identical stimulus evoke such a radically different response in Stan's son? "Meaning" is everything!

The following are some possible "meanings" that pornographic images on the Internet might have for our man Stan:

Possible Meaning: When Stan sees a pornographic image, he immediately accesses cellular-memory groups related to values, morals, integrity, etc. Based on these pathways or links, he rejects the image—considering it disgusting and inappropriate—and exits the porn site.

Possible Meaning: Upon entering the site, Stan feels shocked, awkward, embarrassed. But because Internet porn is so easily and readily available, he is likely to be exposed again in the future. With each new exposure the shock dissipates and the images begin to be routed to cellular-memory groups associated with sexual arousal. Eventually, these sexually-based cellular-memory groups overpower those containing values and morals, resulting in Stan becoming "hooked" on Internet porn.

Possible Meaning: Let's assume that prior to his first exposure to Internet pornography, Stan, like most Americans, has been for years watching not only network television sitcoms, but PG-13 and R-rated movies containing sex, nudity and violence. When he first happens upon Internet pornography, it is easily linked to the cellular-memory groups containing all the sexual images and emotions from his years of program viewing. With these memories firmly ingrained, he at first is not particularly shocked or repulsed.

As a result, he is instantly aroused and proceeds with the viewing. It's true that at the same time he is probably accessing cellular-memory groups related to values, morals, respect, and so on, but, based on the amount of time he has spent over the years watching TV and movies versus learning and practicing values and respect, which cellular-memory groups do you think will win out?

Possible Meaning: If Stan masturbates and reaches orgasm with Internet pornography as the stimulus, his brain/body links the images to the vast network of cellular-memory groups associated with sexual climax. When this network is linked up, the Internet porn becomes overpowering and Stan's addiction increases dramatically. If through the pornographic images he becomes interested in cybersex or sexually-oriented Internet chat rooms, he also can become addicted to sex over the Internet, linking together an even larger network of emotions, biological processes and physiological responses.

Possible Meaning: If Stan was sexually abused as a child, or if he begins to view Internet porn containing violence, the "meaning" of these images can be devastating. He may begin to link nude females and sexual climax to rape, torture, anger, fear, and even murder. When Internet porn takes on this meaning, the innocent bystanders in Stan's world are at risk of becoming victims. Stan can easily start down the path traveled by the "Ted Bundys" of the world.

Step #4

Having established some possible meanings, let's assume that after the initial exposure Stan finds himself strongly stimulated and attracted to viewing porn, and decides to make it a nightly ritual. What is the likely process in his brain and body from that point? The network of cellular-memory groups linked to the pornographic images (or cybersex conversations) will continue to grow in size and strength. Figurative "grooves" will slowly be carved throughout the brain and body.

These cellular-memory groups will carve their way to other related groups. Thus the porn will not only be linked to feelings of sexual arousal, but to other seemingly unrelated emotions: to an increase in heart rate, to the dilation of the pupils, to the release of numerous chemicals in the mind and body, including testosterone, adrenaline, epinephrine and others.

All of these emotions, chemicals and biological processes and events are eventually linked back to the Internet pornography. And even the links normally associated with genuine sexual intimacy will be linked to pornography and its many ills. In other words, links begin to piggyback on or chain with other links.

The feelings of shame, guilt, shock, fear and stress that come from the viewing of Internet porn also are often linked into the network, causing additional chemicals to be released and new biological processes to be initiated, further expanding the cellular-memory network and ultimate power of the porn addiction.

Step #5

In the future, every time Stan views Internet pornography or participates in sexual Internet chat, the same network of cellular-memories and neural pathways lights up. As he becomes aroused, all of the sexual- and stress-oriented responses in the brain and body are triggered, generally ending in orgasm. The cellular-memory groups and neural pathways associated with pornography/sexual chat become so dominant and well-traveled that Stan becomes hopelessly addicted.

As you will learn in later chapters, the human brain and body yearn for growth. Hence, they are not content to remain at one level of experience. Instead, they constantly seek higher "peak experiences." Stan, hooked on Internet pornography, will soon become bored with the same old images and seek out a higher state of arousal or thrill.[24] And the ever-present Internet pornographers are there to oblige. They make available harder and harder pornographic images—often crossing over into formerly taboo areas of group sex, same sex, adult-child sex, live sex, mutilation, torture, rape and bestiality, all designed to propel the brain and body to a higher level of excitement, arousal and shock.

What happens when cellular-memory groups related to sex, intimacy and orgasm are suddenly linked up with cellular-memory groups containing images of violence, rape, torture and debauchery? The results are daily spread across our newspapers and headline our news broadcasts. Incidents of rape, child molestation, spousal abuse, date rape, and even sexually-related torture and murder are skyrocketing.

What happens when a viewer involved in sexually-oriented Internet chat rooms becomes bored with the conversations and his brain and body is screaming for a "higher peak experience"? More and more chat-room participants are meeting for one-night stands, engaging in group sex, and participating in other illicit sexual activities.

FOR THE BRAIN AND BODY, "MEANING IS EVERYTHING"

When we talk about the science of the brain and body, "meaning" truly is everything. The meaning that information from the outside world has for each of us individually will fully determine how our brain and body process that information and how we react or behave as a result.

As you have seen, pornography means different things to different people. To many, porn is offensive, degrading and disgusting. With this meaning, the brain and body of such an individual will rally its forces to avoid, shun and even fight pornography.

But for increasing numbers of people, the meaning of Internet pornography is arousal, excitement, escape, fantasy, sexual climax and absolute obsession. With this meaning, the brain and body of such an individual will rally its forces to find, embrace and experience as much Internet porn as time, resources and availability will allow. He or she will often then move on to other sexual addiction activities when the Internet is no longer sufficiently stimulating.

SOME PEOPLE HAVE LOST CONTROL OVER THEIR CELLULAR-MEMORY GROUPS

A person's network of internal cellular-memories functions like a pair of glasses—lenses through which the porn viewer sees himself and the world around him. This network alters attitudes, values and behaviors in a multitude of ways. Internet porn literally changes a person from the inside-out.

In a number of cases, certain cellular-memory groups and pathways formed in the brain and body are not by choice. Many in our world, through no fault of their own, suffer abuse, poverty, sickness, and other maladies. As a result, the cellular-memories that have become an integral part of their brain and body are extremely difficult to live with.

But what about permanent structural changes brought about in the brain and body as a result of the viewing of pornographic images that are "knowingly and deliberately" distributed to the public? Why would anyone seek to alter another human being's brain and body in this way, knowing the potentially dangerous consequences?

The answer is "greed." Not unlike the tobacco companies, who have deceived the public and hidden the truth for years, porn purveyors are in it for one reason only: because it is extraordinarily profitable.

Key Points

A reference tool for spouses, parents, clergy, counselors and others

- Images viewed for only a few seconds can produce a structural change in the brain and body that may last a lifetime.
- Through the *law of strength*, pornographic images gain immediate entrance into the brain and body and can be allotted enormous amounts of storage space.
- Pornographic images are stored in the **cells** of the brain and body as *cellular-memories*. These images, then, become "tangible" memories, literally changing the viewer on the "inside."
- The brain and body immediately seek to link the stored pornographic images with other cellular-memories. These links are determined by the *meaning* that the pornography has to the viewer. *Meaning is everything* in the human brain and body.
- Because of the powerful meaning and response pornography can evoke in the brain and body, it is often linked to a vast array of other cellular-memories. This vast network of links wields a tremendous impact on the physical and chemical makeup, attitudes and behavior of the pornography viewer.
- Because of this dramatic change in the structure of the brain and body, severe addiction can result and the pornography addict can become a significant burden and risk to family, friends and society as a whole.

9

How Imagination, Memory and Advertising "Hook" Internet Porn Viewers

This Is Called "Imagination"

Cellular-memory groups can be activated without our seeing or hearing something from the outside world. The information contained in a cellular-memory group may be activated independently from any internal or external sensory stimulus. This is called *imagination.*[1]

Once a person has used Internet pornography as the means to heighten his or her sexual fantasies, all he or she need do in order to call up those same feelings and images is express the desire or intention. Once this intention or desire is expressed, a whole network of cellular-memory groups is activated.

The individual can become aroused, fantasize and reach orgasm completely independent of any outside influence. In essence, he keeps stored in his cellular-memory groups his own private porn bookstore or video collection. This collection can be accessed at any time—either by choice or when triggered by some internal or external stimulus.

Many men, women and teens hooked on Internet porn regularly comment how arousal can be triggered by any simple stimulus, i.e., seeing a regularly dressed man or woman walking down the street, catching a glimpse of a billboard, having a brief thought cross their mind.

Some have even talked about how the entire porn cellular-memory network can be suddenly activated in church, at the dinner table, or during a business conversation. The cellular-memory links that crisscross their brains and bodies associated with Internet porn can be so complex, that there is no telling what might trigger arousal.

Unfortunately, there are those who have been exposed to pornography by accident or by force. Long after the initial exposure, they may still be shocked and traumatized by the perverse images, which like recurrent nightmares can resurface in their mind at any time in the future, reproducing the same feelings of trauma. And there are any number of ordinary, seemingly unrelated images around them every day that can trigger this "resurfacing."

PORNOGRAPHY AND YOUR MEMORY

Repetition is one of the best ways to memorize something. For example, if you are studying for a spelling bee, you spell the word over and over until you have memorized it. But, if you understand the way your brain uses cellular-memory groups to store information, you can vastly improve your memory.

It is not only repetition of information that commits it to memory, but ***the number of brain/body cellular-memory groups associated*** with that information. This *mnemonic device* technique is based on "association," where each related cellular-memory group becomes a "hook" to the information that you are trying to memorize. The information can easily be called up when any of the other cellular-memory groups "hooked" to it are accessed. The more hooks, the more easily the information can be re-called.[2, 3]

THE GROCERY LIST

Your spouse calls you on your cell phone and asks you to stop at the grocery store and pick up five items. Since you're driving, you can't write them down.

Using repetition, you repeat the items several times in your mind as your spouse lists them. After you hang up, you continue to repeat them aloud. As you head into the store, you bump into an old friend. After several minutes of chitchat, you stroll down the grocery isles asking yourself, "Now what was I suppose to get?" You can remember some of the items, but not all of them. So much for repetition.

Using the *cellular-memories of association* method, on the other hand, is proven to heighten memory. The next time your spouse reels off a grocery list, you associate the grocery items with other things. For the raisin bagels, you imagine yourself walking into the grocery store with a huge, bagel-like floatation device around your stomach, potato-size raisins, wrinkled, poking out of the dough. (The more outlandish the association, the better. Remember, our brains tend to more readily store images that are absurd, bizarre, arousing, comical or shocking.) You repeat this association process for each of the items on the list.

To take the process a step further, you link each item with the next item on your list. If frozen orange juice is next, then you might see in your mind a huge wave of orange juice coming at you. Luckily, you have a bagel inner-tube on, right? Next on the list is a brownie mix, so you might imagine a little girl dressed in "brownie" uniform, surfing on the crest of the orange juice wave. In this way you are quickly tying the images to one another so that the memory process is filled with linked "hooks."

Again, the more bizarre, unreal or cartoon-like these images are the better. If you can add favorite music, flamboyant colors and vivid emotions like fear (the orange juice wave about to wash over you) to your scenario, all the better. And the more all these things ***do not*** normally belong together, the better you will remember them.

At first, this memory method may make you feel foolish or it may seem too complicated. But once you practice it, it's easy—and effective. You'll never forget another grocery list just because you stop to talk to a friend. In fact, you'll probably be able to recall the items on the list weeks later.

Why does this cellular-memory technique work so well? When you memorize something in this way, instead of accessing and activating a single cellular-memory group, you are accessing and activating many groups. You are associating a single item with a host of other images and emotions, using them as "hooks."

PORN ADVERTISERS USE THIS MNEMONIC TECHNIQUE ALL THE TIME

Advertisers have known for decades about the effectiveness of this technique. They will attempt to engage as many of your existing emotions and memories as possible in order to forge a relationship with their products. Some will use catchy slogans and images that stick with you:

- "You're in good hands with ______________." (Allstate)
- "Get a ____________________ rock." (piece of the; Prudential)

Some advertisers center around musical jingles. You probably can still sing, word for word, many of the TV commercial ditties you heard as a child. And today's advertisers are increasingly using the effective technique of placing their product alongside other images that have nothing to do with it. (Budweiser with its frog and lizard characters is but one example.)

Advertisers have discovered that the more bizarre, shocking, funny, tragic, sensational, violent or sensual their advertisements are, the more easily they attract our attention and will be remembered.

Why? Because the more cellular-memory groups an advertisement can access and activate in your brain and body, the better you will remember the product or service. If a hundred different interconnecting neural pathways are linked to it, the product quickly comes to mind when any one pathway is activated.

Why have I spent so much time on "how we remember things"? Because each of the principles discussed is **directly and powerfully related to Internet pornography/cybersex chat addiction**. In fact, these principles are at the very core of the whole pornography industry and its phenomenal growth.

PORNOGRAPHERS—THE MOST EFFECTIVE AND RUTHLESS ADVERTISERS OF ALL

As we have seen, studies on memory clearly show that when a large number of cellular-memory groups is connected to a single, seemingly unrelated cellular-memory group, this single group is deeply embedded inside us. Pornographic images floating around in a person's mind are very much a part of this cellular-memory group association:

Pornographic images are easily retrieved by the mind because they are linked to so many other images, feelings and ideas that can trigger their retrieval.

The images will be retained in memory longer because they are connected to so many other memories.

Pornography will produce a much more dominant and powerful effect when linked to many other cellular-memory groups than when linked to only a few. This is why Internet pornographers strive to connect their images to sexual arousal, orgasm, fantasy, shock, shame, guilt, anger, and all of the chemical and biological processes that take place throughout the brain and body.

PORNOGRAPHERS COMBINE POWERFUL, UNRELATED IMAGES IN ORDER TO HOOK VIEWERS

Pornographers know that to have their best shot at addicting a viewer to porn, they must access and activate as many cellular-memory groups in his brain and body as possible.

How do pornographers do this? They use the same principles I suggested you use to memorize your grocery list, the same techniques advertisers use every day to get you to remember their products. But pornographers employ these principles in a more sinister and twisted way.

Here are the techniques Internet pornographers use to gain "customers for life," male, female and teen alike:

- Males and females, from an early age, are naturally attracted to each other. Pornographers take unfair advantage of this "built-in" attraction. But, in order to be successful, they have thrown in a twist; this natural attraction is not enough. The twist's effectiveness pivots on being able to access far more cellular-memory groups than just those associated with "male-female attraction."
- Pornographers "piggyback" on images that are already established in the minds of potential customers. This is why they show a porn model with a popular beer logo in the background or one engaging in sex atop a luxury sports car. Internet porn combines nudity and sex with sports, food, the outdoors—"unrelated" images that are already stored in most people's cellular-memory groups. It is the pornographer's hope that the viewer will then link all of these images together with the porn to the vast network of cellular-memory groups associated with sexual climax and orgasm.
- Pornographers want to engage and set in motion as many powerful emotions as possible. So Internet pornography provides shocking scenes of rape, incest, sadism, mutilation, and a host of other

perversions. These images access and activate cellular-memory groups associated with deeply disturbing emotions such as shock, disgust, anger, fear, guilt and shame.

What the pornographer is trying to do is open up as many cellular-memory pathways as possible and associate these to the pornographic images. Remember, the more links, the more easily the image is locked into long-term memory for later retrieval, and the more powerful the response will be the next time the same stimulus (porn) is introduced.

Can you imagine how confused the brain and body are when dozens of emotions—some of them conflicting—are all mixed together? Allowed into this mix, pornography leaves a deep and lasting impression.

- A key ingredient to the pornographer's success is getting the viewer to incorporate masturbation and orgasm into the process. Orgasm is one of the most powerful, singular "peak" experiences the human body can experience. In the process of building up to and reaching orgasm, numerous chemicals are released into the brain and body.[5,6] These chemicals act much like illicit drugs—they produce a "high." If the pornographer can induce the viewer to connect porn images with all of the cellular-memory groups associated with the release and pleasure of these drugs, then he's got the viewer hooked.
- Pornographers often play music when showing pictures, movies and live sex. Studies show that when music accompanies the viewing of images, it opens up a vast array of cellular-memory groups and connecting pathways. Music tends to magnify and deepen the impression of the pornographic images.

So if you add all these things together, what do you have? Using visual images, the pornographer has accessed and activated a huge chemical network of feelings and emotions, and fused them into the neural pathways that run throughout viewers' brains and bodies. Once hooked, viewers will readily return again and again to recapture this all-consuming peak experience.

Pornographers Want To Keep the Viewer From Accessing Certain Cellular-Memories In Their Brains & Bodies While They View Porn

Although pornographers want to activate as many cellular-memory groups as possible in the viewer's brain and body, there are certain existing pathways and cellular-memory groups that they **do not** want the him to access. It is best if his mind is kept as far away as possible from certain images, feelings and ideas.

Nowhere in pornographic materials will you find healthy and normal displays or references to marriage, fidelity, trust, honor, affection, mothers, fathers, families, sons, daughters, God, religion, or any other related concepts. The only time family images are displayed in pornography is when they are perverse, violent and sexual in nature, i.e., incest, rape, child porn, etc. If porn viewers were constantly reminded of normal and healthy images and feelings toward their wives, husbands, marriages, children, religious views, moral values or any such things, the linked cellular-memories would be in conflict and could bring the viewer back to his or her senses.

A pornography producer, during a recent magazine interview, admitted that his pornographic films are geared to the *male viewer*: Rarely if ever does he have the man and woman kiss; there are never any scenes depicting romance—affectionate gestures are a definite no-no. "Our focus is strictly on the geography of genitalia," were his words.

You see, pornographers wince at the thought of their male viewers tapping into cellular-memory groups dealing with affection, tenderness, romance or respect. The focus indeed is on bumping and grinding body parts.

As discussed in a later chapter, the male brain is designed to impulsively focus full attention on a single object. This is why pornography designed to hook male viewers focuses exclusively and narrowly on body parts as opposed to romance and relationships.

But in their persistent effort to attract more viewers, pornographers *have* actually begun to mention—and even feature—mothers, wives and daughters in porn materials geared to men, albeit in the most perverse and twisted ways.

Now on the Internet, men can view pregnant women (mothers) in all sorts of depraved poses and activities. They can view other men's wives (and the sites identify them as such) engaging in adulterous sexual escapades. And men can even witness scenes of incest, where a supposed father is sexually abusing his daughter.

It's not enough to keep men from accessing honorable thoughts of home, family, wife and children. The pornographer wants to disturb these healthy cellular-memories—confuse and twist them, numb and dumb them down—by mixing in pornographic and violent images.

INTERNET PORNOGRAPHERS USE THESE SAME TECHNIQUES TO LURE AN EVER-GROWING FEMALE MARKET

Today's pornographers employ the same kind of tricks to lure the female mind into Internet porn, with much of their effort centering around Internet chat rooms or erotic stories. As we will review later, porn targeted at women does in fact include images and dialogue that elicit romantic feelings. The emphasis is more on relationships, embracing, kissing, etc. This is all in line with the structure of the female brain.

Pornographers are masters at using mind/body science, male/female brain differences, differing advertising techniques, and anything else they can manipulate to gain addicted consumers-for-life.

EXPOSURE TO PORN SHAPES ATTITUDES AND VALUES

Just as thirty-second commercials can influence whether or not we choose one popular soft drink over another, exposure to pornography shapes our attitudes, values and, often, our behavior. Replicated studies have demonstrated that exposure to significant amounts of increasingly graphic forms of pornography has a dramatic effect on how adult and child consumers view men, women, teens, children, sexual behavior, sexual relationships, and sex in general. These studies are virtually unanimous in their conclusions.[7]

When experimental subjects were exposed to as little as six weeks' worth of non-violent pornography, they:

- Began to trivialize rape as a criminal offense, or no longer considered it a crime at all.
- Developed distorted perceptions about sexuality.
- Developed an appetite for more deviant, bizarre or violent types of pornography. (Normal sex no longer seemed to do the job.)
- Devalued the importance of monogamy and lacked confidence in marriage as either a viable or lasting institution.
- Viewed non-monogamous relationships as normal and natural.[8]

Children, too, become desensitized by sexual images they see on the Internet, TV, in movies, etc. *In May of 1998, The Rhode Island Rape Crisis Center asked 1,700 sixth- to ninth-graders about rape. More than half of the boys and girls considered sex to be acceptable after six months of dating—even if rape was necessary to achieve this. Roughly half the children agreed that if a boy spends ten to fifteen dollars on a girl, he has the right to force a kiss. Sixty-five percent of boys and 47% of girls said forced sex was acceptable if a couple dated for six months or more. Perhaps without realizing that "forced" sex is rape, nearly a fourth of the boys and a sixth of the girls felt rape was justified if a boy had spent money on a girl.*[9]

WEAVING THE TAPESTRY OF OUR MINDS

Some of the most beautiful tapestries in the world are created by Navajo women. Navajo women, who meticulously select each colored thread that is woven into a blanket. Threads are carefully added one at a time until each forms the "whole" and the creation is complete.

Such is the structure of the complex network of brain/body cellular-memories. Each image we take in, each thought we allow to play on the stage of our minds is added to the whole and determines "who we are."

What will the finished product be like? Will the threads of pornography, the scenes of sex, violence and nudity, the sexual innuendo and jokes—all woven together in the chambers of our minds—make us who we really *want* to be?

PORNOGRAPHY ADVERTISES, PROMOTES AND TEACHES INCEST

Take the father who is involved with Internet pornography. He covertly begins ogling at pornographic images of "teenage" girls. While most of these girls are of "legal age," still they are selected by the pornographers for their "Teeny-Bopper" or "child-like" features. This father begins fantasizing about having sex with these girls and soon he is masturbating to the fantasy. In his mind, he's back in high school, having sex with the cute cheerleader he secretly had a crush on.

Then one day he comes across an Internet site that promotes incest, portraying fathers having sex with their teenage daughters. (While many of these scenes are "staged," some are actual fathers sexually abusing their own daughters. But remember, our brains and bodies do not distinguish between fantasy and reality when it comes to pornography. Both types of images are stored away for future retrieval.) Before long, the father begins fantasizing and masturbating while viewing these images. He is no longer shocked, but stimulated. The "teen porn" has taught him that teenage girls want to have sex with older men (including their fathers) and that so many are doing it that it is acceptable.

This father's conflict deepens as one evening while walking past her open bedroom door, he catches a glimpse of his own teenage daughter, who is stretched out on the bed in T-shirt and panties, talking on the phone.

The daughter, of course, is an outside stimulus entering the man's brain through his eyes. But which cellular-memory groups will be activated in his brain and body? What neural pathways will the image of his daughter follow?

Some of his cellular-memory groups portray images of his daughter as a little girl; these are linked to other groups brimming with feelings of love, tenderness and protectiveness. After all, this is his daughter and he is her father!

But now after taking in so much Internet teen porn, he has also forged cellular-memory groups containing thousands of images of provocative, "lusting" nude teenage girls. Connected to these images are countless other groups brought into play as he has masturbated to climax while viewing these images. Even as a tinge of arousal is felt as he sees his daughter, a voice keeps screaming "Stop! This is your little girl!"

Which cellular-memory groups will win out? Those containing sentiments of trust, honor, protectiveness, wife, family, religion and tragic consequences, or those carrying fantasized images of sex with teenage girls which have culminated in a physical orgasm? I can give you a hint as to which too often wins out: molestation, parents victimizing children and the like are on the rise.

Note: It also should be pointed out that as more females become habituated to porn, the probability of incest can increase ten-fold, since moms and other female caretakers are often in close cleaning and bathing contact with little children.

In her work *Sexually Explicit Media: Changes In the Structure of the Human Brain & American Law & Public Policy*, Dr. Judith Reisman refers to sexual fantasy becoming reality as "copycat crime." In other words, Internet porn sets up cellular-memory groups that lead people to copy or act out what they have seen displayed on the computer screen.[10]

As will be detailed in a later chapter, it is natural for the human brain and body to seek a higher "peak experience" than the previous one experienced. When the arousal achieved by mere computer images is not enough, the brain and body seek for something more. Unfortunately, this often leads to simulating or "copycatting" porn scenes with real live people.

Pornography advertises, promotes and teaches incest, rape, sexual abuse of children, sadism and a host of other twisted and perverted practices. By viewing pornography, we establish those cellular-memory groups and neural pathways in our brains and bodies that produce behavior to shatter and destroy our own lives and the lives of those most near and dear to us.

THE NEXT WAVE OF INTERNET PORNOGRAPHY ADDICTION—VIRTUAL REALITY AND INTERACTIVE SEX

Just as the drug-dealer is always looking for ways to increase and permanently lock in his customers' addiction, Internet pornographers are developing what may be the most addictive porn of all time: *Virtual Reality and Interactive Cybersex.* Already there are devices a viewer can connect to high-arousal parts of his or her body, and receive remote stimulation from a cybersex chat partner or a live porn actor or actress on the computer screen.

In an article in the March 1995 issue of *Glamour* magazine, Margaret Wertheim, a science writer, comments upon technological advances that are bringing us interactive pornography/sex and virtual reality on the Internet, and poses some very powerful questions:

"Can it be long before more sinister cyberporn fantasies are available? What is to stop anyone from making games in which virtual women are

hurt, tortured or even killed as part of erotic thrill? After all, they would only be collections of bits and bytes.

The prospect of such scenarios highlights a danger of the rapidly increasing realism of computer simulations. . . . Once tactile feedback devices are added (which are now available, by the way), the blurring will become even greater. A not-inconsiderable concern with this technology is that it will be used to give people ever more realistic, simulated experiences of violent and degrading fantasies.

. . . I suggest that the possibility of such "harmless fun" is something we should be concerned about. Just as violence in television drama inures us to real violence, virtual reality has immense potential to inure us to violence and sexual degradation. In virtual reality, your brain experiences the fantasy as reality. . . . With virtual reality, logic takes a back seat to sensual perception. My guess is that it would be a shorter step from violent magazine porn to actual violence—particularly for a viewer who might be a little off kilter.

Even apart from the psycho factor, can we really look with equanimity upon the possibility of a future in which any and all fantasies might be available at the touch of a keyboard? How would you feel, for instance, if you discovered that a male friend or partner engaged in violent sexual acts with a virtual woman? For those who doubt the need for concern here, imagine instead that the friend or partner was engaging in sex with a virtual child. It is no more difficult to visually render a young girl (or for that matter, a young boy) than a grown woman—and in none of these cases would anyone really be hurt."[11]

If you think this author is paranoid or her ideas are farfetched, consider the current court cases dealing with the legality of "virtual" child porn (VCP). VCP is where the visual images of adults engaged in various types of sexual relations have been altered so that one or more of the adults appears to be a young person—in some cases a young child. The Canadian Supreme Court recently overturned two province rulings that made child porn legal. And the Danish legislature fails to legalize child porn and adult/child sex by an ever-decreasing margin every year.

As this level of virtual but very real sex is combined with high-speed Internet access, the devastation increases dramatically. Broadband (high speed) Internet connections are revolutionizing Internet access. Currently, with a conventional modem and phone line, there are limitations on how quickly a person can access and view certain kinds of information. For instance, with standard Internet speed, full motion video does not transfer well; the video footage is often broken up and sporadic. Too much information is trying to come through the line at one time. Like trying to pump large amounts of water through a soda straw, the water will pass through, but only so much at a time.

Now imagine trying to pump this reservoir of water through a fire hose rather than the straw. That is what the magic of broadband allows on the Internet—a fire hose for the information to pass through to your computer screen. Full color motion video images over the Internet, displayed on big-screen TV! No more limitations.

What does this mean? Well, it means that now and in the future you will be able to get motion pictures over the Internet, live footage of news stories from around the world, live transmissions from exotic places—all in vivid color, full clarity, Dolby stereo and *speed.* But it also means that the pornography industry will continue to enjoy a prolonged field day and be able to reach more addicted viewers than ever before.

LIVE INTERACTIVE SEX OVER THE INTERNET—PREPARE FOR AN AVALANCHE OF TED BUNDYS

Industry experts estimate that there are hundreds of thousands of people already experiencing live interactive sex using high-speed Internet connections. With computer video cameras and/or sensory devices at their respective locations, participants can literally engage in full-color, big-screen cybersex.

Now that you understand how the brain and body work, how images and feelings and attitudes are stored in cellular-memory, what impact do you think Internet porn at this new, higher level will have on our society and on our lives? What do you think will happen now that pornographers have found a way to make their wares even "more real" to the mind/bodies of their customers?

Studies of hundreds of thousands of cases clearly show that sexual criminals do not start out raping, molesting and murdering. It starts slowly, over time, as quite normal individuals are desensitized and animalized. In virtually every case, pornography has played a leading role in this desensitization.

Ted Bundy maintained that his road to rape and murder began with *Playboy* magazines he saw as a boy at the corner drugstore. If this constituted **level 1** of his desensitization process, it took years of increasingly graphic materials and activities to bring him to **level 10,** rape and murder. Over those years he continued to add to his cellular-memory groups and seek higher and higher "peak experiences."

Now that virtual reality and interactive sex are possible on the Internet, how long will it take the potential Ted Bundys of the world to pass from **level 1** to **level 10** of desensitization? How many more little-boy Ted Bundys are out there now that the Internet is instantly available to anyone and everyone? And with virtual reality, no longer does one start at level 1 with a *Playboy* at the corner drugstore. Now he jumps directly to level 7 or 8 with interactive sex and direct stimulation!

And live interactive sex is just the tip of a frighteningly destructive iceberg on the horizon. Now with high-speed Internet connections and new computer imaging technology, viewers can request a virtual sex partner be created to their specifications: a movie star look-a-like, a teenager, a child. There is even technology available in which a cybersex participant can place an overlay or composite on top of a video image so as to project him or herself in the appearance of a certain movie star, teenager or child! How long will it be before this individual seeks to copycat his actions with a real person?

We have discussed in detail how the brain and body often cannot distinguish between reality and fantasy when sexually aroused by pornographic images. The brain and body consider the experience "real" and store it in cellular-memories accordingly. Making the jump to acting out the same sexual, violent or depraved scenarios face-to-face with an actual man, woman, teen or child, will be no stretch at all for many people.

For those who manage to control their urges and do not cross the line to committing "copycat" crimes against others, how far *will* they go? Many will consider the Internet's "virtual sex" as merely a great escape. So even if they don't cross the line, still they will have become "zombies" trapped in the world of sexual fantasy.

If you believe such warnings are hogwash or are one man's paranoid exaggeration, consider reading Dr. Kimberly S. Young's book *Caught in the Net*. A world-renowned therapist specializing in "Internet Addiction," (Internet addiction as a whole, not just porn/sex addiction), Dr. Young cites hundreds of cases of people who are using the Internet world as a total escape from the stress and pain of everyday life.[12] With the proliferation of today's high-tech virtual reality and interactive sex, a pervasive, easily-accessed branch of the Internet, the number of addicts is sky-rocketing.

Key Points

A reference tool for
spouses, parents, clergy,
counselors and others

- Once in place, the porn cellular-memory network can be activated and accessed at any time—unintentionally, without conscious directive, and even in spite of the individual's efforts to shut it off.
- Pornographers seek to link as many unrelated images, feelings and ideas to pornography as possible, including sports, food, cars, shock, fear, anger, shame, guilt, etc. This creates in the brain and body, a larger network of links and the potential for stored pornographic images to be activated via hundreds of different outside stimuli that might be encountered on a daily basis. Once the pornographic network is activated, the individual will often seek greater stimulation through Internet pornography or other related activities.
- In order to dramatically increase the allure of their product, pornographers drive the viewer to masturbation. This act releases a host of chemicals into the brain and body, thus greatly intensifying the pleasure, arousal and neuro-chemical "high" of the experience. It also adds a variety of additional cellular-memory links, making the porn network even more diverse and dominant in the brain and body.
- Pornographers purposely keep healthy images and emotions out of their material, i.e., God, marriage, family, fatherhood, fidelity, honor, trust, etc. However, there is a growing trend to include these ideas in pornography in twisted and demented ways—a father

raping his teenage daughter, wife-swapping, porn actors dressed in religious attire, etc. These images **confuse** the viewer's brain and body and link pornography to what would normally be healthy/normal emotions, images and ideas. This technique once again expands the porn network and the chance that it will be activated and accessed under a variety of daily circumstances.

- Pornographers are now using all of the above methods to lure and addict the female market through specific emotions, images and ideas.
- The pornography marketing campaign is radically altering attitudes and behavior toward human sexuality, women, marriage, rape, sexual deviance, etc.
- With constant technological advances, pornographers are utilizing *virtual reality* and *interactive sex* to push porn and sex addiction, deviant behaviors and crimes against the innocent to levels never before witnessed in history.

10

"Just Once" Will Hurt: Why Internet Pornography/Cybersex Is So Highly Addictive

---

Note: Many of the concepts discussed below are a result of interviews with and study of the teachings of Dr. Page Bailey, a leading pioneer in the field of mindbody science. Dr. Bailey is founder of the *Page Bailey Institute for the Recovery Sciences* and creator of the mindbody recovery system known as *Educotherapy.*

Why Your Brain and Body Seek To Turn Everything Into A Habit

I want you to consider what happens when a person is exposed to Internet pornography once, or numerous times. As in Dr. Bailey's writings, I will refer to the brain and the body in tandem as *mindbody,* because the two really **do not** function independently. Information, feelings, experiences, images, sounds, emotions, etc., are stored in cells throughout your brain and body, linked together by a complex highway of electrical and chemical connections. Truly we are one *mindbody.*[1]

HABIT—"JUST ONCE" *CAN* HURT YOU!

Doing anything—even once—provides your mindbody with the foundation for a habit. What role do habits play in your mindbody? Your mindbody innately tries to organize incoming data so that it can function on autopilot, so to speak, or with the least degree of effort. Your mindbody naturally sets up automatic responses to stimuli so it doesn't have to take the time to "think" every time it responds. So, you form habits in order to free up your conscious self to focus on other, more pertinent things. In other words, your mindbody seeks efficiency.[2]

For example, you buy a new car and spend time studying the operator's manual to figure out how everything works. Then after a few days or weeks, you find that you don't need to "think" about how to increase the volume on the CD player or how to turn on the rear defrost. Performing these functions just comes naturally. Your mindbody memory takes over. Can you imagine if every time you got into your car you had to consciously re-figure out how everything works! Your mindbody is designed to turn everything into a habit.

HABITS—WHAT ARE THEY AND WHY DO WE NEED THEM?

Your sitting position as you read this book, the way you hold it in your hand, your ability to concentrate, your reading speed, everything going on inside you at this moment is the result of "habit," or your mindbody seeking to do things efficiently.

Habits are the natural goal of your mindbody. You don't have to announce to your mindbody, "I'm going to form a habit now"; the mindbody is *always* in the process of forming habits. Habituation is the mindbody "standard." Your personality, or "who you are," is the sum total of all of your habits. **Remember**—Never do once what you don't want to do all the time.[3]

When you do something once, your mindbody assumes that you intend to do it again and again. Your mindbody forms habits with the greatest of ease. In fact, everything it does, it does with habit as its main objective. Yes, "just once *can* hurt you!"

WHY DOES THE MINDBODY SEEK TO TURN EVERYTHING INTO A HABIT?

The renowned behavioral scientist Abraham Maslow said that the brain in concert with the body is always hungering after "peak experiences." (For our purposes here we shall continue to refer to the entire human system—the mind and physical body—as one entity or mindbody, meaning that one part does not, and cannot for that matter, function separately from the other.) Maslow identified sex and music as the main ways that the mindbody attains peak experiences. But participating in other enterprises like science, poetry, prayer, dance, extreme sports, and so on, can supply the mindbody with a peak experience.[4]

Why is the mindbody in search of these experiences? The simple answer is that it constantly seeks "stimulation"; it can tolerate anything but boredom. Yet the mindbody finds itself overloaded with too much information all the time, and it craves being able to make order of and organize all the pieces of information it receives. Its natural instinct is to construct the pieces into a whole and then use this whole to achieve stimulation—or a peak experience—of some kind.

A trained computer programmer is able to create a wonderful program and enjoy the accolades of his or her colleagues—a peak experience. One who practices public speaking delivers a keynote address in front of a large audience and receives a standing ovation—a peak experience. You help someone in need, hug a child, overcome a challenge, receive a promotion and you feel warm and full inside—all peak experiences. Your mindbody has set standards that have been met as peak experiences, bringing greater meaning, fulfillment and excitement to your life. Your mindbody has successfully fit together the puzzle pieces it received from the outside world to create a "whole" picture, and now you have obtained the fruits of your efforts: peak experiences.

Is the stimulation or peak experience the mindbody seeks after always productive and positive? At the most basic, instinctive, biological level, the mindbody does not care what type of stimulation is achieved, so long as there is not the "absence" of stimulation.[5]

What determines the type of stimulation or peak experience a person will seek for? This is fully determined by the information, images and input the individual has allowed to be stored in the cells of her brain and body. In harmony with her stored values, beliefs, standards and convictions she will form her intentions, expectations and sincere desires. All these conscious and subconscious decisions and thoughts will be governed by her mindbody.

For example, if a man has spent hundreds of hours in front of Internet porn and has used it as the process to achieve the peak experience of orgasm, then his mindbody will organize all cellular-memories associated with this process so that orgasm through Internet porn can be duplicated over and over in the future with very little effort. All he need do is express the *intention* for this type of stimulation, and the entire network lights up and kicks into gear.

The most effective and efficient way for your mindbody to have as many peak experiences as possible is to form habits that lead to a specific peak experience. Your mindbody is always looking for ways to fit information, events, abilities, etc., together—like the pieces of a puzzle—to form a habit. It will then focus all its abilities and resources toward a *specific type* of peak experience.[6]

A dancer will probably not be able to unify the "parts" of her artistic expression in search of a peak experience by restoring an antique car. Only an antique car buff would find that specific activity "stimulating." Thus, if you are involved in a certain activity, your mindbody seeks a peak experience of "that kind."

Of course, your mindbody seeks out peak experiences in all areas of life, always trying to implement the information it receives in the most effective way possible. When your mindbody achieves a peak experience, it is inclined to always find ways to create a higher experience of that same kind the next time. So if the peak experience your mindbody seeks is in extreme sports, say skydiving or rock climbing, then it will work to achieve a bigger thrill or challenge the next time around. It's kind of like how an expert rock climber would not be satisfied being relegated to climb "kiddy cliffs," or how the pro skier covets the speed and thrill of a steep course rather than the safety of the "bunny slope."

Your mindbody will rally all its resources to practice and perfect its skills, through habit, so that the peak experience is even higher the next time: "I have written this poem, therefore I can write another more tender one." "I have climbed this mountain, therefore I can tackle a higher one."

Scientists have described our mindbody as having "trillions of intelligent cells—all waiting for our intention or instructions."[7] Once our mindbody understands the intention or expectation that we have for a certain peak experience, our cells will do everything they can to bring it about.

USING PORNOGRAPHY TO ACHIEVE THE PEAK EXPERIENCE OF ORGASM

As mentioned, one of the most powerful peak experiences that the human brain and body can experience (some experts says it is *the* most powerful) is orgasm. If the mindbody is always seeking peak experiences, then near or at the top of the list is orgasm.

Nature (or God) did not make us this way by accident. In its proper place and in its proper setting, the natural outcome of sexual union is orgasm. It is a wonderful "high" when experienced between two committed people who have a union, a tie, a marriage that grows to become a flowering love affair.

The power of romantic attraction and sexual intimacy is a big part of what drives a man and woman to accept and carry out the responsibilities of marriage and parenthood. Coupled with love, compassion and selflessness, sexual attraction can be a vital binding force for good.

Pornographers fully understand the power of orgasm as a peak experience, and seek to use this strong attraction for their own greedy, selfish purposes. Many claim that pornography is an innocent form of entertainment, like sports, dancing or music. But men and teenage boys don't masturbate while at a football game or during a symphony orchestra performance.

Yet Internet pornography sites targeted at the male market blatantly announce the fact that their total focus is to lead the male viewer to masturbate and achieve orgasm. Their ads invite men and teens to do just that and even go so far as to graphically portray it!

There are some Internet porn sites that target the female market and encourage masturbation. More common is the push to direct female viewers into sexually-oriented Internet chat rooms, where they are encouraged to masturbate through cybersex with other chat room participants.

Once anyone begins using Internet pornography or cybersex as the means to reach orgasm, his or her mindbody rallies all its resources to make this an automatic response—a habit. And, as discussed, with each porn or cybersex session thereafter the mindbody strives to make the present climax more intense than the last one. Once the mindbody falls into this cycle, the porn or cybersex process leading to orgasm becomes the mindbody's all-consuming focal point.

In order for the easily bored mindbody to achieve a higher peak experience the next time, the Internet pornography or cybersex chat must become harder and more perverse. Some inevitably begin mixing sex with violence, debauchery, mutilation and torture. Cybersex chat discussions become more and more daring and graphic.

Soon, images are not enough and the porn addict begins viewing live sex on the Internet. Many men and teenage boys then "graduate" to strip bars and prostitutes. And, finally, in an increasing number of cases, they work up to rape, and even murder—all in an effort to climb to a higher "peak experience." This was the process that produced a Ted Bundy.

And this process does not afflict men and boys alone. More and more women and teenage girls, bored with cybersex, are meeting their chat-room lovers for one-night stands or extended affairs. Women are leaving long-term marriages and families to run off with their Internet fantasy lovers. And these are not just the so-called "trashy women." Women who have long histories of a committed marriage, several children, active involvement with their church, good neighbors, etc., are falling prey to cybersex.

AN IMPORTANT UNDERSTANDING AND REVIEW

Once you learn how to drive a car with manual transmission, you never forget. Thereafter when you get into a car with a "stick-shift," your mindbody immediately links up all the cellular-memory groups needed for the task. Your left foot operates the clutch in coordination with your right foot, which operates the brake and accelerator. These in turn operate in tandem with your right hand on the gear-shift. The entire "habitual and efficient mindbody network" is in place. It's all virtually automatic—you don't give it much conscious thought.

The next time you hop into the car and express the intention that you want to drive somewhere, in a matter of microseconds that intention triggers an entire series of events. Your mindbody immediately searches out the network or group of linked cellular-memories that are best suited to carry out your intention. It then seeks the network of cells that are most accustomed to working together to drive the car. In other words, it seeks out the most "habitual" network of cells for the desired purpose. Your mindbody will almost always defer to your most powerful habit to accomplish a specific task within the frame of reference of that habit.

When a person has repeatedly achieved orgasm through viewing pornography or engaging in cybersex, his or her mindbody assumes that all the parts of the process are linked together as the most efficient (habitual) way to reach the peak experience called orgasm.

Next time this person feels the need of arousal or sexual release, the mindbody turns on the Internet porn and/or cybersex network almost automatically. There is little need for conscious thought. Suddenly the person is in front of the computer screen headed toward the desired peak experience of orgasm.

This arousal process can be triggered at any time or place. The next time a male Internet porn viewer sees a fully clothed woman, teenage girl or even a child walking on the street, the whole memory-cell network can switch on—like getting into a manual transmission car. What does this do to a man or teenage boy's ability to see a woman for what she really is rather than a collection of naked body parts and a way to arrive at orgasm?

Now you know how viewing pornography literally changes the physical and chemical structure of the human brain and body. But does Internet pornography effect the male brain and body in the same way it does the female brain and body? Are men and women attracted to the same kinds of pornography? Do they behave and react to pornography in the same way?

My research, review of case studies, conversations with therapists, and personal interviews with men and women clearly show that the answer is **NO!** Why? Simply because the structure of the male and female brain and body are different.

Key Points

A reference tool for
spouses, parents, clergy,
counselors and others

- The brain and the body are one system known as the *mindbody*. Pornography's effect is not limited to the brain—it enters and impacts the brain and body (mindbody) as a whole.
- Habits are the natural goal of the mindbody—it is always in the process of forming habits.
- The mindbody's highest use of habit is to efficiently seek increasingly powerful *peak experiences*.
- Sexual climax is one of the most powerful peak experiences that the mindbody can engage in. Combining this experience with pornography creates a habit pattern that becomes deeply etched in cellular-memory networks throughout the mindbody. This habit pattern easily becomes a profoundly debilitating addiction.

11

The Male Brain and the Female Brain: How Men and Women Are Wired Differently

---

A pastor, previously in the Navy, often wondered why ships were addressed as "she" and "her." When he became acquainted with computers, a similar thought crossed his mind: What "gender" was a computer? To answer the question, he pooled two groups of computer experts, the first comprised of women and the second of men. Each group was asked to say whether computers should be referred to in the feminine or masculine gender, and to give four reasons for their recommendations.

The group of women urged that computers be referred to in the masculine gender for the following rather flippant reasons:

- In order to get their attention, you have to turn them on.
- They have a lot of data, but are still clueless.
- They are supposed to help you solve problems, but half the time they are the problem.

- As soon as you commit to one, you realize that if you had waited a little longer you could have gotten a better model.

The men, on the other hand, concluded that computers should be referred to in the feminine gender for the following equally flippant reasons:

- No one but the Creator understands their internal language.
- The native language they use to communicate with other computers is incomprehensible to everyone else.
- Even your smallest mistakes are stored in long-term memory for later retrieval.
- As soon as you make a commitment to one, you find yourself spending half your paycheck on accessories for it.

Though most of the stabs at stereotypes were meant in the spirit of humor, they do make the point that men and women are different. Clearly, understanding these differences is critical if we are to correctly interpret how and why men and women are affected and attracted differently by Internet pornography.

STUDIES OF MALE AND FEMALE RESPONSES

Psychologists R.D. Clark and Elaine Hatfield hired attractive men and women to approach strangers of the opposite sex on a college campus with the line: "I've noticed you around campus. I find you very attractive," then follow up with three questions:

- "Would you go out with me tonight?"
- "Would you come over to my apartment tonight?"
- "Would you go to bed with me tonight?"

Half of the women questioned agreed to a date. Half of the men questioned agreed to a date. Six percent of the women consented to go to the stranger's apartment. Sixty-nine percent of the men who agreed to a date consented to go to the stranger's apartment. None of those women who agreed to go to the stranger's apartment would immediately consent to have sex with the stranger, whereas a whopping *seventy-five* percent of the men who consented to go to the stranger's apartment also consented to sex. Of the remaining twenty-five percent of the men, many were apologetic that they couldn't go to bed with the stranger, asked for a rain check, or offered the excuse that their fiancé was in town.[1]

These results have been replicated in several states with the same results. When the studies were conducted, contraception was available and safe-sex practices were heavily publicized, so the results cannot necessarily be dismissed simply because women might be more cautious about pregnancy or sexually transmitted diseases.

"MEN ARE SLIME"

Men are easily aroused by the sight of a nude woman, not only in the flesh but in movies, photographs, drawings and other media. This would explain a worldwide pornography industry that focuses heavily on male viewers and grossed over $56 billion in revenues in 1999, almost as much as all spectator sports and movies combined.[2]

The majority of pornography depicts in graphic physical detail a succession of anonymous nude females eager for casual, impersonal sex. Men on college campuses demonstrated their attraction to this type of material when a large percentage agreed to engage in sex with a complete stranger. Women, as a general rule, do not seek out the sight of naked male *strangers* or enactments of *anonymous* sex. This fact was borne out when women on college campuses did not wish to have sex with a complete stranger.

In the laboratory, the results of some early experiments claimed that men and women showed identical physiological arousal to pornographic images. However, later, more extensive testing revealed that men demonstrated a much stronger response to a completely neutral image than women showed to actual pornography.[3]

In the past, the closest mass-market equivalent to pornography for women has been the romance novel, in which sex is described in the context of emotions and relationships rather than as a succession of one-night stands. With their added "communication" and "relationship" elements, chat-rooms and cybersex are attracting greater numbers of women. Adult cable channels and certain Internet porn sites cater to the female market by focusing more on romance, tender dialogue and lasting relationships, mixed with soft-core and hard-core sex.

Thus, it appears that with most men, just the image of a nude female body, whether he knows the subject or not, is all that's required for arousal and sexual involvement. But with women this is not enough, and in fact there must be other significant elements added before pornography offers an attraction powerful enough to lead to a sexual escapade.

In one university psychology class, after discussing these issues, one female student raised her hand and said, "I have a simpler explanation of your data. . . . Men are slime."[4]

This would be an "easy out" if not for actual discoveries of the differences found between the structure and function of the female versus the male brain and body. Pornographers clearly understand these differences, which explains why they market so distinctly to men as compared to women, with their greatest focus on the male market.

WHAT ARE THE PRIMARY DIFFERENCES BETWEEN THE MALE AND FEMALE BRAINS?

Significant differences exist between the male and female brains. Although what follows has been meticulously gathered from the research and writings of leading scientists and psychologists, it is by no means a hard and fast rule or description of *every* man and *every* woman. Each person is different and unique.

However, the facts clearly bear out that for nearly all men and women there are *significant* differences between the male and female brain. This means that in most cases, men and women do not behave, feel, think or respond in the same ways, either on the inside or on the outside.

WOMEN ARE "WEB THINKERS" AND MEN ARE "STEP THINKERS"

Helen Fisher in her book *The First Sex*, refers to women as using "web thinking" as opposed to men using "step thinking." Women place an emphasis on the "whole," while males focus primarily on the "parts" of the whole—female multi-tasking vs. a male do-one-thing-at-a-time mentality.[5]

These differences center around how men and women use the right and left hemispheres of their brains. The male brain is narrow and highly specialized; the right side of the brain is used for visual activities, the left for verbal. Women, in contrast, use both sides of their brains for verbal and visual activities.

Tests have measured electrical activity in the brains of boys and girls engaged in the visual task of working out a three-dimensional puzzle. In boys the right side of the brain was consistently activated. In the girl subjects the electrical activity took place in both hemispheres of the brain.[6]

Other studies have confirmed that when emotional information was fed to the male brain, it was only fully recognized when fed to the right hemisphere. Women, on the other hand, recognized the emotional content of the information regardless of which hemisphere it was sent to, and in fact, recognized it over a wide range of both hemispheres at the same time.[7]

Note: Some scientists have suggested that because both visual capability and emotions are bundled together exclusively in the right hemisphere of the male brain, the key perceptual sense in the male is **vision**. Dr. Judith Reisman has indicated that this male dependence on the right hemisphere causes them to respond to visual stimuli with more vigor and speed than females.[8] [This partly explains why the primary market for Internet pornography is male.]

Females, on average, use more of their brain space for specific activities, while men use far less. And women employ a greater spectrum of the brain while men rely more on a specific area of either hemisphere. This results in men naturally focusing narrowly on an issue, while women more naturally see the big picture. Men are able to focus on an issue and be less distracted by anything superfluous going on around them. Ever see a man glued to the TV or the sports page, seemingly oblivious to the chaos around him?[9]

Men tend to be more analytical, extracting the essential from the circumstantial detail—"just the facts, ma'am, just the facts." Women, in contrast, take in the larger picture. They're concerned with context, just as men are forever trying to ignore it for the sake of something they can abstract from it. It's a standoff between brain hemisphere-specific focus vs. wide, hemisphere-diffused focus.[10]

It is true that the female brain is somewhat "lateralized," meaning that some tasks are carried out predominantly on the left or right side. The male brain, however, is far more specialized and lateralized than the female brain. In males, each hemisphere is more rigidly dedicated to performing a single, specific task.[11]

Psychiatrist Mark George of the National Institute of Mental Health proposes that this brain structure difference may enable men to focus their attention more intensely than women. In her book *The First Sex,* Helen Fisher agrees, adding that "women's less lateralized (more integrated) brain probably helps them to embrace the larger view." As psychiatrist Mona Lisa Schultz of the Maine Medical Center puts it: "Because women's brains are less lateralized, they may have access to this area in both the right and left hemispheres. They don't see things as cut and dried, the way men do."[12]

What are the causes of these male/female brain differences? Scientists are still trying to sort it all out, but here are some of the major findings thus far:

THE CORPUS CALLOSUM

One body of evidence explains male/female brain differences by examining the *corpus callosum*, the bundle of some two hundred million fibers that link the left and right sides of the brain. These nerve fibers allow for the interchange of information between the brain's two halves. In the female brain, the *corpus callosum* is different than in that of the male.

In blind tests on fourteen brains obtained after autopsy, scientists found that in women an important area of the corpus callosum was thicker and more bulbous than in men. Overall, this key *message-exchange center* was bigger (in relation to overall brain weight) in women.[13] (Some studies indicate that the corpus callosum may be up to three times larger by weight and density in the female brain than in the male.[14])

The hemispheres of a woman's brain share a larger number of connections, suggesting a greater exchange of information between the two sides. Also, more total brain space has been reserved for everyday activities, so that the information she is receiving from the outside world is processed by a much larger portion of her brain.[15]

In general, women are better at recognizing the emotional nuances in voice, gesture and facial expression, and at interpreting the whole range of sensory information. They can deduce more from such information because they have a greater capacity than men to integrate and cross-relate verbal and visual information.[16]

Men keep their emotions in check by relying on their right-brain thinking, while their power to express feelings in speech resides in the left hemisphere. Because the two halves of their brains are connected by a smaller number of fibers than those of women, the flow of information between one side of the brain and the other is more restricted.[17] Because information is flowing less easily to the verbal, left side of his brain, it is often more difficult for a man to express his emotions.

A woman may naturally integrate emotion with reason because of the way her brain is organized. The female brain is wired with emotional capacities in both hemispheres, plus more information is exchanged between the two halves. Hence, her emotional side is more integrated with her verbal side. She is more suited to revealing her emotions in words because what she feels has been transmitted more effectively to the verbal side of her brain.

MEN CONCENTRATE MORE NARROWLY, WHILE WOMEN SEE THE BIG PICTURE

Studies show that men concentrate more intently on a narrower range of items; they are capable of ignoring distractions because, with a specific part of their brain strictly focused on the task at hand, they are deaf and blind to distractions around them.[18]

Contrarily, psychologists report that women more regularly think contextually; they take a more "holistic" view of the issue at hand. That is, they integrate more details of the world around them, details ranging from the nuances of body posture to the positioning of objects in the room.[19]

Men are good at compartmentalizing their attention. Just ask a man who is reading the newspaper a simple question—often he doesn't even consciously hear you. When he does, he appears to rouse himself as if returning from a different planet. Men tend to tune out extraneous stimuli. Their thinking process is, on average, more channeled.[20]

Women, though, are prone to the opposite. "Whatever they do— even just wiggling their thumbs—women activate more neurons in the brain," reports neuro-psychiatrist Mark George of the Medical University of South Carolina. "When a male puts his mind to work, brain-scans show neurons turning on in highly specific areas. When females set their minds on similar tasks, so many brain cells light up that their bright-colored brain-scans glow like Las Vegas at night.[21]

This observation supports the theory that the male brain tends to be more 'lateral' and divides tasks between its two hemispheres, while the female brain draws more equally on both sides. The compartmentalization of the male brain, researchers theorize, may enhance the ability to focus intensely—an evolutionary essential in many species."[22]

TESTOSTERONE VS. ESTROGEN—ANOTHER KEY MALE/FEMALE DIFFERENCE

Hormones are *mind* chemicals. Acting on the brain, they signal for it to produce certain changes in the body. In the case of males, the hormone principally involved is testosterone.

Testosterone has been shown to have a significant effect on the male brain, a clinical fact that has been well documented. It is a hormone which seems to make the male brain less liable to fatigue—more single-minded. By nature, as we have seen, the male brain can more narrowly focus on a specific issue, subject or goal as well as latch on to that focus more swiftly than the female brain. Testosterone takes the already narrowing male brain and magnifies the narrowing tendency and capacity even further![23]

Testosterone also gives the male brain the ability to focus intensely and narrowly on specific issues and interests for long periods of time without tiring.[24]

ESTROGEN ENHANCES THE COMMUNICATION BETWEEN THE RIGHT AND LEFT HEMISPHERES IN THE FEMALE BRAIN

By contrast, we have discussed how the female brain is more diffused and operates on a wide rather than a narrow scale. Just as testosterone further narrows an already narrow male brain, estrogen, the primary female hormone, actually increases the female brain's diffusing or broadening capability. In *The First Sex*, Helen Fisher writes: "Estrogen builds more dendrite projections or spines on each nerve cell, thereby increasing the number of connecting links between nerve cells. Hence, estrogen facilitates the flow of information among neurons."[25]

The female brain already owns more communication channels between the two hemispheres than does the male brain. With the addition of estrogen in the female brain, these connections are even more substantial.

TESTOSTERONE TRIGGERS THE RELEASE OF EVEN MORE TESTOSTERONE

With men, the impact of testosterone on the brain not only produces aggression, dominance and assertiveness, it also triggers the release of even more testosterone, reinforcing the initial aggressive tendencies. Among male athletes, for example, testosterone levels are higher at the end of a match or of a season than at the beginning. Apparently competition begets competition by the raising of testosterone levels. In other words, rivalry fuels further aggression.[26]

TESTOSTERONE REGULATES SEX DRIVE IN BOTH MEN AND WOMEN

Testosterone, the aggression and dominance hormone, is also the sex hormone—both in men and women. It is the key sexual activator for both sexes.[27] Women who lose their ovaries (which produce female hormones) still retain their full capacity for sexual arousal. At menopause, when the ovaries shut down the production of female hormones, women do not lose their appetite for sex, rather it is fueled by testosterone instead. But if they lose the adrenal gland, which produces and controls the flow of testosterone, their libido collapses. It can, however, be restored by testosterone injections.

There are two important differences, however, in how testosterone affects men vs. women. First, a man's brain is better attuned to the effects of testosterone upon it, quite simply because it has been so made through the impact of testosterone in the womb. Secondly, after puberty, a man has 20 times more of the substance in his body than does a woman.[28]

This means that the blend of aggression, dominance and sexuality is a headier, much more controlling mixture in men. The more testosterone, the greater the sexual urges are made manifest, be they homosexual or heterosexual, orthodox or deviant.

Key Points

A reference tool for spouses, parents, clergy, counselors and others

- The male brain is highly specialized, using specific parts of one hemisphere or the other to accomplish specific tasks. The female brain is more diffused and utilizes significant portions of both hemispheres for a variety of tasks.
- Men are able to "focus" on narrow issues and block out unrelated information and distractions. Women naturally see everyday things from a broader, "big-picture" vantage point.
- Men can narrowly focus their brains on specific tasks or activities for long periods of time without tiring.
- Men are able to separate information, stimulus, emotions, relationships, etc.,into separate compartments in their brains, while women tend to "link" everything together. Men see individual issues with "parts" of their brain, while women see holistic or multiple issues with their "whole" brain (both hemispheres).
- Men have as much as 20 times more testosterone in their systems than do women. This makes men typically more aggressive,

dominant and more narrowly focused on the physical aspects of sex.

- In men, the dominant perceptual sense is "vision," which is typically not the case with women. All of a woman's senses are, in some respects, more finely tuned than those of a man.
- Pornographers incorporate male/female differences into the design and marketing of their wares. Just because something might not appeal to a man doesn't mean that a woman won't be attracted to it, and vice-versa.

12

How Male and Female Brain Differences Affect the Way Each Views Human Intimacy

Perhaps the greatest impact of the differences between the male/female brain is how men and women view sexuality and intimacy. It is important to understand the contrasts in these views in order to comprehend the vulnerabilities men and women have to Internet pornography and cybersex chat rooms. Internet pornographers are cognizant of these differences and market specifically to each set of potential customers.

Again, the insights that follow are not absolutes, but represent what most therapists, psychologists and scientists consider to be the "majority" of men and women. The facts are not listed in any particular order and are not intended to be a complete study. Rather, they are presented to help you understand the unique male and female views of sexual intimacy as a result of the differences in their respective brain structures.

Special Note: The descriptions that follow are the findings of professionals who have dedicated their lives to the study of male and female sexuality. You will note that some of the male descriptions are not very flattering; many paint a downright cold, animalistic picture. Unfortunately, the descriptions represent a large cross section of the male population in our society. And with Internet porn and cybersex, these common attitudes are growing.

Let me clearly state that I ***do not*** believe that men (or women) are locked into these negative stereotypes. We each have the inner capacity, strength, and innate goodness to rise above "animal/sexual" instinct if we choose to. We are not dogs; we are not forced into the "reactive-impulse" mode from which the Internet pornographers profit. I believe that we are so much better than that. I believe that the potential of human intimacy is light-years ahead of what is portrayed on the sterile screen of Internet porn.

WOMEN SEE RELATIONSHIPS, MEN SEE BODY PARTS

Anne Moir & David Jessel, in their book *Brain Sex: The Real Difference Between Men & Women*, write: *Women are not, in the main, turned on by pictures of nudes. . . . Women may be aroused by pictures of couples coupling—because what they are seeing, in however sterile a sexual context, is a relationship in action. Women are not excited by a picture of male genitalia by itself. . . . Men like female genital close-ups in porn magazines because it is a thing to which they can imagine doing things. Sex for men is vastly impersonal—pornography is simply meat for men. Do they ever wonder who the nude is? Not for a moment—they wonder what they would do to her.*[1]

In her book *The First Sex*, Helen Fisher writes: *In a 1920s study of several hundred American men and women, 65% of the men said that they had done some peering through a bedroom window. Only 20% of the women had done any stealthy ogling. Men are more turned on by visual stimuli. They use pornographic materials of every kind more frequently than women do. When they fantasize, they conjure up more images of coitus and body parts, the explicit details of sex itself.*[2]

Helen Fisher continues: *Women, too, are excited by visual erotica, although women are not as turned on by it as men are. Women are much more aroused than men by romantic words, images, and themes in films and stories. Women's sexual fantasies include more affection and commitment. Women often dwell on their own emotional reactions. And they are more than twice as likely to think about a sex partner's emotional characteristics.*[3]

Diane Hales, in her book *Just Like a Woman*, quotes Beverly Whipple, president of the American Association of Sex Education Counselors and Therapists, and mixes in her own insights: *"Women have a variety of sexual responses, and not all fit in with the monolithic pattern described by Masters and Johnson," says Whipple. "Female sexual response may be much more complex than anyone ever guessed." Men, she notes, tend to view sex—like many other things—in a linear way. To them, a sexual encounter is like descending a staircase that leads step by step to only one endpoint: ejaculation. Woman's sexuality, like our ways of taking in and thinking about the world, is more holistic.*[4]

"I see female sexual response in a circle, with every aspect of sexual interaction—touching, kissing, hugging—as a pleasurable endpoint in itself," Whipple says. For women, the process of making love—the holding and the hugging and the tenderness—can be as emotionally gratifying as orgasm itself, and sometimes even more so.[5]

When women experience sex not as a ten-nine-eight countdown to climax, not as quest or test, but in terms of sensing, knowing, and feeling what one poet calls "the song of life singing" through them, then Eros offers more than mere physical gratification. This may indeed be what sex was meant to be—an experience that touches the essence of who we are in ways not unlike a spiritual revelation.[6]

Anne Moir & David Jessel, in their book *Brain Sex: The Real Difference Between Men & Women*, state: *The female mind is organized to place priority on relationship, the male on achievement. Men keep a tally of their sexual conquests. The female brain is not organized to keep sex in a separate compartment. This is a male model—as if his brain has a specific filing cabinet for sex, completely unrelated to emotion.*[7]

This ability to "compartmentalize" is why a man can put his involvement with pornography in one compartment (or cellular-memory group) in his brain, and his relationship with his wife in another. He may consider the two to be completely unrelated. Many men can't understand why their wife makes such a big "emotional fuss" when she finds out he has been viewing pornography.

Helen Fisher sums up: *Flowers, oils, candlelight, satin sheets, fluffy towels: when women fantasize about sex, they conjure up the textures, sounds, and smells, all of the ambience surrounding sex, more regularly than men. Women also like more kissing, hugging, stroking, and cuddling during sex. In short, women place the act of intercourse within a wider physical context.*[8]

"Men think having orgasm is having sex. That's the difference," remarked one woman in the Prodigy survey. There is a kernel of truth in what she says. Female sexuality is nested in a broader lattice of emotions, a wider range of physical sensations, and a more extensive social and environmental context—all reflections of feminine web thinking. Men's sex drive is far more focused on the act of copulation itself—yet another example of men's propensity to compartmentalize the world around them and focus their attention on specific elements.[9]

And David Jessel and Anne Moir in their book *Brain Sex: The Real Difference Between Men & Women*, have this to say: *Men want sex, and women want relationships. Men want flesh and women want love. Just as boys wanted balloons, toys, and carburetors, the girls have always wanted contact, and communion, and company.*[10]

In a 1996 survey of 720 American teenage girls, the majority concluded that girls engage in sex because they think they will lose their boyfriends if they don't, or because boys pressure them into sex. "Girls trade sex for love, and boys say they love them to get sex," says Deborah Tolman of the Wesley Center for Research on Girls and Women. "Girls don't realize they are entitled to have their own feelings and desires and to expect others to take them into account."[11] (Just the opposite of what porn teaches boys.)

With a clear understanding of the differences between the male and female brain and their opposing views of human sexuality and intimacy, you don't have to be a genius to figure out why and how pornographers market differently to men and women. Before we talk about how pornographers are targeting these polar-opposite markets, it is important that you understand one final, critical segment of mindbody science: ***The Funnel of Sexual Arousal***.

Key Points

A reference tool for
spouses, parents, clergy,
counselors and others

- The structure of the male brain vs. the female brain is very different. As a result, men and women, teenage girls and boys, do not react to nor view sexuality and intimacy the same way.
- Pornographers approach the male and female markets differently. What seems harmless, uninteresting or meaningless to a woman may be extremely powerful and addictive to a man, or vice-versa. We must be aware of what materials, stimuli and circumstances make men and women, teenage boys and girls, most vulnerable and at greatest risk when it comes to pornography, chat rooms, movies, TV programs, etc.

13

THE FUNNEL OF SEXUAL AROUSAL AND THE "NARROWING PROCESS"

THE FUNNEL OF SEXUAL AROUSAL

As we have already seen, our mindbody is persistent in its mission to seek to link information, experiences and knowledge together, and thus achieve a "peak experience." Orgasm is one the most intense peak experiences the mindbody can experience. And one orgasm cannot take place without what is called the "narrowing process."

Our mindbody is like a narrow landing strip—only one plane can set down at a time. For example, if you are in conversation with someone, and the TV is blaring in the background and children are screaming and playing outside, in order to clearly make out what the children are up to you must "let go" of the conversation first. Of course, if you do so, then the conversation becomes background.

Yes, there are those that can pull the "stunt" of performing multiple tasks, but the natural tendency of the mind is to focus on only one thing at a time. In fact, the mindbody craves a singular focus. Why? Because it is by way of a singular focus that it has the greatest access to all its own learning resources.[1]

The mindbody assumes that its number one responsibility is to *learn.* It is there to acquire new experiences, learn from them, then turn them into habit so it can go on and focus on new tasks, habituate them—and the cycle continues. How does the mindbody access its highest ability to carry out this function? By a *single focus*—one plane at a time on the landing strip. The mindbody is a master of focus.

Orgasm requires a "one plane on the landing strip" type focus in order to take place.[2] As with any sexual activity, this focus by a man or woman as they move toward orgasm is legitimate and desirable **in the appropriate setting**. The following discussion of the "funnel of Sexual Arousal" and the "narrowing process" provides an explanation of sexual functionality without any implied moral commentary.

NARROWING DOWN THE FUNNEL INTO THE TUNNEL OF ORGASM

If orgasm is one of the most intense, single-focus peak experiences that the human mindbody can experience, but it can only take place through a "narrow focus," how does the mindbody do this? In order to understand this process, consider the following illustration:

The Funnel of Sexual Arousal

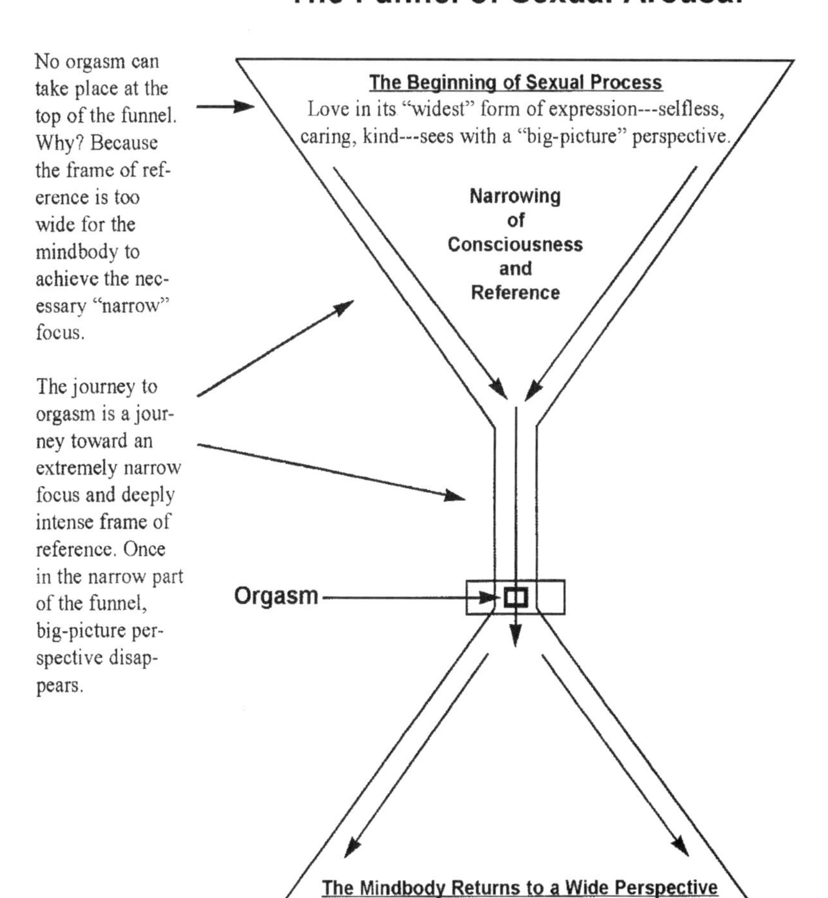

No orgasm can take place at the top of the funnel. Why? Because the frame of reference is too wide for the mindbody to achieve the necessary "narrow" focus.
The journey to orgasm is a journey toward an extremely narrow focus and deeply intense frame of reference. Once in the narrow part of the funnel, big-picture perspective disappears.
The Beginning of Sexual Process
Love in its "widest" form of expression---selfless, caring, kind---sees with a "big-picture" perspective.
Narrowing of Consciousness and Reference
Orgasm
The Mindbody Returns to a Wide Perspective
Love in its "widest" form of expression---selfless, caring, kind---returns to its "big picture" perspective.

At the top of the funnel, we are in control of our thoughts, perspectives, beliefs, morals, etc., and keep them in check in the "widest sense." Keep in mind that women more naturally think at the top of the funnel much of the time, while men can narrow down to the bottom of the funnel very quickly and stay there for longer periods of time.

When a person "lets go" and moves from the top of the funnel, narrowing toward orgasm, everything at the "big-picture" level of thought starts to fade away as the mindbody begins to narrowly focus on the attainment of a powerful peak experience. Our wide perspective and full mental faculties are not accessed again until after orgasm, when we emerge from the tunnel at the base of the funnel. This narrowing process is where the powerful differences between the male and female brain structure really manifest themselves.

THE MALE BRAIN IN THE FUNNEL

When a man or teenage boy uses pornography as the process to arrive at the peak experience of orgasm, the results are usually mind-boggling.

Remember, because of testosterone and the structure of the male brain, a man or boy can focus intensely on a single subject for long periods of time. He also can block out all other thoughts and distractions.

Men typically do not think in terms of the big picture, but rather on the specific issues at hand. They tend to be more goal-oriented and can focus intensely on getting to the finish line, completing the project, winning the trophy, while blocking out all other thoughts not related to the end goal. This is not to suggest that a man cannot see things from a wide perspective. If he makes an effort to do so, he can see the big picture. But, given a specific task, goal or purpose, he tends to narrow rapidly and utilize a specific area of the brain on one hemisphere or the other.

What do you think happens when a man begins to focus on pornographic images with the **intention** or **goal** to achieve the peak experience of orgasm? The male mindbody *races* down the funnel and narrows at an amazing rate.

After orgasm and exiting the narrow opening at the base of the funnel, the male mindbody returns quickly to the wide part of the funnel. With their senses restored, men often ask themselves after a porn-viewing session,

"How could have I forgotten my wife and children, my religion, my convictions?"

How can a man, staring at pornography, with all of his focus on attaining the culminating peak-experience of orgasm, possibly be thinking about his wife and children at the same time? He can't. Having descended into the narrow base of the funnel, he surrenders his ability to see the "big picture" and what ought to be most important to him.

As a man narrows his mental consciousness, chemical and hormonal responses are triggered in the brain and body that would not be triggered if he stayed at the top of the funnel. When a man viewing pornography begins his descent into the funnel that leads to orgasm, this narrowing leads to "switches" that are not accessible at the wide perspective level of thinking. Remember, the mindbody can only experience orgasm on a "narrow landing strip." Once he heads down the funnel to where the switches of arousal and orgasmic focus are tripped, there is little hope of him being able to turn back. (In a similar way, we counsel teenagers not to start down the funnel of sexual arousal in the first place, because they will reach a point where their bodies take over and rational thought is lost.)

COMMENTS FROM MALE PORN ADDICTS ABOUT THE FUNNEL

In gathering research for this book, I conducted interviews (both formal and casual) with men who have been or are now addicted to Internet pornography. As soon as I show them the funnel illustration, it's like a light going on. The standard comment is, "That's exactly the way it is!"

Without exception, these men talk about how rapidly their focus and perspective narrows with Internet pornography. But the amazing and frightening thing is, the narrowing process usually began before they actually turned on their computer!

John, a man with a typical Internet porn addiction problem, said, "I would be going through a normal day and then suddenly I would get this urge to look at porn. Once the urge hit me, it was like everything around me became unimportant. All I could think about was getting to a computer. It was like I was being pulled by some powerful force. I would cancel meetings, or make up excuses, do anything necessary to get to the computer. Once there, I blocked out everything else. I would spend hours looking at porn on the Internet. It was like I was in a cave and the rest of the world didn't exist. These sessions always ended with masturbation, after which it was like I was suddenly coming out of a cave and seeing the world again. I remember being shocked when I would look at my watch and realize how long I was out of commission. It was almost like I didn't know where I'd been—like waking up from a dream or something."

With virtually everyone I spoke it was the same story. They described being pulled or pushed down the funnel—almost as if its sides were greased and once they had begun their downward plunge, pulling up was nigh to impossible.

They all talked about being trapped in the narrow tunnel, glued to the images, riveted by desire, completely consumed, out of control. They referred to everything around them as being blocked out, blurred or of little significance. And in every case they described the sensation of emerging from the narrow tunnel after masturbation and suddenly coming to their senses, stepping out of the dark, once more being aware of everything around them.

The desire to experience a sexual encounter and orgasm is triggered in the male very quickly because the brain narrows very quickly. The sexual stimulation of pornography floods directly into the male brain stem where higher reasoning is eliminated and automatic response or animal instinct takes over.

In *Brain Sex, The Real Difference Between Men and Women,* Anne Moir and David Jessel state the following: *Male lust is blind. High testosterone acting on the male brain increases the narrow focus and "single-minded" approach to the "object" of his desires. After orgasm, testosterone levels subside and the male brain starts to receive a wider input of information without the "narrowing" effect of larger amounts of testosterone present during arousal.*[3]

An Interesting Side Note

It isn't only pornography that pulls men into such a narrowing process. Since the beginning of time men and boys have enmeshed themselves in dangerous, foolish, careless and crazy things in the "narrow tunnel" at the base of the funnel. But instead of the peak experience being orgasm, it is something else such as the thrill of danger, the heat of competition, the enticement of mischief.

How many times after pulling some really dumb or dangerous prank has a boy or man been asked, *"What on earth were you thinking?"* And the response has usually come, *"I don't know,"* or *"I just had the sudden urge to do it."*

And you know what? When you ask, "What on earth were you thinking," you can already assume that they "weren't thinking at all," but were acting on instinct in the narrow passageway at the bottom of the funnel, in hot pursuit of a peak experience. With a narrow "male" focus on a single end goal, the wide-perspective and logical-reasoning mechanisms were completely blocked out.

Some have suggested that this "blocking out" of logic and reason is due to the fact that the male brain recognizes emotion and visual stimuli in the right hemisphere, while logic and reasoning are located in the left. And remember, the left and right hemispheres of the male brain do not act together or communicate very effectively in performing tasks.

What happens then when a man looks at porn? The visual images race to the right hemisphere where the emotions of arousal, and excitement are located. The right hemisphere "narrowly" focuses on the nude images, and as a result of the accompanying sexual arousal, more testosterone is released, narrowing the brain's focus even further.

Where is the logical, left side of the brain during all of this? Once a man heads down the funnel and narrows beyond a certain point, the logical side doesn't even come into play. Or if there is faint communication of reason, it is totally overpowered by emotion and arousal.

To better understand the male narrowing process, consider the following analogy:

THE HIGHWAY AND THE NARROW TUNNEL

Imagine you are driving along a well maintained highway. You enjoy a clear and wide view of the rolling countryside around you. There are many options for you to choose from: other highways to merge onto, exits to take, you could even turn around and go back the other way. You see an interesting landscape in the distance and decide to explore it "for just a minute."

You exit the highway. Suddenly the sides of the road begin to taper inward and a dark tunnel looms up ahead. You are losing your view of the countryside around you and there are no more exits. You try to stop the car, but the gas pedal is stuck and the brakes won't work. You try to turn back, but the steering wheel won't budge.

Your car roars steadily ahead. With all your options exhausted, you have no choice but to drive straight into the darkness. You don't know how long you are in the tunnel. Time seems to stand still.

Then in a burst of light you emerge from the darkness into the light. You take the on-ramp and get back on the highway. Once again you can see the wide expanse of the countryside, the exits, the side roads. Your brakes, gas pedal and steering now are all operating normally.

But something happened back there in that tunnel. You glance down at your watch. "Four o'clock!" You were in there for over three hours! But how? Suddenly you feel ashamed; regret and guilt wash over you like a wave. Something happened in that tunnel—something you're not particularly proud of, something you wish you hadn't done.

Knowing what you do about the male brain and its attitudes toward sexuality and intimacy, can you see why it does what it does when trapped in the funnel? The rapid narrowing, the intense focus for short or long periods, the singular goal on visual arousal leading to orgasm, blocking out all other thoughts, distractions or surroundings, and suddenly regaining reality after climax. All of these are perfectly matched to the structure of the male brain. The funnel is an addictive nightmare for the one who is trapped and a money-making dream come true for the Internet pornographer.

THE FEMALE BRAIN AND THE FUNNEL

How does the female brain operate in the funnel of sexual arousal? With every woman I spoke to about this issue, including those who were presently involved with Internet porn and cybersex chat rooms, the response was universal: Yes, a woman does slip and slide down the funnel, but with some very important differences:

- None of the women indicated that they had ever been pulled uncontrollably down the funnel with no way to stop. Each of them used *one* word to describe their slippery descent into the funnel: "choice." They each said that narrowing toward orgasm was a conscious choice rather than an uncontrollable compulsion. They only descended down the funnel when they wanted to and at their own pace.
- They all agreed that they had never narrowed to the point where everything else was completely blocked out. None of them had experienced suddenly emerging from the tunnel after orgasm and exclaiming, "What just happened? Where was I?"
- The women maintained that although orgasm was highly enjoyable, it was not their singular focus and be-all/end-all goal. In fact, they contended that if the other important elements of intimacy were experienced, and orgasm was not reached in a given situation, they could be just as satisfied with the experience. (With all of the men I interviewed, the attitude was entirely opposite—the funnel

experience could not be complete without orgasm; orgasm was the total focus.)

- None of the women were interested in Internet porn images all by themselves as *the* way to narrow down the funnel to orgasm. Each insisted that there had to be more to it than that.

Each of these areas of response from women make total sense when measured according to the structure of the female brain. The female brain is not organized so as to keep sex and the process leading up to orgasm in a separate, narrow mental compartment like the male brain does.

A woman is exerting both sides of her brain when she steps into the funnel. She also connects the process with a wider variety of emotional information against a background where relationships, communication and emotional fulfillment are more important than the single, narrow event of orgasm.

FOR WOMEN, THE RIGHT SETTING IS PARAMOUNT

Because she is so much more aware of her emotions, thoughts and feelings at a much wider perspective, it takes the right setting and a longer period of time for a woman to allow herself to get to the place in the funnel where she begins "throwing the switches" leading to orgasm. This, of course, is completely contrary to the classic porn flick scenario, in which the woman plays the willing victim, the ravenous nymphomaniac, the office hussy.

Porn also shows women writhing in pleasure, achieving orgasm at the drop of a hat and under all circumstances. These responses are obviously staged. Few if any women could become aroused so easily, especially in such situations. Remember, porn seeks to create fantasy women who respond sexually the same way a man might—or in the way a man *wishes* his fantasy woman would respond.

In the female brain the centers of logic, reason, arousal and emotion are well connected. A woman thus will not typically narrow down the funnel unless she has considered the big picture and deems the journey to be in line with her overall values, reasoning and goals.

And even when she does slide down the funnel, a woman's narrowing is not nearly on the same level as that of a man's. Again, remember, even when focusing on a single issue, such as intimacy and climax, a woman is still exerting her entire brain and on a wider scale when compared to the male. A woman's reasoning is still intact at some level, which is why all the women I interviewed used the word "choice." And this would explain why they did not suddenly "regain their reasoning when coming out of the tunnel"—basic reasoning was connected to the process all the time.

In *The First Sex,* Helen Fisher writes the following: *Women are more likely than men to be distracted during coitus. If a woman hears a baby cry, recalls something that happened at the office, or wonders if she turned off the stove, her concentration can be interrupted. She has to reset her focus and rebuild her sexual excitement. Men are better able to keep their attention riveted on sex. . . . Women tend to assimilate many disparate thoughts at once—web thinking. Web thinking may disrupt their concentration as they make love.*[4]

Several of the women I interviewed proposed that the funnel of intimacy be rendered slightly differently for women. They offered the following adjustments:

1. The female funnel should be wider at the top, indicating that women start out using more brain space and taking in a wider range of information, emotions, etc.

2. The female funnel should narrow more gradually, with "exits" or "rest stops" along the way, suggesting that women more slowly narrow toward orgasm and can halt the process at will. Further more, they can be completely satisfied if the process is put on hold, if other important elements are present.

3. The tunnel at the base of the funnel should be wider than that of the male's, indicating that, even in its narrowed state, the female brain still maintains a wider perspective and is continuing to consider a wide range of choices, emotions and information.

Dr. C.Y. Robi, a psychologist with over 20 years' experience counseling thousands of male and female sex offenders and sex addicts, compares the difference in male and female sexual arousal as follows:

Regardless of which model is used, suffice it to say that men and women do not approach nor experience sexual arousal in the same way. Through a more habitual, mindbody process, a man may use Internet porn

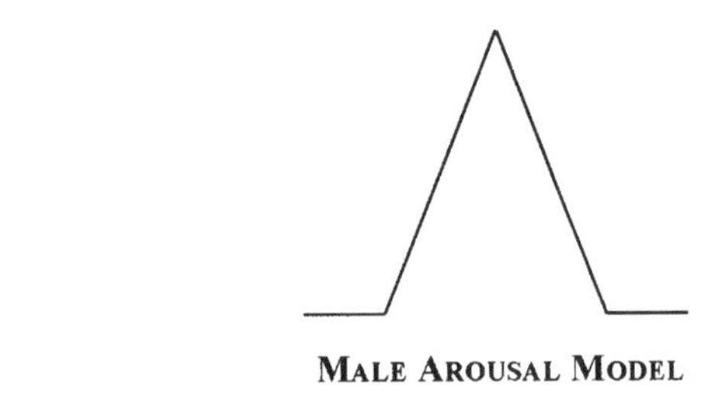

MALE AROUSAL MODEL

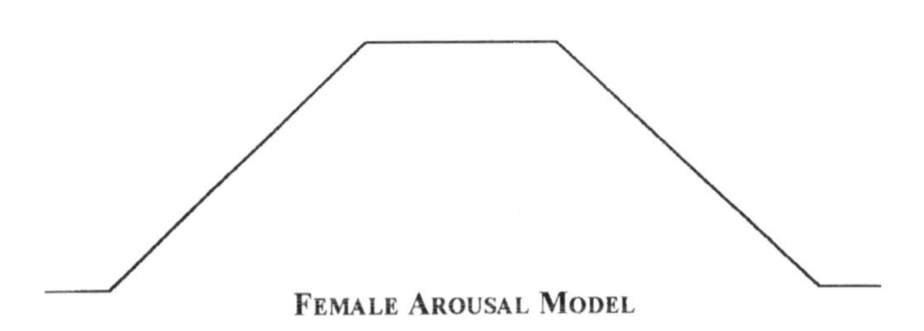

FEMALE AROUSAL MODEL

as the process to achieve orgasm. And each subsequent time he expresses that intention, his mindbody is trained to seek out the network of cellular-memories that activate the process and he quickly begins the slippery slide down the funnel.

When a woman expresses an intention for a sexual experience, her mindbody requires much more than some pornographic images. Since she must receive a much wider range of stimuli in order to be fulfilled, her mindbody will seek for the network of cellular-memories best equipped to make her intention a reality. This network generally will be much larger and more complex than in the male, and so her journey down the funnel is necessarily wider, slower, and much more of a "consciously-directed" process.

Given what I have learned about the female brain and based on numerous interviews and discussions, I would have to agree that the female funnel of intimacy should be rendered differently than that of the male. However, there is a disturbing trend with Internet porn and cybersex chat rooms that indicates a growing number of women may be approaching the funnel more like men do—traveling down the funnel more quickly and more narrowly! Women are becoming addicted to their cybersex relationships as surely as men are addicted to cyberporn.

Now that we have thoroughly explored the differences between the male vs. the female mindbodies, with these differences in mind, let's take a look at how Internet pornographers entice each separate market.

Key Points

A reference tool for spouses, parents, clergy, counselors and others

- The Funnel model depicts how porn-viewing men narrow their focus to achieve orgasm. This model is a key to understanding the male porn addiction process.
- When women are introduced to this model, they usually begin to understand for the first time how their husband, son, brother or boyfriend can get so caught up in pornography—and how they could abandon values and loved ones.
- The Funnel model is also extremely valuable in helping pornography addicts finally understand why they lose all perspective and reason in the addictive process, and what creates the *hopeless dialogue*.

14

How Internet Pornographers Target the Male Brain

Internet pornographers are some of the most cunning, degenerate marketers and salespeople in the entire world—real or virtual. They know their craft and have devised laser-focus techniques to capture each of their target markets.

Based on the structure of the male brain, how do Internet pornographers market to men and teenage boys? Let's review the typical attributes of the potential male Internet porn consumer in the cold, hard terminology the pornographers use. How do they seduce their customers?

1. Vision is the key perceptual sense in males—they "like to look." They typically respond with far more vigor and speed to visual stimuli than females do.
2. Males are able to descend down the funnel of arousal lightning fast and block out all thoughts and attached emotions of wife, romance, tenderness and love. Their total focus is on the physical act of sex. They typically yearn to see "body parts" and things being done to those body parts.

3. Males are more attracted to anonymous, nude females for casual, impersonal sex. They are usually less interested in relationships, romance, foreplay or anything connected with these. Instead, they are more prone to "get right down to business"—the explicit physical sex act.
4. Males can have up to 20 times more testosterone coursing through their mindbody than a female. Testosterone fuels sexual drive and aggression. As a result, it's a turn-on for most viewers to see males dominate, be aggressive or even violent during the sex act.
5. The male brain can focus narrowly for long periods of time on body parts and the physical act of sex. Therefore, a variety of changing material and an increase in stimulation are required or male viewers can become bored. The pornographer must lure them into the site, keep them there, then bring them back for more the next time.
6. The end goal for males in viewing Internet porn is masturbation and orgasm. Pornographer's must be sure that their male viewers complete this process to assure addiction and the powerful imprinting of the images in the cells of the male mindbody.

With all of this in mind, how do Internet pornographers provide content that taps into the male brain at the highest level possible? Consider their techniques:

VISUAL STIMULATION AT THE HIGHEST POSSIBLE LEVEL

Knowing that the typical male viewer's primary perception is vision, pornographers have crammed the Internet with every visual stimulus that exists—photographs, videos, live-camera, cartoons, virtual reality. These appear as "banner ads" even before the male viewer ever enters the porn site. Like billboards, banner ads display graphic porn and words of every kind designed to **visually** lure in male viewers. Such banner ads are attached to standard search engine home pages for men, women and children of all ages to see.

Once inside the porn site, the viewer is splattered with a visual overload. Thousands of explicit photos, hundreds of hours of explicit videos and 24-hour live cameras, all instantly available at the click of the mouse button. An unending stream of visual stimuli as fast and constantly changing as the male viewer desires—a critical element, because without a constantly changing visual display, the male brain quickly grows bored. Truly, pornographers are masters at tapping into the male desire "to look" at the highest level possible.

MALE VIEWERS WANT TO SEE BODY PARTS

Pornographers know full well the male brain's predisposition to narrowly focus on parts rather than the whole—to objectify and compartmentalize everything. Internet porn geared to the male audience is a continuous wave of one specific male body part *doing* everything imaginable to every conceivable female body part, from head to toe. Much of this material involves extreme close-ups of one body part after another. This is always completely devoid of any emotion, romance or tenderness. Rather, it is designed to be sexually intense but without commitment or emotion—the perfect visual male stimulus.

THE MALE VIEWER WANTS TO VISUALIZE HAVING SEX WITH THE PERFECT FEMALE SEX PARTNER

Most Internet porn geared to the male market shows the "man in control." The female is "servicing" the male, subservient to whatever he wants done to him or to whatever he wants to do to her. And she is nearly always shown as completely lusting after him and enjoying every moment of their sexual activities, even though in real life many of these activities would be painful and/or distasteful to most women.

This *"male-in-control/female-wanting-and-enjoying-it"* combination, in effect creates a female that is responding sexually the way a male would, which in turn supplies the male viewer with his "perfect sex partner" fantasy. He is in total control, while having done to him, or doing, exactly what turns him on most. This is male sexual fantasy at the highest level of stimulation.

DOMINANCE, AGGRESSION AND VIOLENCE IN MALE-CENTERED PORN

As discussed, the more cellular-memories (biological and physiological) to which pornographers can link their porn throughout the male brain and body, the greater chance they have of addicting their viewers. And the more naturally-occurring drugs/hormones (especially testosterone, but also adrenaline, epinephrine and others) flowing in the male mindbody during viewing, the more narrow will be his focus, the more intense his sexual/mindbody arousal, the more deeply the images will be imprinted in his memory, and the greater his addiction.

Pornographers achieve this combination of high numbers of mindbody links and maximum drug/hormone release by mixing sexual images with male dominance, aggression and violent images, all simultaneously intended to shock and stimulate. Porn scenes ranging from simple "male in control" to aggression, rape, torture and murder, abound in Internet porn geared to the male viewer.

These kinds of images link sexual arousal in the male mindbody with emotions of shock, anger, confusion, violence and domination, designed to cause the male mindbody to release enormous amounts of additional testosterone, in turn further increasing male narrowing, loss of reason, feelings of aggression, and sexual drive and arousal.[1]

High amounts of adrenaline and other chemicals are released as the male mindbody switches into "fight or flight" mode. Why does this happen? Because the mindbody is experiencing so much stimulus and physiological activity at once, that it cannot adapt to it fast enough. In other words, the male mindbody goes into stress-mode. Internet porn of this ilk creates a chain reaction in the male mindbody with hundreds of hormonal, chemical, emotional, physiological and biological processes all converging at once.[2]

The male viewer is not only addicted to simple sexual arousal, but this arousal is linked to mindbody processes that would normally never be linked to the sexual process. Talk about addiction at a whole new level! This would be like a drug addict shooting up with a dozen different hard-core drugs all at once.

THE MALE VIEWER CRAVES VARIETY

The mindbody is always seeking stimulation, a peak experience of some kind. Once a certain level of peak experience has been reached, the mindbody will naturally seek to then achieve a higher peak experience in that same frame of reference. Pornographers know that if they show the same images again and again, the male viewer will become bored and seek greater stimulation elsewhere. Thus, Internet pornography geared to the male audience is an ever-changing array of images, objects, actors and scenarios providing links to associated websites containing increasingly depraved material. A viewer could literally stay on the Internet many hours each day and never see the same image twice!

Internet pornographers also know that as time goes by male porn addicts seek increasingly greater stimulation. Internet pornographers oblige by offering everything from the partially nude pin-up girl to the hardest, most perverse images. With Internet porn, nothing is considered out of bounds or taboo. It is all there at the push of a button from anywhere in the world.

As the male viewer addict's appetite continues to heighten, these pornographers are there with instant gratification, like drug lords waiting with the next "harder kicking" strain of crack cocaine.

Pornographers also know that not all males are "turned on" by the same images, so they strive to appeal to as many types of viewers as possible.

They offer the male audience anything and everything including children, animals, objects, fetishes and settings—literally hundreds of thousands of different kinds of porn. What the male porn viewer's mind can conceive (and not possibly imagine), the Internet pornographers can achieve and deliver.

MAKE SURE THAT IT ALL ENDS IN MASTURBATION AND ORGASM

Internet pornographers want to make certain that virtually every male viewer ends his pornography session with masturbation and orgasm. Why? Think about it:

- Orgasm is one of the most (many say the most) powerful peak experiences the mindbody can undergo. Any activity that gets linked in the mindbody to orgasm will be adopted and become a habit of the most powerful and permanent kind. If you want to addict the male viewer to Internet porn at its highest level, then make it part of the habitual process leading to orgasm! Orgasm releases chemicals into the mindbody that permanently imprint whatever process was used to arrive at that end. If Internet porn was that process, guess where the male viewer returns again and again every time he desires sexual release?
- The be-all and end-all culminating event of sexual activity for virtually all males is orgasm. The Internet pornographer's aim is to lead every male viewer to this end, thus reinforcing this already-present end goal. So what's the problem? Many male viewers begin to substitute the porn process leading to orgasm for normal, healthy human intimacy. Internet porn can greatly disturb, interfere with, or literally replace healthy sexual intimacy. Pornographers seek to make the porn process the dominant sexual activity in the male viewer's life.
- The male Internet porn viewer can achieve orgasm quickly and effortlessly, anytime, and anywhere there is a computer. No need

to waste time with affection or romance; no worrying about creating the right atmosphere, whether it's a good time for a liaison, if she's "in the mood" or not, all the other "annoyances" and delays, or even if his partner is present or not. The "females" of Internet porn are always there, always ready, always eager for more. Literally hundreds of thousands of willing "females" whose sole purpose is to give the male viewer anything and everything he could possibly want or imagine. He doesn't have to take out the trash, do the dishes, or be polite for them to be sexually available. They just want him, on *his* terms, period.

MAKING MEN STUPID!

Increasing numbers of professionals in our public education system are paying closer attention to the different "learning styles" of children. Slowly they are coming to the realization that, in general, male and female students learn differently. After our review of the principal differences between the male and female brain, you can probably deduce what some of these learning styles might be. Educators are now adjusting teaching techniques and tools to more closely match the brain structure and learning styles of their students, efforts that are paying dividends in the form of increasing the powers of intellect and reasoning in thousands of students across the country.

But with Internet pornography geared to the "base animal instinct" of the human male brain, men and boys strung out on Internet porn are not becoming smarter. Rather, the more time they spend with Internet porn, the more ***stupid*** they become. As one 12-year-old youth told me, "Pornography makes you stupid."

Key Points

A reference tool for
spouses, parents, clergy,
counselors and others

- Pornographers specifically target the male mindbody in the design and marketing of their materials. If they can't lure the male viewer in through one method, they have a dozen others uniquely geared to his physiology.
- Men and teens must be careful not to be lulled into the complacency trap that says, "That stuff doesn't attract me at all—I can handle it with no problem." There are literally thousands of different varieties of porn on the Internet from all over the world. If such an individual engages in viewing Internet porn long enough, eventually he will encounter something that does push his button, triggers arousal and has a high potential for addiction.

15

How Internet Pornography Makes Men Stupid

Rather than re-examine the mass of convincing mindbody science showing why Internet pornography makes men stupid, I will present a sampling of the millions and millions of men who have done some of the most wildly stupid things as a direct result of pornography consumption.

Of course, you need not go any further than the headlines of the past few years in which prominent world leaders have abandoned all values, responsibility, reason and logic, and under the influence of porn and sex addiction, have engaged in behavior that rightly would be considered stupid, vulgar and depraved.

Among this cross section of examples are stories from men I have interviewed; other examples are taken from reports in the media.

MEN ON A DIET OF PORNOGRAPHY DO WILDLY STUPID THINGS

Internet Porn Led Man to Rape Tot:

(From the *Deseret News*, Salt Lake City, Utah, December 21, 1999)

Kenneth Rodger Hardy started experimenting with pornography on the Internet. Once the high-tech, sex superhighway got rolling, he couldn't stop. Before long he was stockpiling pornography on videotapes and computer disks and videotaping himself performing sex acts on a 15-month-old female relative.

"It got away from him," said Hardy's attorney, Lee Rasmussen. "That's the root of the problem."

Hardy pleaded guilty Monday to rape of a child, sodomy of a child and aggravated sexual abuse of a child, all first-degree felonies, for raping and sexually abusing the 15-month-old girl while he was baby-sitting her.

The charges surfaced after Hardy's son-in-law discovered the videotape, filmed sometime between Aug. 1 and Oct. 8. The son-in-law showed the tape to the baby's mother, who turned it over to Grantsville police.

. . . Rasmussen, who worked in the FBI 23 years before becoming a defense attorney, has also seen the tape. He said Hardy has no explanation for why he sexually abused the girl or videotaped the act. [Remember how male narrowing at the base of the funnel contributes to the loss of all reason, values, logic, etc.?]

"He feels terrible," Rasmussen said. "He has a lot of remorse. It's been devastating to him. It is an egregious case, and he realizes that."[1] [Remember the "hopeless dialogue" and that takes place when one

emerges from the narrow base of the funnel and full perspective, values and reasoning return?]

Mayor Arrested:

The 46-year-old Deputy Mayor of the City of Los Angeles attended a West L.A. porn theater one afternoon a few years ago. While engrossed in the sex film, he became so aroused ("narrowed"—all logic and reason blocked out) that he started to sexually assault a patron seated next to him.

The individual turned out to be an undercover city vice-squad officer. The Deputy Mayor was arrested, booked, and found guilty in a subsequent trial. This *distinguished* public-servant resigned his office, shamed and humiliated, his career in shambles.

Man Exposes Himself On Freeway:

One morning after spending hours on the Internet surfing pornography, a successful executive drove to a meeting across town. While on the freeway, he noticed a pick-up truck ahead of him with two teenage girls inside.

A great deal of this man's Internet porn viewing had been at sites that featured "teen porn," i.e., teen girls engaging in sex acts with older men. The image of the girls in the truck went straight to the neural pathways and cells where the Internet porn images were stored. This triggered a series of connections in his brain and body and he immediately became sexually aroused.

Pulling up next to the truck, he pulled his pants down to his knees, exposed himself and honked his horn. The two girls looked over and were so startled by what they saw that the driver gunned her engine and swerved away from the man's car, nearly causing an accident.

Jolted back into reality by the girl's reaction (he pulled out of his narrow focus and began seeing things at the "top of the funnel" again), the executive slowed down and managed to get his pants back up. Afraid that the girls or someone else might jot down his license plate number, he pulled off the freeway at the next exit. He was late for his meeting.

Man Enters the Narrow Tunnel of Porn the Day Before His Wedding:

In the wedding video shot by his father-in-law, John doesn't smile or even look at the camera. He shifts his gaze and his eyes drift downward. The day that was supposed to be a highlight of his life is among his darkest memories more than 20 years later.

The wedding went according to plan. A minister from John's church performed the ceremony in a sacred edifice he had always revered. But it was John's actions the day before that haunted him. "Stressed out" by the magnitude of the vows he was about to take, John "medicated" himself by indulging in the addiction that had plagued him since his early teens. He drove to a park, walked to a restroom, and acted out sexually with a man who remains nameless and faceless in his memory. Though John doesn't recall all the details of what went on, the shame he felt afterward is still glaringly clear in his mind.

You may be tempted to judge John harshly. "What a pig he is—a sleaze, a real pervert. How could he do that to himself and to his future wife?" And of course you'd be right. The *act* was disgusting, grossly irresponsible, a vile betrayal of his bride-to-be. But only John and those like him know the dark and overwhelming power of porn. John is no different than the alcoholic or the cocaine addict, who under the stress and pressure of getting married just has to have one more "fix."

Former Disney Executive Seeks Sex with 13-Year-Old Girl:

Aside from the assumptions and stereotypes many people have adopted, many Internet porn addicts are college graduates, are in the upper income brackets, and often are prominent, successful citizens.

Such was the case of a former Disney Studios executive. Convicted of possessing child pornography and of crossing state lines while seeking sex with a 13-year-old girl with whom he had made arrangements over the Internet, he reaped the sad fruits of his addiction. His career, his marriage, his life was ruined.

GRANDFATHERS AND PORNOGRAPHY—A HUMAN TRAGEDY

As men grow old and grey, most become wise to the trappings of the world. They develop greater perspective, self-discipline and self-control. Most people think Internet pornography is a young man's problem. Grandfathers are above this sort of thing; they are too mature and wise to be lured in by such juvenile trash.

As much as I would like to tell you that this is true, statistics don't bear it out. The male brain and body are structured in a way that make them susceptible to pornographic images. It makes little difference whether a porn viewer is a 12-year-old boy or a 70-year-old grandfather.

I have the deepest respect for our senior citizens. The more time I spend with them, the more impressed I am. I often think to myself, "This woman has a lifetime of experience and knowledge. That man is a walking, talking library on life. These people are our most precious natural resource. We must not let them go to waste. Let's tap into their wisdom and knowledge and really use it!"

I marvel as I see elderly couples who have been together for half-a-century or more, and are more deeply in love than ever. I reverence the elderly as they age with grace and dignity. What great wells of wisdom; what a tremendous gift they are to our society.

So it pains my heart deeply when I see loving grandfathers fall into the pornography trap. With their distinguished grey hair, their deep wrinkles of experience, their quiet wisdom, it seems all the more tragic to see one of them shot down by porn's poisonous dart.

Out of my deep respect for grandfathers, I hesitate to share the following stories. But I feel compelled to do so as a cautionary voice of warning. No matter what your age, you cannot afford to indulge your curiosity when it comes to the highly addictive drug called *Internet pornography*.

Grandfather #1:

An acquaintance recently told me of a grandfather in the family who had discovered pornography on the Internet and had begun viewing it on a regular basis.

One afternoon when the family was off running errands, it was just the grandfather and his 12-year-old granddaughter in the house. The grandfather was in his bedroom with the door locked, getting his Internet porn fix, consisting of images of naked "teenage-looking" women.

Having descended to the narrow bottom of the funnel in his arousal, he rose from his chair and proceeded to the room where his granddaughter was. He doesn't remember what he said to her, but he exposed himself and attempted to sexually molest her, whereupon she fled to the house of the next-door neighbor. I'm sure you can imagine the sequence of painful events from that point.

This example isn't so different from hundreds of others. But there are several facts about this case that I will never forget. First, there was no denial, no deception or concealment on the part of the grandfather, only total and complete despair, humiliation, regret, shock and disbelief.

"Shock and disbelief?" you ask. "Wasn't this grandfather accountable for his actions? Didn't he make a conscious decision to do what he did?" Yes. The grandfather acknowledged that he was responsible. He made no excuses. The shock and disbelief he suffered emanated from how quickly it all had happened and how he could not remember exactly why he had risen from the chair in the first place. It was like he had been in a "trance," like he was a different person.

At the moment his granddaughter screamed and ran from the house, it was as if he had been shocked back to his senses (regained his big-picture perspective at the top of the funnel). He just stood there in total horror at what had just occurred.

In fact, I was told that the family found him sobbing uncontrollably when they arrived home later that day. This distinguished, dignified and loving gentleman had been cut down by the crushing force of pornography. The pain, shame, guilt and regret of that moment will follow him for the remainder of his life.

Here is a grandfather who would never harm one of his grandchildren for anything in the world; on the contrary, he would give his life for any one of them. Yet, in a moment of sexual indulgence he temporarily abandoned everything he loved and violated his values, his morals, his beliefs. How could this happen?

His initial mistake came in the moment he took that first peek at his first porn site. For this grandfather, at least, from that first glance the tragic outcome was set. He didn't understand the power of what he was looking at. He knew it was wrong, but he probably figured he could give it up just as easily as he had embraced it, and it would be no big deal. After all, he was a grandfather, an old man, a religious family man. He was in control. It wouldn't hurt to indulge his curiosity just a little bit.

This tender grandfather didn't realize beforehand how pornography "narrows" the male brain and robs the viewer of his logic, reason and sound judgement (regardless of his age); how it forces him into a narrow tunnel where nothing else matters but satisfying the fiery urges the porn has ignited. It was in this "narrow tunnel" that this grandfather lost his way for but a moment—a moment that would haunt him and his family for the rest of their lives.

Grandfather #2:

This second incident was related to me by a colleague of mine who is in law enforcement. I cannot adequately describe the sea of emotions that wash over me as I call it to mind.

My colleague and his partner received a call from a woman complaining of an awful stench coming from the house next door. She said that an elderly man lived there alone, but she hadn't seen him for several days. Upon entering the house, it didn't take the officers long to locate the source of the smell.

As the officers cracked open the bathroom door, the full impact of the dreadful odor washed over them like a pungent wave. On the bathroom floor lay a pornographic magazine opened to a page displaying a graphic image. And there, seated on the toilet, was the decaying body of an elderly man, stiffened by rigor mortis.

Judging from his frozen position, it was obvious how he had died. An autopsy later confirmed the officer's suspicion—the man had died of a heart attack while in the act of masturbating.

During his life, pornography—a true thief if there ever was one—had apparently taken much from this man and his family. And in the end, the thief even robbed him of dignity in death.

The horrific image of this elderly man is forever etched in my mind. His frozen body, magazine at his feet, is like a statue, a testimony to the insidious and wretched nature of pornography.

Alongside this horrid image, I would create a monument to all of pornography's tragic victims: the women, the children, the wives, mothers, sisters and daughters, the little boys, sons and brothers—all innocent bystanders—and the men, fathers and husbands who could have been so much more and given so much more, were it not for the thief called "pornography."

So, as you can see, my 12-year-old friend was right—pornography really *does* make you "stupid." However, the examples I have given, horrific though they be, represent only the beginning of the carnage and catastrophe that pornography addiction can create.

IN SOME MEN PORNOGRAPHY BRINGS OUT THE DARKEST EVIL

We have seen that under the "narrowing" influence of pornography, men momentarily forfeit their reasoning and judgement. As a result, they do stupid things that bring shame, embarrassment, broken marriages, scarred families, ruined careers and lost opportunities.

Many of these men could have made significantly greater contributions of love and service to those around them and to the world, if they had not spent so much time trapped in their own "narrow world" of pornography.

But porn's ability to make men do stupid things is only the tip of the proverbial iceberg. The industry, with the Internet as its primary ally, is now leading more and more men and women, teens and children down a dark and sinister path. It is seducing them to become part of a world where innocent bystanders bear the hellish, hideous impact of pornography's progeny.

In his work *Pornography's Effects on Adults & Children*, clinical psychologist Dr. Victor Cline reports:

In research conducted by Dr. W. Marshall, almost half of the rapists that he studied used pornography depicting consenting sex to arouse themselves preparatory to seeking out a victim to rape. Another investigator, Dr. M. J. Goldstein, found that far more of the sex offenders than the non-offenders he studied wished to, and often did, emulate the acts they saw depicted in pornography.[2]

In still another study, most of Dr. E.G. Abel's sex offenders said that pornography increased their appetites for deviant activities (and these were the men who reported the least control over their deviant activities). Other investigators have reported that rapists and child molesters use pornographic materials fully, both immediately prior to their crimes and during the actual assaults.[3]

Still another type of evidence comes from a study conducted by Darrell Pope, a former Michigan State Police officer, who found that of 38,000 cases of sexual assault on file in Michigan, 41% involved pornography exposure just prior to the act or during the act.[4]

Porn users don't live in a vacuum; they live among people, real, living, breathing people: spouses, children, neighbors, co-workers. Any or all of these can be hurt when a porn addict spins out of control.

COPYCAT CRIME

Those who make it a habit to view porn or engage in cybersex of any form often begin to imitate what they have seen. Dr. Judith Reisman terms this acting out in a deviant, illegal nature "copycat crime."[5] Based on what we know about cellular-memories and the mindbody using these memories to bring about our desires for a peak experience, this makes perfect sense.

If a man or teenage boy has been masturbating while viewing porn, the images he sees are linked by the mindbody as the way to arrive at the highly desirable peak experience of orgasm. The mindbody links these images with pleasure, release, arousal and climax. And what are these images? In their obsession to capture as many viewers as possible, to appeal to every fetish and appetite, no matter how twisted or deviate, Internet pornographers display an incredible variety of images—from the traditional pin-up girl to the bizarre, depraved, debauched and vile; sexual images mixed with traditional fantasy, but also co-mingled with images of children, animals, rape, torture, murder, expectant mothers, and many other shocking connections.

Do you recall that the mindbody does not distinguish between reality and fantasy when it comes to material that is highly erotic, violent or shocking? When men look at Internet porn photographs, videos and live transmissions, their mindbody accepts the images as "reality."

An Internet site shows "girl-like" women dressed in girl scout uniforms being raped; a few weeks later a local newspaper reports the brutal rape of a girl scout while selling cookies door-to-door. After viewing a graphic video on the Internet portraying little girls in their school uniforms, a porn addict kidnaps, rapes, tortures, mutilates and murders two children in their Catholic schoolgirl uniforms. Mere coincidence? Sound too far-fetched? These are actual cases! They are only two of the thousands of such copycat crimes committed by porn addicts each year.[6]

Taking into account the litany of sexual perversions linked to acts of violence that can be accessed on the Internet, can you begin to pinpoint the source of grizzly sex-murders, tortures and mutilations occurring with increasing frequency around the world?

In the past, the most extreme examples of porn-related copycat crime were men like Ted Bundy and Gary Bishop. With the Internet now exposing tens of millions of men and teens to pornography day in and day out, in what direction and magnitude will the number of copycat crimes committed against innocent women and children go?

CHILDREN COMMITTING COPYCAT CRIME

It isn't only men, women and teens who are viewing explicit/degrading/violent porn and committing copycat crimes. A rising number of children are now acting out what they see.

Dr. Judith Reisman states:

Children practice adulthood by careful imitation of adult activity. As with adolescent sex offenders, youngsters commonly imitate what they see in films, video, television, and still photos. That means that, if they can, many will light the brand of cigarettes, drink the beer, eat the candy or food, wear the clothes, and do the sex acts—as shown.[7]

Clear back in 1984 during the widely publicized Senate Hearings on the "Effect of Pornography on Women and Children," Senator Jeremiah Denton affirmed the St. Petersburg, Florida, account of the nine-year-old boy who was convicted of first-degree murder, aggravated child abuse, and three counts of sexual battery in connection with the torture death of an eight-month-old girl. The brother of the boy testified that, in sexually assaulting the infant with a pencil and coat hanger, they were imitating what they had seen in their mother's sex magazine.[8]

In early February 1991, the Department of Justice sent out a mailing that included a chilling report of "a ten-year-old boy . . . who learned to have sex by watching X-rated movies . . . arrested on charges he raped and sodomized an eight-year-old girl and her four-year-old sister. . . . Medical tests showed evidence of sexual intercourse. . . . 'Whoever is responsible for letting the boy see the movies' [police said] 'should be arrested for endangering the welfare of a child.'"[9]

With every kind of explicit pornography instantly available to children over the Internet in homes, libraries and even some schools, how many more copycat crimes will we see committed by children?

"But These Cases Are Unusual"—Bill's Story

There are still those who claim that men acting out based on their viewing of pornography is unusual, extremely rare. They say this simply does not happen to normal men with normal jobs, marriages and families, living in normal communities. I've even heard people say, "Besides, I can recognize a pervert when I see one."

Really?

Let me share with you a recent interview I had with a "normal man." He was a good father, a loving husband. He had a good job and was successful at it. He was respected—a religious man with high moral values and deep convictions. He lived in an average small town in America and enjoyed an average American lifestyle. But pornography forever changed his life and the lives of everyone around him. We'll call him "Bill."

In the 1960s, at the age of 22, Bill picked up his first piece of pornography at the neighborhood drug store. He told the clerk, an older woman, that it was for a college research project—to see if the material was as bad as people said it was.

After that first magazine, Bill was hooked (just as millions of teens are after their first Internet porn session). He began purchasing more magazines from the same store and found others with additional magazines for sale. When he didn't have enough money to buy them, he would steal them.

About a year later Bill went on a business trip to a city located some two hours away. It was on this trip that he saw his first X-rated movie. He described this experience as one that accelerated and locked in his porn addiction at the highest level imaginable. Going from photographs on a magazine page to witnessing graphic, open sex on a motion picture theater screen was like making the jump to light-speed.

For several years, whenever he would travel on business, he would attend X-rated movies. Bill recalled, "One thing I remember is that during the movie, you could go downstairs to the bathroom and find other men down there masturbating to what they had seen. I know that on several occasions, with just two of us down there, I masturbated one of the men while he masturbated me."

Bill was married in 1970. For almost a year prior to the marriage, he quit viewing pornography of any kind. "I finally thought that I had this type of behavior licked and behind me," he said. "After all, I would be getting married and wouldn't need to masturbate or watch other people having intercourse on a movie screen. I would be able to have the real thing this time." But Bill did not fathom the power of his pornography addiction. He did not realize that the male brain places intimacy with a wife in one compartment and porn in another. Within a year of marriage Bill was back, submerged in pornography.

And he found that it wasn't just a pastime, but instead a source of ruin. "I was disillusioned with our marriage, unsatisfied with our sex life—I felt I needed more than my wife could give . . . and I went back into pornography. Pornography became my escape from all the stress and strain of everyday living. No matter how sexual my wife could have been, she could not have filled my appetite for sex."

When pornographic video rentals became available, Bill began to bring them into his home and watch them late at night when the family was asleep, or on other occasions when the family was gone. Bill describes the cycle of guilt and shame he felt after porn sessions and masturbation, which just added to his stress and pushed him to seek even more porn.

Bill described needing harder and harder pornography to arrive at the same intense arousal necessary to achieve orgasm. To that point, the porn he was involved with was all adult, with no children or teens of any kind portrayed. This cycle of porn viewing and masturbating continued for several years. Then the unthinkable happened.

Bill tells of the events leading up to his disaster: "Though I had all of these fantasies about adult women, though I was deeply entrenched in pornography, I could not follow through with any of those desires. For years I had put on the appearance of being a happily married man. I was going through the motions of being active in my church, a professional businessman in the community. Adultery was against my moral values. It was alright in my mind to read about it and fantasize about it, but to actually do it was against the rules." (A classic example of the male brain's ability to narrow and compartmentalize.)

Bill began fantasizing about having sex with some of the neighbor women. But he refused to act out these fantasies on moral grounds and because he did not want to ruin his reputation in the community nor his relationship with his wife and children. So, instead, Bill made a terrible and bizarre decision: He began sexually molesting the *children* of these women! He could have sex with the child while fantasizing about his or her mother!

How could a truly good person, a truly understanding man, do such a vile thing? Bill claimed that somehow in his brain, twisted and filled with pornography, he rationalized that sex with the children was not adultery, and therefore it was okay. Only in that way, he reasoned, could he retain his reputation and standing in the community, in his church and in his family, because the children would keep it all a secret. He also mentioned that when he was with the children, "it drew warmth from my childhood back into my life." [The phrase *pornography makes you stupid* comes to mind!]

Over the course of many months, Bill sexually molested more than a dozen children. Finally, a child let slip a comment to a parent, which led to further inquiries. Within hours Bill was arrested. He spent the next ten years of his life in the state penitentiary. He lost his marriage, his business, his reputation and his freedom, all because he picked up a *Playboy* magazine at age 22.

What Bill did was despicable, perverted and terribly cold and cruel. But before we pass final judgement, sentence and execute this man, let me give you some additional insights.

I went to interview Bill feeling extremely uncomfortable, uneasy about how I would talk to a convicted child molester. With six children of my own, I'm very sensitive to this issue. How would Bill look? How would he act? Just how do you approach your average run-of-the-mill child molester? I'm not sure I had formed a definite image of him in my mind, but I knew there had to be something sinister or "slimy" about his appearance or mannerisms.

When Bill opened the door I was totally unprepared for what I saw. Whatever preconceived notions I had of a child molester, he was not it.

Here was a humble man, in all respects. If I were to pick a child molester out a crowd of a hundred men, he would be one of my last three choices. He spoke softly, intelligently, candidly and without excuse or blame. He spoke of regret, remorse, the destruction of his life and of all those he had pulled down with him. He described his despicable behavior with innocent children. As he did so, the emotion that raked at his voice and the tears that welled up in his eyes told of his painful regret, even now, over a dozen years after the culmination of those dark events.

Though Bill knows he can never repair the damage done to those innocent children, he hopes he can at least help prevent such tragedies in the future. He presently travels with law enforcement officers to participate in training seminars for educators and parents. When he first stands at the podium, most of those in the audience assume he is a police officer, a government official or a counselor. He looks and acts the part of an intelligent, gentle, kind man.

In sessions described most simply as "unforgettable," he teaches audiences about the tools and techniques of a pedophile and offers first-hand advice in how to protect children from sexual abuse.

Now some would still dismiss Bill's story as "rare." They might say, "Most men who look at porn don't end up like Bill."

So, I asked Bill about his experience in federal prison, and invited him to tell me about the other convicted child molesters and sex offenders he met there. What kind of men were they? His response was astounding: "The 80 or so sex offenders in prison with me were business executives, religious leaders, fathers, husbands, and virtually all were successful and well respected in the communities they came from. Most of them were college graduates and very intelligent."

Then I asked, "How many of those who were in prison with you admitted to regularly viewing pornography prior to committing their crimes?"

Bill's response? "Every single one of them."

WE ALL MUST LEARN FROM BILL

I learned a critically important lesson from Bill: No one is immune from the mind- and behavior-altering effects of pornography. Anyone is a potential "pornoholic."

It is interesting to note that Bill never looked at child-pornography, an area in which virtually all pedophiles are heavily involved. I use Bill as an example to demonstrate how powerful pornography is in establishing cellular-memory links throughout the brain and body. Porn can link sexual arousal and orgasm to virtually any other activity, including using children to act out sexual fantasies derived from pornography.

I asked Bill, "What would've happened if Internet pornography had been available to you?"

He responded without hesitation: "My porn addiction would have skyrocketed and I would have begun 'acting out' with children a whole lot sooner."

Bill was limited in the amount and variety of pornography he could access. Today, with the Internet, no such limitations exist. Anything and everything is instantly available at the click of a mouse-button, much of it absolutely free.

How many future "Bills" are out there? How many men and teenage boys will get hooked on Internet porn, radically altering the chemical and physical structures of their brains and bodies? These pornographic images are permanently stored in the cells of these individuals' brains and bodies. How will this "warped pair of glasses" affect the behavior of these Internet porn addicts? The wave of stupid, violent and depraved behavior committed by men and teenage boys under the influence of Internet porn will continue to grow in size and strength, until it becomes a tidal wave of pain and destruction. Millions of "Bills"—and far worse—are out there. Internet porn is unleashing the "Mr. Hyde" in these otherwise normal, everyday "Dr. Jekyll" citizens.

I recently spotted an article on the AP news wire that I fear will become all too common. It was like an eerie and unnerving real-life manifestation of the fictitious *Doctor Jekyll and Mr. Hyde*. In big bold letters the title announced: ***Prosecutors say doctor led double life***. The article offered the grim description of a well-respected allergist who took a morning stroll with his wife in the pine-needled woods near their home. Only the doctor came out of the woods alive. His wife was bludgeoned with a hammer and stabbed with a knife. After 31 years of marriage, the doctor, age 59, has been charged with his wife's murder. Authorities say that he killed his wife after she learned he led a *secret* life to indulge his desire for pornography and prostitutes.

Key Points

A reference tool for spouses, parents, clergy, counselors and others

- Even the most intelligent, respected, prominent and successful citizens find it almost impossible to control their actions once they slide down into the narrow bottom of the porn funnel. No one, regardless of education, wealth, position or status can escape the devastating effects of pornography addiction once it spins out of control. To say "It could never happen to me" is an arrogant and foolish statement.
- Because of *instant-access* on the Internet, millions of men, teens and boys are being exposed to the mindbody/behavior-altering effects of pornography. Copycat crimes are increasing at an alarming rate. Even children are replicating what they have seen in pornographic images.

16

How Internet Pornographers Target the Female Brain

Women View Pornography Differently Than Men Do

Internet pornographers know full well that they cannot have any significant degree of success marketing to females using the same techniques they use for the male market. Male and female brains are different; the Internet pornographer's marketing approach must also be different.

Still, the purveyors of porn have begun paying closer attention to their potential female audience. There are profits to be made, and Internet pornographers are all about profits.

In August of 1998 the "World Conference on Pornography" was held under the sponsorship of California State University at Northridge. For three days conference directors presented an unending stream of explicit pornography, all under the guise of "academic analysis."

At the close of the conference, awards were given out to the producers of films, to the actors and actresses of same, and to the various exhibitors who had "pioneered" the introduction of hard-core pornography throughout the world. (Of course, the keynote address for the event was given by the president of the ACLU.)

Speaking of this academic farce, John Harmer points out that "Among the most stunning aspects of an event that could only be described as 'beyond comprehension' were the number of *women* faculty members who actively participated, and the significant amount of pornographic material being produced *by* women *for* women. The conference left no doubt that in the United States women have become more than equal with men as they have aggressively entered into the production and distribution of pornography."[1]

It is obvious that Internet pornographers, some of them women, have openly chosen to pursue the female porn market. Let's examine the female mind—the way pornography producers already have. Let's review the typical attributes of the potential female porn consumer in the cold, hard terminology pornographers use:

1. The key perceptual sense for females is not vision, or any one sense. Instead, females place high priority on the entire sensory package as a whole. No one sense is given significant value over the others. For porn to be addicting, there must be more to it than just a bunch of ever-changing visual stimuli.

2. The female mindbody does not typically descend swiftly down the funnel of arousal with a total focus on body parts and the physical sex act. She descends more slowly, taking into account a wide variety of sensorial factors. Her focus is not only on the whole-body experience (as opposed to parts), but also upon the whole of the relationship, where the partners are in love, engaged in tenderness, carry on a romance. With these things in place, she can become highly aroused by images of couples coupling, but rarely by the mere act itself or by close-ups of body parts.

3. The male is interested in images of casual, impersonal sex, in getting right down to the physical sex act. The female, in contrast,

yearns to see the interplay of relationships, caring, love, foreplay, communication and tenderness that lead up to and culminate in the physical act of intercourse.

4. Females do not typically enjoy seeing images of women being dominated, aggressively treated or abused in sexual situations. Rather, they prefer sex where a man and a woman have mutually agreed to the encounter and both are enjoying it, with the man showing consideration for her feelings and desires.

With all of this in mind, how do Internet pornographers provide content that taps into the female brain at the highest level possible? Consider their well-devised techniques:

PORN BASED ON RELATIONSHIPS AND MUTUAL CONSENT, RATHER THAN BODY PARTS AND DOMINATION

In a private screening room at the University of Amsterdam, 47 female volunteers watched two sexually explicit clips from pornographic movies. One film, made by a male director, presented the standard "male fantasy" scene in which the woman "services" the man, with an emphasis on body parts and little romance, kissing, etc.

The second film, directed by a woman, offered a more romantic context for its hard-core sex. The woman in the scene was rather ordinary looking. Prior to sex there was a tender scene showing the couple kissing and embracing. The woman appeared to be sincerely enjoying herself.

When asked, those who participated in this experiment said they were aroused only by the second, woman-directed video, not by the first film, which they described as gross, repulsive and disgusting.[2]

Pornographers, having learned their lesson well, are using clever methods to lure women into a world that they formerly were repulsed by. Romance novelists and soap opera writers have used these techniques for decades, showing sex, but showing it in a more "holistic" way, preceded by romantic settings, communication, hugging and kissing, knowing that this approach attracts a larger portion of the female market.

Internet pornographers often use "average looking" females as their subjects so that the female viewer can more easily relate by fantasizing or imagining herself playing the role. Likewise, they portray both the male and female pleasuring each other equally. More and more Internet porn caters to the lesbian viewer as well.

In essence, the Internet pornographers have taken the successful "soap opera/romance novel" genre and wrapped it around pornography in order to seduce the female viewer.

THE REAL KEY IS THE CYBERSEX CHAT ROOM

Even with a romantic twist or feel, many women still are not interested in Internet porn. And so the pornographers have found a "decoy" to lure them into this dark world: Internet chat rooms. Chat rooms consist of informal groups of people who "talk" with one another by typing messages which are sent over the Internet. While two people chat, others can eavesdrop on the conversation and interject any time they wish. If two people want to talk privately, they can enter a "private" chat room where no one else can see their conversation.

Knowing what we do about the female brain, the chat room is the perfect model to attract women to the Internet. They can engage in "innocent" conversations with men, develop relationships, express their emotions, and become part of the Internet "community" or chat group to which they belong. Women encounter friendly, interesting men (and women) who really listen to them; people who pay attention to them. They develop innocent friendships which deepen quickly as they talk about those subjects that matter most to them. All is done behind a "shield" of anonymity that lends itself to full disclosure beyond that of most marriages.

Before the woman realizes it, she has achieved an artificial intimacy that she perceives to be superior to that in her marriage. Just as a porn-addicted husband is no longer satisfied by participating in sex acts with his wife, the cybersex- or chat-addicted wife is no longer satisfied as she compares the intimacy level of her marriage to the artificially intense depth of intimacy with her cybersex companion. Over time, her conversations can become more bold and sexually explicit. All the while, her cybersex relationship remains anonymous and safe—or so she is led to believe.

In her groundbreaking book *Caught in the Net*, Dr. Kimberly S. Young describes how many women (and men) initially turn to Internet chat rooms as a form of escape. She writes: *Sooner or later, the explanation points to the desire to escape. No matter who they are, where they live, or how solid their lives may appear economically or psychologically, Internet users who turn to the faceless community for company, happiness, or relief usually are trying to avoid something or someone they don't want to confront.*[3]

The Center for Online Addiction reports its findings regarding why women seek out chat rooms:

Women more often than men commented on how they sought out support, acceptance, and comfort through online relationships formed in chat rooms. Virtual communities gave women a sense of belonging and the ability to share the company of others in a non-threatening environment.

As men tended to look more for Cybersex, women tended to look more for romance in Cyberspace. In virtual chat areas . . . a woman can meet men to form intimate relationships. But like a soap opera, tender moments with a romantic stranger can lead to passion and progress into sexual dialogue. I should note that it is not usual for women to engage in random Cybersex, but many times they preferred to form some type of relationship prior to sexual chat.[4]

Internet pornographers lure women into chat room relationships through one of two methods:

1. The woman starts out with friendly conversation, which eventually leads to romantic talk, then to sexual conversation and hard-core sexual dialogue. Soon the woman finds herself desensitized, leaving her vulnerable. The man on the other end will often lead her to the viewing of Internet porn. Exposed to such graphic images right off the bat, most women would reject them. But, in the context of a "relationship," after proceeding through the steps of building a friendship, forging a romance, and finally engaging in sexual dialogue, the woman is slowly coaxed into the world of Internet porn.
2. Out of curiosity, a woman may experiment with Internet porn to see what it is all about. This will often lead her to sexually-oriented chat rooms, where she will undergo the process of desensitization as described above, and become immersed in the porn viewing/sex addiction cycle.

YOUNGER AND YOUNGER WOMEN ARE TURNING TO CYBERSEX CHAT ROOMS

In a recent survey of over 9,000 MSNBC.com readers, it was found that a significant number of younger females are turning to cybersex sites. In contrast to their male counterparts, most of these women are bypassing the titillating erotica sites in favor of interactive chat rooms. The reason is the "three A's" of the Internet: Accessability, Affordability, and Anonymity. Together, they are allowing young adult women to be more comfortable experimenting with their sexuality online than almost anywhere else. In chat rooms they can engage in new relationships without fear.[5]

CYBERSEX LEADS WOMEN TO ADOPT A MORE MALE-LIKE FUNNEL OF INTIMACY

From the previous chapters on mindbody science, you know that repeated exposure to pornography can lower a woman's defenses and diminish her initial "shock" to explicit images. This can cause a woman or teenage girl to become fascinated with pornography, chat rooms and cybersex, and lead them into the cycle of addiction.

Caught up in the romantic/sexual fantasies brought on by Internet pornography and cybersex chat, women more and more will allow their mindbody to narrow its focus to progress from a romantic/sexual conversation to more dangerous actions, such as an actual sexual rendezvous.

Women caught in this trap begin to focus "narrowly" on sexual fantasy, illicit sexual encounters and masturbation. Many "short-circuit" their female brain and adopt a more "male" mind-set.[6] Further, pornographers, Hollywood, and magazine media are influencing women and teenage girls to view sex more like men do—body-part-centered, physical sex act-centered, "narrow"-centered.

Recently while shopping at our local grocery store, I noticed the title of the feature article splashed across the cover of a prominent woman's magazine. *"The Sex Game"—Playing it like a **Man**—and Winning!"* it read. With constant reports of rape, date-rape, spousal abuse, molestation and the like being committed by men, that's just what we don't need: women acting like men when it comes to sexual addiction.

Key Points

A reference tool for spouses, parents, clergy, counselors and others

- Most women would consider it absurd that they could ever be addicted to such "disgusting trash" as pornography. They must understand that pornographers market very differently to females as opposed to males. The same female mindbody characteristics that can attract a woman to *romance novels* can also lure her into cybersex chat rooms, Internet pornography and, eventually, sex and/or porn addiction. The process is much more subtle and seemingly innocent than that of male addiction, but just as debilitating and devastating.
- With movies, TV, magazines and other media constantly bombarding them with a "male-dominated" presentation of sexuality, women must be careful not to adopt a *narrow* male-like mind-set.

17

How Cybersex Chat Rooms and Internet Pornography Make Women Stupid

Just as porn-addicted males do some really stupid things, women under the influence of Internet porn and cybersex chat rooms are engaging in some stupid behaviors of their own. In her book *Caught in the Net*, Dr. Kimberly Young cites the following examples:

"From an e-mail—*'Read your article on Internet addiction . . . took the quiz . . . got the worst possible score . . . but know what? Don't really care. . . .Yes, I am TOTALLY addicted but having the best time of my life. . . . I'm mother of two kids, 13 and 11 . . . used to be very devoted, but now I live for the Internet. . . . I hide a lot of dirty laundry, make quickest meals possible . . . could go on and on. Online lovers? Met a few . . . even planning a vacation with one. . . . Everyone in my family is worried sick. . . . My husband is ready to throw the computer out the window. . . . Poor guy, he's suffering . . . gotta go . . . Bye, Paula.'*[1]

"Another e-mail: *'My name is Dennis. I have been married for eleven years, and my wife, Melinda, and I have three children. We bought a new computer a few months ago, and Melinda got very interested in chat rooms.*

Soon the friendly chat turned to cybersex, and from there it escalated into phone sex. Finally, she started driving to meet a couple of these guys hundreds of miles away, taking the children with her! When I found out about this and confronted her, she refused to admit she had a problem . . . .'"[2]

And finally, Dr. Young offers this description of a woman addicted to cybersex on the Internet: *It's almost midnight and the lobby of People Connection [an Internet chat room] is bursting with people, excitement, and anticipation. Leah has just clicked on and already is engaging in a little harmless flirting. Then she sends a bolder message: 'Any guys out there looking for a foxy babe tonight?' Instantly, her screen fills with invitations from eager men from all over the world who urge this 'foxy babe' to come to a Private Room for a more intimate conversation. The erotic dialogue that ensues resembles what's found on 900 phone sex lines, except that no one is paying for this service and both parties enter the exchange as equals.*

Dr. Young continues her description of Leah: *A 32-year-old single librarian from upstate New York, Leah is shy and overweight. In real life, she feels intimidated by men and hasn't had much success attracting them. Now when Leah enters the People Connection seeking quick sexual encounters, she finds herself desired by dozens of men. She's amazed at how brazen she's become, hopping among several 'partners' in one night and indulging in virtual sex acts she had never previously imagined."*

For Leah, the best part is the morning after. She had no fears of pregnancy or sexually transmitted diseases; she hadn't spent any money beyond her basic Internet access cost; she wasn't concerned about one of the men knocking on her door someday or sending unwanted love letters or flowers, because she never shared her phone number or any specifics about where she lived. Her reputation in her real-life community remained intact. No one knew where she had gone, what she had done, or the language she had used the night before. She was still the same shy, quiet, responsible librarian. And after work she could go home and play the vixen again, engaging in dominance and submission under handles like "Super Vixen" or "Madam X."[3]

CATHY'S STORY—THE FUTURE OF WOMEN AND INTERNET PORNOGRAPHY

I took the opportunity to conduct a telephone interview with a woman whom we will call "Cathy." Before this interview, I had all but completed this book and titled it *How Internet Pornography Makes Men Stupid*. As a direct result of this interview, together with my interaction with Willie Draughon, retired Assistant Chief of Criminal Investigations with the State Attorney General's Office, I returned to the drawing board.

Since then, this book has been revised to include the rising and devastating problem of female Internet porn and cybersex addiction.

The following is a brief overview Cathy provided me prior to our telephone interview:

My first contact with the Internet is an experience that I will never forget. I was ***curious*** *about how far a person would go to expose their body for all the world to see so I got on a pornography site. . . . The more I saw the more I wanted to see. I found myself looking for time when no one was around so I could get on the Internet. I began having sexual fantasies about what I saw there (sometimes involving masturbation). Before long I realized that I didn't want to just imagine sex with a partner, I wanted to physically have sex with someone.*

One day I got bold enough to find a person online and we arranged to meet for the sole purpose of having sex. I didn't know this person. I had never met him before in my life and that is the way I wanted it. For six months I forgot what life was. All I wanted to do was live for myself and fulfill my selfish physical desires. My circle of friends changed. I now wanted to hang around the people who wanted a life such as mine.

I began going to bars. I didn't drink or smoke but I went there to ***socialize*** *with the kind of people that I could take home and have a one-*

night stand with. . . . My life was one of sex and gratification, and all because of curiosity about porn sites.

I know of many women who have fallen in the same trap that I did for one reason or another. It's a slow, subtle process that takes you on a trip to hell. I was addicted to sex, fantasies, physical desire, and I didn't even know it until it was too late.

The detrimental effects that those six months had on me are too great to mention in detail, but I can tell you the worst of them. My family was nearly destroyed. My children have lost respect for their mother. Somewhere along the way I contracted Chlamydia, a serious sexually transmitted disease. But worst of all, I lost respect for myself and it took a lot of time to get my life back.

Internet pornography is a world of subtlety. It is the first lurid step in a long staircase that leads both men and women into a life of misery.

Cathy stated very clearly in our telephone interview that she was "heavily involved with cybersex chat rooms." *My initial curiosity with Internet porn led me to the chat rooms, which in turn led me to actual face-to-face sexual encounters. Chat rooms had a much more powerful attraction to me than the pornography itself. I spent many hundreds of hours in sexually graphic conversations with men in cybersex chat rooms. The Internet porn was simply a convenient tool that aided in my romantic/sexual fantasizing.*

There are those reading this who might assume that Cathy was simply a loose woman, slutty, not unlike a prostitute in her mind-set. Actually, prior to her introduction to Internet pornography and her subsequent addiction to cybersex chat rooms and illicit sex, she was an exemplary wife and mother, a model citizen in her community, an active participant in her church. Now she lives alone, divorced, virtually ignored and despised by her children.

Like it has done to so many men, Internet pornography/cybersex chat takes decent, intelligent, respected and successful *women* and **makes them**

stupid! Just as it does for men, Internet porn/cybersex becomes a "drug of choice" where women find pleasure, relief and escape (self-medication) from the pain, stress and realities of everyday life.

In fact, retired sexual crimes investigator Willie Draughon asserts that "females are more inclined to pursue the communication aspect of the subculture after their initial intro through visual porn. The argument can be made that females may spend even more time in the porn underworld—i.e., chat rooms, phone sex, and eventually personal encounters—than males since their world of intimacy involves the need to have more stimulation than just the visual alone to reach the fantasy of fulfillment. The Internet provides this type of environment for women more than any other vehicle in history."

Key Points

A reference tool for spouses, parents, clergy, counselors and others

- Just as the male mindbody by its very nature can be pulled into Internet pornography, women are just as susceptible to the allure of cybersex chat rooms, which then often lead to pornography and live encounters.
- Because of the unique structure of the female mindbody, a woman's addiction can be more time-consuming and life-consuming.

18

THE VICTIMS OF PORNOGRAPHY

THE LAW OF GRAVITY

A common argument in favor of pornography is that it negatively affects only a few people. "The Ted Bundys of the world are sick and rare," cries the pro-porn camp. "For the rest of us, porn is no different than any other hobby."

Whether this pro-porn elite wants to admit it or not, there are "Universal Laws" that apply to all of us. Let me give you an example of this. A dear friend, Bruce Wright, author of *The Wright Exit Strategy,* often cites the "Law of Gravity" to illustrate this point. He tells of a family member who was debating the concept of "universal laws and principles" applying to everyone. Like the pornographers and their minions, this family member claimed that "perceptions are reality," that such universal laws do not exist.

Bruce took this family member aside and suggested that together they climb to the top of a ten-story building. Out on the roof, they sidled over to the edge and gazed down. Bruce said, "Let's assume that you perceive there is no law of gravity. If you believe that your 'perception is reality,' then jump!"[1]

Fortunately, Bruce's relative did not jump—and perception *is not* reality. There are certain laws and realities that apply to us all no matter how we perceive them.

Whether you're a man, woman, teen or child, viewing pornography exacts serious consequences. Even though pornographers and those who support them insist otherwise, they cannot change this reality.

SILENT ALARMS

"Silent" alarms are going off all around us as a result of the effects of pornography—on us, on our children, and on society as a whole. But few are responding to these alarms. Why? Because too many are allowing their attention to be diverted by the much louder alarms being set off by the pornographers themselves.

"Censorship!" "First Amendment Rights!" "Freedom!" scream these "ravening wolves in sheep's clothing," all the while quietly collecting their enormous profits. Pornographers deliberately trigger these alarms just as the bank robber who sends a decoy to rob the teller while he empties the main vault and waltzes out the back door!

The tragedy is that while much of America is buying into and being distracted by these alleged "assaults" on our constitutional rights, the pornographers are robbing millions of their freedom through addiction to pornography. Along the way they are stealing the most precious treasure we have—the future legacy of goodness and decency that we want our children and grandchildren to enjoy.

The waves of pornography pouring freely from the Internet have become destructive shockwaves. Their aftershock rumblings will wreak havoc at a level and intensity of destruction never before experienced in the history of mankind.

Key Points

A reference tool for
spouses, parents, clergy,
counselors and others

- Viewing Internet pornography is not "just a harmless pastime"—it results in serious consequences for the viewer and those around him or her. As the popularity and proliferation of Internet pornography increases, so will the number of its victims. Pornographers and their supporters can't change this reality.

19

PORNOGRAPHY DESTROYS WOMEN'S RIGHTS

THE MAN OF LA MANCHA

In Miguel de Cervantes' *Don Quixote de la Mancha*, when the retired country scholar Don Quixote looked upon the young village woman Aldonza, he saw more than just a prostitute. While other men viewed her as an object of lust, a thing to be used and then cast aside, Quixote saw more. He was able to look past a mere collection of female body parts to the inner worth, beauty and potential of the woman. In fact, he gave her a new and honored title: "Dulcinea del Toboso."

He helped his sweet lady love to see herself for who she truly was—a valuable human being with intrinsic worth and tremendous capacity. His kindness, gentleness, encouragement and the "absence of a lustful motive" helped her begin the process of a wonderful transformation.

Later, as Quixote lay dying, she came to see him one last time. She was doubting her newfound identity and value. He tenderly took her hand in his and, with his last breath whispered, "Never forget who you truly are. You are Dulcinea. Never forget."

As she left the house where his body lay, a man she passed on the street recognized her from her life as a prostitute. "Aren't you Aldonza?" he said.

She held her head high and with grace and dignity exclaimed, "I am Dulcinea!"

What if Cervantes had cast his protagonist as a pornographer or as a "pornoholic"? Would he ever have seen beyond the physical body of this woman and discerned her true worth and inner beauty? The answer is painfully obvious—No! The question is, "Why is this so?"

When a man views pornography, he establishes a network of deep cellular-memories in his brain and body. Stored in the cells within this network are all the images, attitudes and ideas that he has taken in during his aggregate porn viewing sessions.

What do you suppose the stored images and attitudes regarding women are within this network? Pornography teaches that women are objects, pieces of meat used to satisfy the sexual desires of men; that all women are insatiable—they want sex all the time and from all men. This is the network of beliefs piped into the porn viewer's brain and body. So, if Don Quixote were a regular viewer of porn, what would he have seen when he looked upon Aldonza the prostitute? Only a physical object of male sexual gratification.

Pornography Promotes and Portrays Women As "Objects"

Pornography is degrading and humiliating to women as a whole. Women should be honored for their tremendous value and contribution to our society in all fields of study, talent and ability. They should be treated with dignity and respect, as valuable human beings. No man alive exists except that a woman substantially sacrificed herself to give him life. We should be sensitive to their rights, their needs and their feelings.

Pornographers and the pornography they produce demonstrate a frightfully wanton, callous disregard for women. Pornography portrays women as a collection of body parts, objects of lust who enjoy being dominated and used solely for the purpose of sexual gratification. Or it portrays them as sex-crazed—willing and anxious to have sex with virtually any man at the drop of a hat. These images and attitudes degrade and demean all women.

Internet Pornography Entices Men To Commit Violence Against Women

Pornography portrays and promotes violence against women. It also supports the so-called "rape myth," which leads men to believe that women really enjoy being sexually abused—a flawed farce if there ever was one. Pornography acts as both a "training manual" and a catalyst for rapists and predators, who act out their vicious pornographic fantasies on innocent women, teens and children.

A former Surgeon General, Dr. C. Everett Koop, summed up the "Rape Myth." After examining all of the facts,. Dr. Koop stated: "I am certain that pornography that portrays sexual aggression as pleasurable for the victim is at the root of much of the rape that occurs today. Impressionable men, many of them still in adolescence, see this material and they get the impression that women like to be hurt, humiliated and forced to do things that they do not want to do. It is a false and vicious stereotype that leads to much pain and even death for victimized women."[1]

Pornography brings many men who view it to the point where they think violence against women is socially acceptable or even secretly desired by women.

The Rape Myth

Dr. Victor Cline, in his work *Pornography's Effects on Adults and Children,* sites the following: *Drs. Neil Malamuth and Edward Donnerstein noted in their research-based book, Pornography and Sexual Aggression, that "Certain forms of pornography can affect aggressive attitudes toward women and can desensitize an individual's perception of rape. These attitudes and perceptions are, furthermore, directly related to actual aggressive behavior against women."*

Drs. Malamuth and Donnerstein also found that when men watched films that depict women enjoying being raped, it increased male acceptance of interpersonal violence against women and tended to increase the male's acceptance of the rape myth (i.e., even when she said "no" to sex or being sexually assaulted, she really meant "yes.")[2]

The following is an insight taken from Dr. Judith Reisman's revolutionary book *Soft Porn Plays Hardball*:

In 1984, Neil Malamuth and James Check reported on a study in which they showed UCLA college males a series of films depicting three common rape myths: (1) the victim enjoyed the rape, (2) the victim deserved the rape, and (3) the victim was not harmed by the rape. Prior to viewing the films, the students had expressed normal, non-violent sexual attitudes. After the films, more than half of the college men claimed they would rape a woman—if they were sure they would not get caught.[3]

Dr. Reisman concludes: *It is common knowledge that rape is now practiced sexual "etiquette" for many college males. In campus rape, "Joe College" acts out suggestions which are historically found in pornographic materials.*[4]

Now with most college males having a computer and the Internet right in their dorm or apartment, "rape myth" porn images are instantly available.

Contrary to what its proponents claim, porn does provide a "script" for the viewer to follow, offering instructions in such things as campus rape, boyfriend rape, date rape, acquaintance rape, gang rape, and, the newest craze, "wilding" (a combination of gang rape, battery and mutilation inflicted on a female victim by a group of teenage boys or young men).

Dr. Reisman declares: *The nature of these attacks indicates that Joe College knows many of the women he rapes—the very "nice girls" whom, in the past, he protected.*[5] (With Internet porn images of nymphomaniacal college girls fed into his cellular-memories, should we expect anything less from Joe College?)

Again, Dr. Reisman: *Now the conventional rapist frequently knows not only the co-eds he rapes, he is also well-acquainted with the families of his victims, suggesting a whole new middle-class script that reflects a conventional twist to rape and retribution. Victims are often left with the sense that not even the father, brothers, and the police themselves will serve as her protector.*[6]

And what if her ideal protectors are all involved in some type of Internet pornography viewing, just like the Joe College who raped her? What neural pathways are in place with these men, and how much empathy or protection can she expect?

The "Denmark Experiment"

Pornography proponents love to discount the rape-porn connection by referencing the "Denmark Experiment." In 1969, Denmark's government lifted pornography restrictions. Studies in the early '70s by Berl Kutchinski of the University of Copenhagen claimed that easy access to pornography had reduced sex crimes by providing a "safety valve" for potential offenders.

In 1977, in the International Journal of Criminology & Penology, 5, p.129, John H. Court published a research paper titled *Pornography & Sex Crimes*. In this report Court indicated that the Copenhagen police had committed a gross error and now had released new rape statistics which were considerably higher than the figures originally reported. In the words of Court: " . . . the trend since 1969 indicates that there has been a new level higher than anything in the previous decade."

As expected, porn advocates have remained quiet about the results of similar studies in Sweden, Great Britain, New Zealand and Australia. In his work *Criminal Neglect: Why Sex Offenders Go Free* (Toronto: Doubleday, p.141), John Court comments on the studies in these countries, stating: ". . . as the constraints on the availability of pornography were lifted . . . the rates of rape in those countries increased. For example, in two Australian states between 1964 and 1977, when South Australia liberalized its laws on pornography and Queensland maintained its conservative policy . . . over the thirteen-year period, the number of rapes in Queensland remained at the same low level while South Australia's showed a sixfold increase."

(**Author's Note:** For more information regarding other findings and studies of this nature, please go to www.enough.org and see the article titled *Just Harmless Fun? Understanding the Impact of Pornography.*)

Clearly, in light of this evidence, and contrary to the rhetoric of pornography proponents, the Danish experience and that of other countries throughout the world shows a direct correlation between the legalization of pornography and the increase of sexual assaults against women. Knowing what we do about pornography and its effects on the male mindbody, there could have been no other result.

Internet Porn Inflicts Suffering Upon the Male Viewer's Wife

When married men regularly view pornography, their wives always suffer. After feasting upon the exaggerated/manufactured bodies of porn stars and the sexual acts they eagerly participate in, a man can easily become dissatisfied with his wife, whom he suddenly considers physically and sexually inadequate. As a result of this trend, the wife begins to feel inadequate, and may try to "measure up" by enhancing or changing her body via assorted surgical procedures, make-overs, etc.

At the insistence of their husbands, some women subject themselves to the perverted, bizarre and uncomfortable sex acts their addicted husbands have witnessed via the Internet. Many women's lives are turned upside down and their marriages destroyed as a direct result of pornography.

Pornography Can Change Women's Attitudes Toward Themselves

With so many men lending their attention to the fantasy women posing on computer screens, what impact does this have on the "real" women in their lives? Here are some ways individual women might feel and react:

- One woman becomes disgusted and angry. She feels like she is being exploited and used. She sees exposed breasts, buttocks, perfect faces and slim bodies on magazine covers in grocery stores, on TV, in movies, and wonders, "Is that all we're good for, to be sex objects?" She wants to scream out, "There's more to me than just a collection of body parts!"
- Another woman sees the same magazines, movies and men paying attention to porn models and suddenly feels totally inadequate. Unlike these women her husband or boyfriend ogles over, she doesn't have the perfect face and slim body. She wants to be loved, valued and considered attractive. As she considers the plastic women that men seem to be so attracted to, she wonders, "Maybe I should get breast implants so that my guy will find me more sexy." (By the way, over 120,000 women a year are getting breast implants.) Or in frustration she throws her hands in the air and exclaims, "I'll never look like that!"
- A third woman knows what men want. She has bought into the whole "sex sells" mind-set. Her hair, lips, nails and makeup are flawless. She wears tight-fitting clothes that reveal her well-proportioned body. She looks something like the models on the magazine covers—or at least tries to. She is always interested in ways to be more attractive and enticing to men. When she catches them looking her over, the attention makes her feel good, as if she is of value and worth. But then there are those times when she feels hollow and lonely inside, when she feels cheated, when she feels

like she wants to value herself for something more than just her looks.

- A fourth woman shrugs it all off and thinks, "Men will be men; it's no big deal. He can look all he wants, so long as he doesn't touch." She has no concept of cellular-memories or neural pathways in the male brain and body. She doesn't understand the potential for disaster when her man starts spending his time in the narrow part of the funnel. It is almost certain that, unchecked, the man in her life who is addicted to porn will cause her heartache and misery. And when it's all over, she'll wonder, "What went wrong?"

Pornography Can Place Tremendous Stress and Anxiety On Women

Dr. Judith Reisman, one of the world's leading authorities on the psychological and neurochemical effects of pornography, has done extensive research on the effects of pornography on the innocent bystander.

Imagine you are a woman or teenage girl who is doing some research at the public library. You notice a man at the computer terminal engrossed in viewing pornographic images—in essence, filling his cellular-memories with sexual perversions.

Aware of how pornography escorts the male mind directly into the narrow base of the funnel, you view this man as he is: you know his logic, decency, self-respect and compassion are blurred. He regards women not as whole human beings, but as a collections of naked body parts created solely to satisfy his sexual urges. You know how pornography triggers copycat crime—men mimicking what they have seen. Quickly you move to another part of the building.

Later you are bothered by the feeling that someone is watching you. You glance up and see the same man, his cold eyes staring at you. What is he thinking as he looks at you? What is he imagining? A shiver runs up your spine.

Dr. Reisman's research clearly shows that women and girls experience tremendous stress and anxiety under these circumstances. As a result, many no longer frequent stores where any form of pornographic magazines are on display, or have stopped visiting shops near porn bookstores. Soon they may balk at going to public libraries as well.[7]

With Internet pornography available at the push of a button on nearly any computer terminal, how will women know what any man she sees might be capable of in his "narrowed condition"?

Talk Shows Fuel the "Women Are Sex Objects" Mystique

Over the last year or so I have noticed a disturbing trend. Talk shows like "Jenny Jones" and "Jerry Springer" promote with vigor the concept of women as sexual "objects."

As I was recently taking a break from writing, I began flipping through the channels (a dangerous practice these days) and I caught one of the Jones/Springer-type daytime shows. The program illustrated so well the concept that I was trying to impress upon my readers that I had to include it here.

It began with a picture of a little girl, about nine or ten years of age. The host delivered a heart-wrenching account of how this girl had grown up in abject poverty under pitiful conditions—no shoes, going without food for days at a time, living in an orphanage, etc. Then the host declared, "This is a 'Rags-to-Riches' story."

My first thought was, "This is great. They're going to bring out this person, now an adult, and spotlight her as a successful businesswoman or doctor or mother."

Well, there I sat, expectant. The suspense builds and finally she emerges from backstage. The men in the crowd are on their feet, cheering. Most of the women are just sitting there, dumbstruck. This woman looks like she has just won the award for best actress at the annual "Porn Film

Festival." A skin-tight miniskirt barely covers her behind, while two spaghetti straps strain to hold in her oversized breasts.

Now the host announces that they're going to bring out the bully, also now an adult, who used to tease her as a child. At this point I turn off the TV set because, number one, I'm thoroughly disappointed and disgusted, and number two, the rest of the program is totally predictable. The guy comes out on stage so that the "little girl" he once teased can get her revenge by saying, "Look at what you could've had if you'd been nice to me," and he sits there chagrined, drooling over her exposed body. The explicit message sent to the audience and to all the viewing public is "This woman is a success. This is a real rags-to-riches story. This is what all you girls and women out there should strive for." *And* the equally odious message to men is, "If you treat us right, we'll reward you with our bodies. If you don't, you won't 'get any.'"

All I could think of after witnessing that daytime circus was, "What a wasted opportunity" and "Another blow to the perception and rights of women." The producers of the show could have used the success of a "little orphan girl" to lift and inspire. They could have invited any one of literally hundreds of thousands of women across America who have lifted themselves out of similar backgrounds of poverty and hardship, women who rose above dire circumstances and overcame tremendous odds to become first-rate teachers, mothers, professionals and business-owners. Such a story would have given the show's female viewers a sense of hope and pride, both individually and collectively. And it would have instilled in the male viewers an appreciation for the true dignity and value of women.

Instead the producers followed the script that much of Hollywood—and all pornographers—have been promoting for years. Once again, a woman is put on stage as a "sex object," and one more perverted sexual image is added to the already crowded cellular-memory groups and neural pathways of each and every male viewer. Almost as tragic, each woman in the audience is once again shown what she must look like and act like if she is to draw the attention and "affections" of men.

Women As Primary Victims of Pornography

Many of the comments thus far have had to do with women as "secondary victims" of pornography. But as a result of Internet pornographers creating porn sites geared to women and the proliferation of Internet cybersex chat rooms, increasing numbers of women are falling prey to porn and cybersex addiction.

All of the tragedies afflicting male porn addicts are also heaped upon these female addicts; hours, days, weeks and years of wasted time, talents left undeveloped, marriages and families destroyed, self-respect laid waste, and many other even more devastating consequences.

But perhaps a tragedy at least as great as them all, is the fact that these women surrender themselves to the trappings and lies of the Internet pornographers, the Hollywood smut peddlers, and the whole male-oriented-and-dominated "sexual attitude." If women, with their gifts of intuition, perspective, reasoning and host of other "whole brain" attributes, buy into the pornography agenda and campaign and adopt an "If you can't beat 'em, join 'em" philosophy, "then as a society I fear we have little hope of restoring anything that resembles a healthy and sacred human intimacy.

Key Points

A reference tool for spouses, parents, clergy, counselors and others

- Pornography turns women into objects—a collection of body-parts. This fuels the infamous "Rape Myth," directly increasing the incidence of violence and sexual abuse against women. Thus, pornography places all women at risk.
- This "objectification" focuses solely on the physical, diverting attention away from the many gifts, talents and abilities women possess as human beings and contributors in society.
- The "Denmark Experiment" and others like it, were a dismal failure. Rather than providing the expected *safety valve* for potential sex-offenders, the legalization of pornography actually increased the number of sexual assaults against women.
- Pornography destroys *healthy* intimacy in marriage.
- Sexualized media is all around us and is having an extremely powerful effect on the way women see and feel about themselves.
- With hard-core pornography readily accessible in homes, offices and libraries, many women are feeling the stress of being around men in a "narrowed state" following porn viewing. In this narrowed condition, otherwise normal, decent men become potential sex-offenders.
- Growing numbers of women are falling into the trap of Internet porn and cybersex chat addiction.

20

PORNOGRAPHY TRIGGERS CHILD ABUSE

Children Are Severely Victimized by Pornography:

- The combination of pornography and the pedophiles it produces is deadly for children. The brutal abuse of children by pedophiles pumped up on porn is tragic, shocking and heartbreaking.
- Men who view pornography portraying 18-year-old women dressed to look like young teens, often act out their prurient sexual cravings by raping "real" young teens.
- Children and teens who are exposed to pornography have these images etched in their memories for the rest of their lives. These images can be triggered and surface without warning, leaving the potential for numerous problems in future life.
- Internet pornography is often the first exposure that children and teens have to sexual images. This plants in them a twisted and perverse view of human intimacy that is difficult or impossible to weed out. These early learning experiences can lead to sexual deviancy and crime, and at the very least hampers their future relationships and marriages.

- When a father or mother is involved with pornography, the children will suffer in one way or another ranging from something as simple as a parent who is often moody, angry or "in his or her own world," to a father or mother who commits incest. Pornography hurts husband-and-wife relationships and breaks up marriages, which of course seriously impacts the children in the family. Only pain is in store for children with a father or mother hooked on pornography.

Fatherless America

Countless studies have proved conclusively that at the center of many of American society's most serious problems is the trend of fatherless families. Due to divorce or abandonment, an ever-increasing number of American homes are without fathers. The problems associated with a father's absence are myriad, certainly the topic of countless other books.

But of equal calamity, and in far greater numbers, are the homes in America that have a father who is there physically but absent emotionally and spiritually: fathers who are constantly moody, angry or physically and verbally abusive; fathers who say very little, seldom express their love verbally, rarely engage in casual, friendly conversation, and just seem to be living in their "own little world."

Perhaps not surprising, most of the attributes I have just described are the same ones that manifest themselves when a father is hooked on/preoccupied with pornography. Now with the floodgates of porn thrown wide open by the Internet, how many men will be consumed by addiction, spending much of their time in front of their computer screens at the office or in the den at home when they normally would be interacting with their wives and children?

And when they are not overloading on porn, how fit will they be mentally and emotionally to love and care for their family? Pornography robs parents of healthy parental emotions. Internet pornography will accelerate the plight of "fatherless America" in a way never before witnessed in society. The incidence of fathers (and mothers) just "taking off" will increase, as will the divorce rate. And in more certain and terrifying numbers, fathers who are at home physically but absent emotionally and spiritually as a direct result of Internet porn will increase at an explosive rate. Heaven help an America that is "fatherless."

As incredible as it may seem, there is also a growing trend toward a "motherless" America. More and more women are becoming addicted to Internet porn/cybersex chat rooms, and are found to be demonstrating many of the same behaviors and attitudes of men who are porn or cybersex addicts. This is inflicting an even greater devastation on children than the loss of a father to Internet porn. A woman, with her female brain and attributes, is often better equipped to nurture and communicate with her children in ways that most men cannot. Indeed, her loss in the home is a tragedy of the highest proportions.

Pornography Can Scar Children For Life

In her work *Mind & Brain*, Dr. Gilinsky discusses the fact that humans pass through well-defined stages of development when they are maximally sensitive to certain kinds of stimuli.[1] An infant imprints on his or her mother's voice even while in the womb; a two-year-old may be hypersensitive to a parent leaving him or her with a new babysitter.

We all know how deeply impressionable small children are. They possess a huge number of cells in their brains and bodies, all just waiting to soak up and store information, experiences, emotions, etc.

Cellular-memory groups are being formed and linked together with other cell groups with great rapidity throughout a child's mindbody. These cellular-memories will act as a pair of glasses through which the child will see herself and the world around her.

What happens if during a critical developmental period in a child's life she is exposed to pornography on the Internet or in some other way? Or what if she is sexually abused by an older friend or relative who has been exposed to pornography? Part and parcel with this abuse, cellular-memories will be formed in this child that will effect her for the rest of her life. And because she is so impressionable and at such a sensitive developmental stage, the cellular-memories and linking pathways forged will be especially wide and deeply etched. Hence her future growth and development—especially in the emotional/spiritual and healthy human intimacy vein—may be greatly retarded.

Can you see why adults carry so much baggage from abusive childhoods? What they bring with them into their adult lives are the cellular-memories that were established during their sensitive, deeply impressionable "learning" years as children. Many have been left severely emotionally stunted.

As adults, outside stimuli are still being processed and recalled through precisely formed cellular-memory groups. Thus, children who were sexually abused, for example, often find it difficult to enjoy healthy sexual intimacy with their spouse. Can you imagine what might happen when in an intimate moment with a spouse, stimuli is processed through those cellular-memories that were formed during sexual abuse as a child? These cellular-memory "filters" are for some a lifelong burden.

Special Note: In his heroic book *A War We Must Win*, John Harmer points an accusing finger at a media that deny that pornography, sex, nudity and violence inflict any long-term damage to adults or children. He quotes a well-known liberal columnist, Nicholas van Hoffman:

Why is it that liberals who believe "role models" in third grade readers are of decisive influence on behavior when it concerns racism or male chauvinist piggery, laugh at the assertion that pornography may also teach rape? Every textbook in every public school system in the nation has been overhauled in the last twenty years because it was thought that the blond, blue-eyed suburban children once depicted therein taught little people a socially dangerous ethnocentrism.

If textbooks, those vapid and insipid instruments of such slight influence, can have had such sweeping effect, what are we to surmise about the effects on the impressionably young of an R or X-rated movie, in wide-

screen technicolor, with Dolby sound and every device of cinematic realism?

Network television executives who deny the likelihood their programs can alter human behavior lie, and they know it. All you have to do is listen to what these same gentlemen say to their advertisers. They boast, they brag, they bellow about what an effective sales medium their networks are—how good they are at getting people to alter their behavior and part with their money.[2]

Children Often "Act Out" What They See In Pornography

Children are notorious for imitating what they've seen, read or heard. Studies suggest that exposure to pornography can prompt kids to act out sexually against younger, smaller or more vulnerable children.

Experts in the field of childhood sexual abuse report that any premature sexual activity in children always points to two possible stimulants: experience or exposure. This means that the sexually deviant child may either have been molested or simply exposed to sexuality through pornography.[3] In a study of 600 American males and females of junior high school age and above, researcher Dr. Jennings Bryant found that 91% of the males and 82% of the females admitted to having been exposed to X-rated, hard-core pornography. Over 66% of the males and 40% of the females reported wanting to "try out" some of the sexual behaviors they had witnessed. And among high schoolers, 31% of males and 18% of females admitted to actually *doing* some of the prurient things they had seen in the pornography within a few days of exposure.[4]

Copycat crimes committed after exposure to pornography are beginning to manifest themselves even among children. More headlines like this one are showing up in our newspapers: ***Boy, 12, blames X-rated videos—officials searching for rape motive***. . . *A 12-year-old boy accused of raping a 10-year-old girl may have learned some of the behavior by watching pornographic videos, police say.*

According to a report in the Buffalo News (April 24, 1984), mimicking photographs found in their mother's pornography magazines, a nine-year-old boy and his seven-year-old brother in St. Petersburg, Florida, penetrated and killed an eight-month-old baby with a pencil and coat hanger.

Similarly, the *Washington Post* reported on a boy, age ten, who after watching an X-rated film, raped an eight-year-old girl and her four-year-old sister.[5]

Children are highly impressionable! Most incidents like those cited above occur after extremely limited exposure to pornography, in some cases only once or twice. What will happen now that pornography of every kind imaginable is instantly available over the Internet? And, believe it or not, organizations like the American Library Association and the ACLU are doing everything in their power to prevent libraries from protecting children from pornography on the Internet![6] They actually have the audacity to label "protection of children" as "censorship!"

Child Pornography The Most Dark and Sinister of All

We have established the fact that the producers of pornography are predators, seeking to addict their prey by whatever means they can get away with. These "online" predators hide behind the cloak of anonymity, not unlike a shark lurking beneath the surface of the water. If the producers of pornography are sharks, then the producers of "child pornography" are the Great White Sharks—the most dark and sinister, the deadliest predators in all of porn's inky ocean.

Most porn producers avoid getting mixed up with child pornography. They prefer to employ young women who are age 18 and above, and dress them up to look like "teeny boppers" to suggest that the viewer is seeing a 12- or 15-year-old engaging in sex. This results in some viewers attempting to "act out" what their mindbody *thought it saw*, by seducing or raping young teenage girls.[7] (Remember, the mindbody is always seeking to piece together input, images and information stored in cellular-memories, to have a peak experience. It does not distinguish between a woman made to *look* like a teenager and an actual teenager.)

Again, most pornographers don't risk the chance of using actual children for their material. They're afraid of being prosecuted by the law. Why risk prosecution when they can achieve the same end result with "virtual" children?

Child pornography is the most tragic of all because it requires the actual sexual abuse of children. Produced in the form of still pictures, video or movies, child porn is literally a permanent recording of a heinous and despicable crime in progress.

The producers of true child pornography are almost always "pedophiles." Pedophiles, or "child molesters," have one primary focus in life: to engage in sexual relations with children. They have warped their mindbody to use children as a center of the process to arrive at the peak experience of orgasm. Over the years their mindbody has become twisted and confused, a result of storing pornographic images of children in their cellular-memory groups.

As a result of strong federal prosecution in the United States, child pornography is not freely available over the counter. But in many countries there are no laws against child pornography. Pornographers in those countries, therefore, can pipe it into the U.S. through—you guessed it—the Internet. With the Internet, there are no borders and few laws.

With the development of the Internet, child pornography has become a thriving underground industry for pedophiles, primarily because the Internet allows them to remain hidden and anonymous. Pedophiles traffic their products by exchanging them over the Internet with other pedophiles.[8]

Pedophiles also use these same advantages and tools to engage in their overwhelming fixation and addiction—interaction with children that they hope will lead to a sexual encounter. They use the Internet to share "trade secrets" with others of their kind, i.e., how to change identities, forge passports, and smuggle children.[9]

By way of the Internet, pedophiles help other members of their circle feel accepted and promote the idea that their sexual interest in children is normal.[10] Pedophiles are constantly prowling children's chat rooms in pursuit of new prey. In recent years there has been an alarming increase in the number of pedophiles using the Internet chat rooms to arrange face-to-face meetings with children.[11] When you consider the number of children online, it is no wonder pedophiles are using the Internet to seek out their prey. An estimated 26.8 million children will have Internet access by the year 2001, and 77 million by 2005.[12] In a *USA TODAY* article dated 6/09/2000, Karen Thomas reports: *One in five adolescents and teens who regularly socialize on the Net have encountered a stranger there who wanted "cybersex," says a government-financed survey to be released Thursday.*

Children left to fend for themselves on the Internet may be victimized by pedophiles. This is done with virtually no prior warning. A pedophile may show a child a picture of naked adults and say, "See, this is what mommies and daddies do." Or he may flash on the screen a photo that to him is sexually stimulating and ask, "Did you know that this is how boys and girls have fun?"

A Los Angeles Police Department study of every child molestation case referred to them over a ten-year period, found that in 60% of the cases adult or child pornography was used to lower the inhibitions of the children molested and/or to excite and sexually arouse the pedophile. Once the pedophile lowers his victims' defenses, the children are stripped of their precious innocence and subjected to brutalities that defy description. These children suffer tremendous guilt, shame and anger, especially as they grow older and more fully understand the enormity of their abuse. These emotions are further compounded when they realize that there is a permanent record of their nightmare circulating out there for all to see—perhaps by future friends, or, years down the road, even by their own children.

Mike Brick, head of the Florida Department of Law Enforcement, has said, "Child molesters are using the electronic superhighway to look for victims. They've got to go to other places where the children of the '90s play."[13]

To illustrate how vulnerable our children are to the scourge of pedophiles on the Internet, I cite a recent case: A grand jury recently charged 16 people in the United States and overseas with participating in a child pornography ring. The members of this ring shared home-processed photographs, recounted their sexual experiences with children, and held conversations over the Internet while two men molested a ten-year-old girl, broadcasting their sexual abuse "live" via video camera over the Internet. Other pedophiles tuning into the live scene on their own computer screens, transmitted requests back as to what they wanted to see next. Prosecutors said that members of the group produced and traded child pornography involving victims as young as five years old![14]

The marvelous non-profit organization Enough is Enough, cites the following facts about child molestation in the United States:

- One in three girls and one in seven boys will be sexually molested by age 18.[15]
- 87% of convicted molesters of girls and 77% of convicted molesters of boys admit to using pornography, most often in the commission of their crimes.[16] More children contract sexually transmitted diseases (STDs) each year than all the victims of polio in its 11-year epidemic (1942-1953).[17] "One of the most popular pornographic video series in America is based upon incest."[18]
- 29% of all forcible rapes are against children under the age of 11.[19] The median age of abuse is 9.9 for boys and 9.6 for girls.[20]
- 22% of boys and 23% of girls who are sexually abused are molested before the age of eight.[21]

Enough is Enough also cites the following recent news stories documenting "Sexual Violence Against Children" that was fueled by pornography:

- "After gaining the trust of a 14-year-old boy on computer, Donald Matthew Deatherage arranged to meet him. Police say he shackled, tortured and molested the boy, whose father discovered sexually explicit e-mail messages between the two."
- "A Houston man who adopted two sex abuse victims and then began sexually abusing them himself has been sentenced to 90 years in prison. Police said their investigation of Mr. Layne turned up sex devices, women's lingerie and so much pornography that it took an 18-wheeler truck to haul it away. . . . The boy is now in a mental facility and the girl is in intensive therapy. . . ."[22]
- "One of the young girls David Lee Thompson molested made him cry. He assaulted the five-year-old several times along the 100-mile drive from her Illinois home. She asked God to help Thompson, and she told him he could help himself by throwing away pornographic magazines that were in the van. He talked about how he sat up front and cried." (In other words, he emerged from the narrow part of the funnel to see his horrific actions with a big-picture perspective.)

But, in this latter case, what happened after the girl fell asleep? The article indicates that Thompson scanned through the pornographic magazines in his van, slid back down into the narrow part of the funnel, lost all perspective and went back and molested her again. "He has told police he was molested as a child, which he claims pushed him toward a youthful fascination with pornography."[23]

(For more information on this organization dedicated to protecting children and helping citizens organize in the battle against the porn trade, visit www.enough.org.)

Key Points

A reference tool for
spouses, parents, clergy,
counselors and others

- Growing numbers of children are losing their fathers (and in some cases, mothers) to Internet porn and cybersex chat addiction. These parents are in the home *physically*, but often are absent emotionally and spiritually. Addict parents are often guilty of emotional, physical and even sexual abuse of their children. Many children are dragged through the mire of divorce as a result of these addictions.
- Through the Internet, an alarming number of children are being exposed to incredibly depraved and explicit images. These are permanently stored in the mindbody as cellular-memories and can cause significant trauma and dysfunction, now, and in the future.
- More and more children are "imitating" the pornographic images they see on the Internet and in the media.
- With the Internet, child pornography has become a thriving underground industry for pedophiles. They use the Internet to create a "community" where they traffic their insidious products, share "trade secrets" and prey on innocent children.

21

INTERNET PORN IS DESTROYING OUR TEENS—OUR FUTURE

PORN SEEKS TO PLACE TEENS AND ADULTS IN THE SAME SEXUAL CATEGORY

Pornography makes no attempt to separate the sexual development and maturity of teenagers from that of adults. It places teens and adults in the same general category. In fact, pornographers go to great lengths to satisfy the "young teen sex" fetish by making their models appear to be as young as possible.

Pornography fosters the message that as soon as a boy or girl reaches puberty, he or she should be having sex and viewing pornography right along with the adults. Likewise, Hollywood movies are geared to push teens prematurely into an adult world.

I recently read an article in the movie section of a local newspaper. Headlined *"Teen Movie" is becoming a sexual euphemism*, it read:

Nobody, apparently, was asked to vouch for the under-17s who made up at least half the audience at last week's preview screening of "Cruel Intentions," which opened Friday. The version of the novel, "Les Liaisons Dangereuses" stars Sarah Michelle Gellar and Ryan Phillippe as bored, rich high schoolers who make a bet as to whether Phillippe can seduce a committed virgin. The wager? A night with Gellar.

It's difficult to imagine anyone too far beyond 17 having any interest in "Cruel Intentions." And it's even harder to conceive that any parent could sit through this movie with a teenager without squirming. It's as raunchy as they come, with references to sexual practices of every variety. Yet it represents a trend.

Of the five teen-oriented films released by a major studio this year, four have been rated R, primarily for language and sexual content. "Cruel Intentions" was released by Columbia, which also released "Jawbreaker," about teens who conspire to cover up the accidental death of a girl in their clique.

It sports a sequence in which their ringleader asks a boy to show her how he'd like a sex act performed. This scene elicited squeals from the girls in front of me at the screening, who were probably around 14. But maybe they were older. I could've been mistaken. What is not mistakable is that the major studios, emboldened by the pervasive sexualization of teen culture in advertising, magazines, pop music, and television, are upping the ante. . . .

The teenage audience has become increasingly important in Hollywood because movies like "Cruel Intentions," with their young casts, inexpensive directors and low production overhead, usually cost less than Harrison Ford's salary. "I Know What You Did Last Summer" earned almost 10 times its production cost, while "Six Days and Six Nights" barely broke even.

So the rating system, designed to protect children, becomes another code for kids to crack, while the term "teen movie" becomes another sexual euphemism, like "adult bookstore" and "mature audience." Perhaps it's time to add yet another rating: GR—for Get Real.[1]

And so, what are the results of teens involving themselves in adult sexual activity? In the U.S., approximately one in four sexually-active teens acquires a sexually transmitted disease (STD); infectious syphilis rates have more than doubled among teenagers since the mid 1980s,[2] and one million teenage girls become pregnant each year.[3]

Males who are exposed to significant amounts of porn before the age of 14 are more sexually active and engage in more varied sexual behaviors as adults than males who are not exposed.[4]

Pornography's menacing message to teens is clear: ***Sex without responsibility is not only acceptable but preferable and desirable.***

One In Five Kids Solicited For Sex Online

On June 20, 2001, the *Journal of the American Medicine Association (JAMA)* featured an article titled *Risk Factors For and Impact of Online Sexual Solicitation of Youth.* In the article, Drs. Kimberly J. Mitchell, David Finkelhor and Janis Wolak reported the results of their extensive study.

The researchers found that one in five U.S. teenagers who regularly log on to the Internet say they have received an unwanted sexual solicitation via the Web. Nineteen percent of the 1,500 surveyed youths aged 10 to 17 reported getting solicited, presumably by adults. Solicitations were defined as requests to engage in sexual activities or sexual talk, or to give personal sexual information.

"In terms of risk, girls and older youth (14-17 years) were more likely to be solicited. Risk was higher for youth who were troubled. It was also higher for those who used the Internet more frequently, participated in chat rooms, engaged in risky behavior online, talked to strangers online, or used the Internet at households other than their own," wrote Kimberly Mitchell of the Crimes Against Children Research Center at the University of New Hampshire, in Durham.

One quarter of the children who were solicited for sex—some of whom were subsequently approached in person or enticed on the telephone or by regular mail—reported being extremely upset or afraid.

Neither parental oversight of children's online activities nor filtering or blocking technology had much impact on whether children were solicited, the study found. "Add Internet solicitation to the list of childhood perils about which (authorities) should be knowledgeable and able to provide counsel to families," said the report. "At the same time, the concerns are not so alarming that they should by themselves encourage parents to bar children from accessing the Internet," it said. (6/20/2001, JAMA 2000; 285: 3011-3014, as quoted from ZDNet News, www.zdnet.com)

TEENAGE GIRLS AS VICTIMS OF INTERNET PORNOGRAPHY

When it comes to Internet porn, one of the most vulnerable of any group, are teenage girls. As discussed several sections ago, there are certain times in a person's development when she is more impressionable and sensitive to outside stimuli. When cellular-memory groups and neural pathways are laid down during these times, they are large, deep, dominant and cast in concrete. The person's attitudes, emotions, self-esteem and core beliefs are swayed for life.

Let's consider how two teenage girls might react after observing that teenage boys and men like viewing pornography:

- This teenage girl is immediately turned off by the thought of pornography. She has been taught and believes that her self-worth and value go far beyond her physical body. She feels good about herself as a "whole person" and has confidence in her talents and abilities both as a woman and as a human being. She believes that sexual relations are only appropriate in marriage. She is convinced that if a man truly loves and cherishes her, he would never attempt to "use her body" for his own selfish purposes. She is waiting for the man who will make a total commitment to her through marriage. Then they can share "everything" together, including sexual intimacy.

- Another teenage girl is struggling with her self-esteem. In the grocery store she sees the perfect model posing on a magazine cover. *"10 sex pointers from women, GUARANTEED to drive your man wild."* Of course she wants boys to like her. But then she looks down at her own, comparatively pathetic body and decides she doesn't like it very much: she thinks her nose is too big, her cheek bones aren't high enough; her hips are too big, her breasts too small. She gazes at the magazine cover again. "That's what boys want," she thinks to herself. "I see them staring all the time at girls who look like that. Maybe if I change my hair or make-up, or wear tighter clothes or shorter skirts, the boys will like me more."

I'm not trying to describe all the possible reactions a teenage girl might have to the messages of pornography. I am trying to cause you to think. We live in a time when increasing numbers of teenage girls are going in for plastic surgery—nose jobs, chin jobs, eye jobs and breast implants. Why are they so dissatisfied with how they look? How are these ideas getting into their brains and bodies? Just look at the magazine covers on the grocery store rack, the sitcoms on TV, the movies at the theater, and the Internet porn that men and teenage boys (and increasing numbers of women) are obsessing over.

Some teenage girls begin trading sex (their bodies) for affection and acceptance from teenage boys. I address this issue in greater detail in other chapters. Suffice it to say, teenage girls are constantly being sent the message through magazines, television, movies and pornography that teenage boys and men want to look at sensuous, voluptuous female bodies and engage in sex with them.

Sexual Violence Becomes Acceptable and Fun

At the core of many pornographic fantasy scenarios is the sexual assault of the "girl next door." Standard fare includes jokes about raping women after drugging them or plying them with alcohol; scenes showing women taking pleasure in being gang raped; and "entertainment" depicting the rape of coeds, girlfriends, students, secretaries, maids, neighbors and children. In fact, *Playboy* publisher Hugh Hefner once bragged about his success in tearing down the barrier erected by Judeo-Christian beliefs that at one time protected "good girls" from being viewed as "bad girls."

Hefner said: *In the prudish moral climate of the Fifties,* Playboy *unabashedly championed sexual liberation. Before* Playboy, *women were typeset either as Madonna or as a whore. But the wholesome, unselfconscious sexuality of Playboy's "girl-next-door" Playmates conveyed—to men and women alike—the unsettling and exciting message that "nice girls" like sex, too.*[5]

This "wholesome (?!), nice-girls-like-sex" message has also helped change the "nice boy's" attitudes toward sexual violence against "nice girls." In fact, it's now common to hear rape euphemistically referred to as "rough sex."

As previously stated, in May 1988 the Rhode Island Rape Crisis Center asked 1,700 sixth- to ninth-grade students to share their attitudes about rape. More than half the boys and girls considered sex to be acceptable after six months of dating—even if rape was necessary to achieve this. Roughly half agreed that if a boy spends $10 to $15 on a girl, he has the right to force a kiss.

Sixty-five percent of the boys and 47% of the girls said that forced sex was acceptable if a couple dated for six months. Without realizing that "forced" sex is rape, nearly a quarter of the boys and a sixth of the girls saw rape as acceptable if a boy had spent money on a girl.[6]

What does it mean when boys and girls grow up believing that "rough sex" is merely erotic or flirtatious play? According to the *Washington Post* (May 6, 1988), of 1,035 rapes reported to the Rhode Island Rape Crisis Center in 1987, 79% of the victims were raped by someone the woman or girl knew. Moreover, experts estimate one in four girls and one in seven boys will be sexually assaulted before they are 18 years old, generally by a relative or another trusted acquaintance.

In 1988 Michigan reported an astounding 681 juveniles convicted of sexually assaulting younger children. The average age of the victims: seven! Almost 60% of the assaults involved penetration, and further, "93% of the [juvenile] offenders were acquaintances, friends, baby-sitters, or relatives of the victims."

The horror of this new wave of juvenile sexual assaults is just the tip of the iceberg. On October 11, 1984, the *Washington Post* reported an instance in which a high school girl was raped in a boys' school bathroom while at least ten other boys looked on, cheering.

The *Boston Herald*, on June 28, 1984, ran a story about a 12-year-old Pawtucket, Massachusetts boy who raped a ten-year-old girl on a pool table in a "reenactment" of the infamous "Big Dan" pool table gang rape of a woman. The "Big Dan" pool table case had recently received wide media coverage in the Pawtucket area.

With every type of sex act and perversion involving female children, teens and women being displayed, glorified and promoted over the Internet, the type of atrocities cited above will become commonplace.

Porn Encourages Anorexia and Bulimia

In her book *Soft Porn Plays Hardball*, Dr. Judith Reisman states:

Porn subtly communicates that the value of a woman is determined by her body shape and size. Only those women with a perfect physical appearance are valuable and worthy of being admired, desired and loved. This can have detrimental effects on how women and girls view themselves.

I often wonder how many young girls who struggle with anorexia, bulimia, and other eating disorders are unknowingly struggling to measure up to the perfect "10" image projected by the airbrushed centerfold.[7]

TEENAGE BOYS AS VICTIMS OF INTERNET PORNOGRAPHY

Teenage boys are extremely vulnerable to pornography's seductive allure. In her book *Kids Online*, Donna Rice Hughes shares some valuable insights:

Print and movie pornography tend to trap males more often than females. It would be easy to believe that males are more visually oriented than females, but the evidence is less clear than we need to make that assertion. What we do know is that the male's hydraulic sex system and the exterior genitals keep him more aware of his sexual feelings than the typical female is.

His ejaculation pattern, once begun, will continue, and his psycho-social sexual appetite tends to be fully developed within thirty-six months after that first ejaculation. The "porn" market, therefore, exploits this normal development of male sexuality, with the tragic effect that addiction to pornography tends to desensitize the male, such that a bonded heterosexual relationship is not only unlikely to develop, but the genuine relationship with one exclusive person is not even desired.[8]

Giving porn to a teenage boy is like giving crack to a baby: addiction is almost guaranteed. No wonder boys ages 12 to 17 are the porn industry's core target, as determined by the 1986 Attorney General's Commission on Pornography. Instant addiction—customers for life. With 20 times the normal amount of testosterone suddenly coursing through a male teen's system at puberty, how can one say that "He has the presence of mind and the self-control necessary to decide on his own whether or not to continue looking at porn once he is exposed to it"? Come on! This is no choice at all. Again, it's like feeding crack to a baby, then expecting him to wean himself from it when he becomes older. Not likely that it's gonna happen.

Pornographers Use Nature Against Men and Boys

The power that drives men to procreate, to mate, to commit themselves to a wife and family is one of the most powerful forces in the universe. Couple this with the fact that teenage boys and girls are equipped at puberty with dormant cells containing sexual commands and instructions, just waiting to be activated, and the situation becomes one of sexual overdrive. How these cells are activated and the images, emotions and attitudes stored there initially will have a direct impact on the teenagers' future sexual attitudes and practices.

Pornographers use this natural biological phenomenon to their advantage. In order to sexually arouse, their products show females that appear to be in *estrus* or *heat*[9] to excite the male mating instinct. Pornographers don't want males to *think*, they want them to *react*. Instinct is the key to unlocking the male appetite, not rational logic and thought, so females are erotically posed with their lips glistening in red lipstick, their genitals exposed, their bodies assuming a mating position so that the viewing male will instinctively be aroused.[10]

But it isn't simply sexual drive that impels teenage boys to get hooked on Internet porn and masturbation. There are countless things going on in the brain and body of a teenage boy, any of which can trigger his need to "self-medicate." Think about the teen years—zits, extreme self-centeredness, bodily changes, peer pressure, girl problems, shyness, and the list goes on. The entire male teen mindbody is in upheaval, a state of constant flux. And then, Bam! Like the marijuana, crack or heroine dealer, the Internet pornographer is there to "make it all better." This faceless porn-dealer offers the already vulnerable and troubled teen an instant and easy recipe to escape.

The teen is given all the "drugs" he could ever want, all at his beck and call, and in the privacy of his own room or home study. He can completely immerse himself in the fantasy filth world of nudity, sex, perversion and the self-medication of repeated masturbation.

This teen, trapped in the blurry world of puberty, quickly becomes a "client for life," assuring the Internet pornographers of gaudy profits well into the future.

Teen-in-a-Box Tragedy

When teens get sucked into the porn trap, they suffer the same dark consequences that men suffer when they view pornography. But teens undergo a misery that seems to have an extra sharp bite. With the images permanently stored, they may find themselves slaves to a cruel master who will suck every bit of life out of them.

I remember years ago reading a most tragic and heart-wrenching account of human suffering. It was written by the victim himself, now a man, recalling the horrific experience of his youth.

From the time "Matt" was a tiny child, his mother had kept him confined 24 hours a day in a large cardboard box! This was his entire world; this was all he knew. I cannot recall the exact details, but I believe that Matt remained in the box until he was eight or nine years old. His situation—and his mother's treachery—was finally brought to light, and he was released and placed in foster care.

As I read his account, tears flowed down my cheeks and I thought my heart would break. Matt spoke of the wonder and awe he felt upon seeing and experiencing things for the very first time—things you and I take for granted: seeing a blue sky, touching the leaves on a tree, rolling in fresh-cut grass, tasting a freshly baked chocolate chip cookie. And how surprised he was when he discovered that all children don't live out their early lives inside a cardboard box. The exhilaration and joy he must have felt the day he was set free into a world that wasn't dark and smothering!

I often think of that child and his tortured beginnings. I grieve at the marvelous experiences and wonders he was deprived of during those formative years. What an awful tragedy! Then I think of all the teenage boys in this country who are trapped inside their own "cardboard box" of

Internet pornography addiction. This is a tragedy of monumental proportions.

I also ponder the sad state of the pornographers, who, like the deranged and demented mother, are obsessed with the profit potential of luring young men into the box and then keeping them there, sealed off from so many of life's beauties, deprived of hope for the future, stifled by the disabling captivity of such an insidious addiction.

The Boy Who Couldn't Give Blood

The young college student's mother was in the hospital, literally bleeding to death. A blood transfusion was desperately needed to save her life. Her son recruited his college friends and they all drove to the hospital to donate the needed pints.

The young men were first tested for blood type. Several proved to be a match for the dying mother. One young man's blood, however, was found to be unfit, in that it tested positive for venereal disease. He was unable to aid the woman—his own mother.

Earlier in his life this young man had become addicted to pornography. His addiction escalated to the point where he began "acting out" his fantasies with dozens of women, including prostitutes. Walking the pornographic path rendered this young man unable to give much-needed help to a loved one in her time of crisis. In fact, he added to her pain and suffering when she learned of his diseased condition.

Key Points

A reference tool for
spouses, parents, clergy,
counselors and others

- Pornography and sexualized media push teens to become sexually active.
- Growing numbers of teens are being solicited for sex on the Internet. Most of these solicitations are from adults (many of whom have undoubtedly been viewing the plethora of "teenage-looking" porn models on the Internet).
- Pornography and sexualized media distort the way teens view themselves and others: many teenage girls attempt to alter their dress and physical appearance to correspond to the sexualized models they see in the media; Anorexia and Bulimia are on the rise; growing numbers of teenage boys see sexual violence (i.e.., date-rape) as acceptable and fun, etc.
- Pornography and sexualized media are teaching teens that *sex without responsibility is not only acceptable but preferable and desirable.* Teenagers are being bombarded with "adult" sexual images and situations long before they have the emotional maturity, wisdom, and life experiences to make <u>informed</u> decisions and choices.
- Just like cigarettes, alcohol and drugs, pornography addiction is robbing teens of reaching their full potential and future opportunities.

22

MEN ARE PORN VICTIMS

THE MEN WHO VIEW PORNOGRAPHY

We have discussed how pornography's scourge scorches the soul of the innocent—the children, the teen, the brokenhearted wife or husband. Theirs is the most tragic situation of all because they suffer needlessly as a result of the lust, greed and selfishness of others.

But what about the men who get sucked into porn's cauldron of lust? I certainly would never suggest that their suffering is anything like that of innocent women and children who lay in the wake of pornography addiction. Nor am I suggesting that their actions should be excused or justified. But I do submit that the suffering and misery experienced by men who get pulled into the pornography trap are real and excruciating.

- Nearly all men who view pornography use it as the stimulus for masturbation. As a result they frequently suffer feelings of guilt, shame, regret and humiliation.

- Many men become addicted to pornography and lose their freedom. They feel trapped, "out of control," and in despair. They literally become slaves to their own lust.
- Pornography places men on emotional roller coaster. One minute they're happy, the next they're sad; calm, then angry; kind, then cold. These moods change without warning, causing stress and pain for wives, children, friends and neighbors. Feelings of estrangement ensue, further isolating and alienating them from their loved ones, which often drives men even deeper into the "self-medicating" escape of pornography.
- Men isolated on the slippery slope of pornography typically fail in their families and marriages, and in their relations with people in general. They are less effective, less reliable, less creative, and more prone to meanness and fits of anger. In essence, pornography turns men into "zombies" who are but a shadow of their true selves and potential. They waste their time, talents and resources, caught up in their own dark little world of pornography viewing.
- In the advanced stages, pornography addiction can lead a man to commit rape, incest, violence, exhibitionism, other sex-related crimes and even suicide. Millions of men have lost their families, their careers, their reputations, their good names, and their freedom just to satisfy their addiction.
- Pornography can take an immensely good, talented, enthusiastic man and turn him into one of the "walking dead."

Porn is a purely "selfish hobby"—it gives nothing to anyone but the viewer and the porn producer. In that way it is not at all like other hobbies, such as painting, writing, playing a musical instrument, woodworking or gardening, which give something of value to others and make the hobbyist a more generous, well-rounded person.

With rare exception, porn for the male viewer has a "singular purpose": It is a process that leads to orgasm. In marriage, the process leading to orgasm at least has the potential to be a binding, loving, giving experience for both the man and the woman. No such benefits exist with porn. And, in fact, when a husband is locked into the porn process leading to his private orgasms, this selfish attitude will nearly always spill over to his marriage. Over time, he will be less of a soulmate and more of an isolationist. Plus, sooner or later he will begin seeing his wife as an object similar to the porn images he views in order to achieve orgasm. Thus, pornography often turns intimacy in marriage into a totally selfish and narrow experience.

Each of us has an obligation or "stewardship" to develop the talents, abilities and gifts that have been given us. Much of the pain and suffering in this world of ours can be traced to the "takers," the greedy, the selfish—those who keep all and give nothing back.

There Are Two Seas

Writer Bruce Barton inspires us with a powerful and appropriate metaphor:

One is fresh and fish abound in it. Splashes of green adorn its landscape. Trees spread their branches over it and stretch out their thirsty roots to sip of its life-giving waters. Along its shores children play, as children played when He was there. He loved it. He could look across its silver surface as He spoke His parables.

And on a rolling plain, not far away, He fed five thousand people in the miracle of the loaves and fishes. The River Jordan forms this Sea with sparkling waters from the hills. It laughs in the sunshine, and men build their houses near it, and birds their nests, and every kind of life is happier because it is there.

The River Jordan flows on south into another Sea. Here there is no splash of fish, no fluttering leaf, no song of birds, no laughter of little children. Travelers do not pass, unless on urgent business which might take them there. The air hangs heavy above its waters, and neither man nor beast nor fowl will drink of it.

What makes this mighty difference in these neighbor Seas? Not the River Jordan—it empties the same good water into both. Not the soil in which they lie, nor the country round about. The Sea of Galilee receives and gives but does not keep the Jordan water to itself. For every drop which flows into it, another drop flows out. The receiving and the giving go on, day after day, in equal measure. The other Sea hoards its income jealously. Every drop it gets, it keeps. The Sea of Galilee gives and lives. The other Sea gives nothing. It is named "The Dead Sea."

So it is with men who immerse themselves in the "me-first/pleasure/orgasm-centered" world of Internet pornography. They keep everything for themselves. They even "have sex" with themselves, filling the role of both man and woman to reach sexual climax. Like the selfish sea, they can become truly "dead" in their desires and capacities to love, lift and serve those around them.

Those Who View Pornography Lose Their Sight

The more a man or teenage boy views pornography, the more he loses his sight, until finally he is, figuratively, completely blind. Not that he can no longer see with his physical eyes, but he becomes blinded emotionally and spiritually.

As a man or teenage boy gets lured into pornography's dark prison, he begins to lose his ability to see and appreciate women for who they truly are. He becomes blinded to women as valuable, gifted and contributing human beings. As the nature of the pornography viewing increases in frequency and hardness, the cellular-memories storing these images become larger and more dominant in the male brain and body.

The neural pathways linking these cellular-memories become chasms, wide and deep. Eventually, the neural pathways and cellular-memories that allow a man to see and appreciate a woman as more than just a sex object are overpowered, then shut down completely from non-use.

Pornography Viewing Causes Brain Damage In the Male Internet Porn Addict

Gazing At the Grand Canyon Through a Straw

Imagine you are a tour guide leading a column of tourists up a winding path to a point overlooking one of the vast natural wonders of the world. Upon reaching the summit, a curious thing happens: Each tourist takes out a drinking straw and, closing one eye, places it up to the open eye and looks through it. There they stand, your little group, taking in the beautiful vista spread before them through soda straws! You hear comments like: "What an interesting rock," "That's a lovely leaf on that tree" or, "There's a beautiful patch of blue water." Finally, in total exasperation, you holler, *"For crying out loud, get rid of the straws and look! This is the Grand Canyon, folks!"* As ridiculous as this may sound, this is how men and teenage boys hooked on pornography often see their own life and other people (especially women)—through the narrow conduit of a drinking straw. Pornography fosters the most insidious form of "tunnel vision."

The Story of Jack

A person hooked on pornography develops a "one-track mind." His focus in life becomes single-minded and his view of others, especially of women, narrows.

In her book *An Affair of the Mind*, Laurie Hall shares the true-life story of her husband Jack, who had been severely addicted to pornography for over 20 years. She writes:

After indulging in fantasy for more than 20 years, Jack lost his ability to think about anything else. Dwelling so much on that which wasn't true made him unable to think about that which was true. He lost his common sense and his ability to solve problems.

My husband, once a brilliant engineer, couldn't even figure out how to turn a freezer so it would fit through the door into the cellar. He was absentminded in the extreme. He'd turn on the stove to make tea, forget to put the kettle on, and just walk out of the kitchen with the burner glowing red. He'd put wood into the wood stove and leave the door open, causing chimney fires. In the morning, it wasn't unusual to find the outside door standing wide open. He'd have gone out for something the night before and forgotten to close it when he came in.

Sometimes, when someone would ask him a question, he would start to answer, only to stop halfway into the reply and then freeze with his mouth open. His mind had gone completely blank.

Jack always said he wanted other people to think he "had it all together." So, for a long time, when other people were around, he'd manage the herculean effort of staying focused enough so that only the most alert could see that he wasn't tracking well. In the end, though, his "checking out" became apparent to people besides the children and me.

Too much time fantasizing meant that he also lost his ability to do his work well. Finally, the man who was recognized three times as an outstanding employee was fired for being incompetent and lying to his boss. Once a regional manager for a large company, overseeing millions of dollars worth of equipment and managing half a dozen men, Jack had an expense account, a cellular phone, a company vehicle, and a comfortable middle-class salary.

Today, he is doing production work, packing 12-ounce bags of chocolates at $7.25 an hour. He stands at an assembly line seven-and-a-half hours a day, catching bags that come off the machine at a rate of 71 a minute. Then he puts them into boxes—24 to a box. Sometimes he scrapes chocolate off the factory floor. And every day when he leaves home, he carries his briefcase.

If he forgets it, he comes back in to get it. He needs to remember what he was before he was brought to a piece of bread by means of a whorish woman.[1] *(Proverbs 6:26)*

Laurie felt strongly that her husband had somehow damaged his brain and lost touch with reality through his pornography viewing and fantasizing. Of course, having no scientific backing for this theory, most people thought it was a ridiculous assumption. Still she writes:

It wasn't until Jack and I were separated and we met with Dr. Ron Miller that my observations were verified. After examining Jack, Dr. Miller looked at him and said: "You've destroyed your mind by fantasizing. You've dug a deep channel going in one direction. The rest of your mind is atrophied!"[2]

When I first found Laurie Hall's book on the Internet, I read some reviews that had been submitted by readers. All were extremely positive and complimentary, except for one. And that one negative response was so typical of the complete ignorance and arrogance regarding the effects of pornography on the male brain and body, that I must quote it here. This reader's critical comments were as follows:

What a waste this book was. It is certainly horrible when a man destroys his life for pornography! But the majority of people who look at pornography do not destroy their lives over it! Porn is a hobby just like any other hobby!

Does that mean that all pornography is bad and should be banned? Thousands of people die every year in automobile accidents, so does that mean that automobiles are bad and should be banned? She thinks that her opinion is right and that anyone who disagrees with her is wrong! This book presents a very ignorant view of pornography! The author has a lot to learn! What a waste of time!

I find it fascinating that this reader-critic would refer to the author as an "ignorant" woman who "has a lot to learn." It seems to me that after living with a porn addict for 20 years, Laurie Hall has experienced firsthand the "true nature" of pornography and its highly toxic effects.

The reader-critic also asserts that porn does not destroy the lives of the "majority" of people who look at it. With the overwhelming personal examples, facts and research results that we now have, this reader is most definitely the one who has a lot to learn.

What's more, this reader-critic claims that porn is a hobby, similar to stamp collecting, rock climbing, oil painting—there's no difference, right? Of course, when compared against a standard of what benefits our society, porn fails to measure up. This reader-critic is like the person who points at the perfectly healthy, 90-year-old codger who has smoked cigarettes all his life and exclaims, *"See, I told you that cigarettes only harm a few people!"*

I've just two words to say to such nonsense: Wake up!

How Does Pornography Viewing Cause Brain Damage?

I want to share with you a body of scientific facts that supports Dr. Ron Miller's diagnosis of Laurie Hall's husband, when he said, *"You've destroyed your mind by fantasizing. You've dug a deep channel going in one direction. The rest of your mind is atrophied!"*

Dr. Gary Lynch, a Neuro-scientist at the University of California at Irvine, in discussing how the human brain processes information received from the outside world, said: "What we are saying here is that an event which lasts half a second, within five to ten minutes has produced a structural change that is in some ways as profound as the structural changes one sees in [brain] damage."

Further commenting on how a word or image can immediately alter the brain structure, Dr. Lynch says, " . . . in a matter of seconds, taking an incredibly modest signal, a word . . . which is in your head as an electrical signal for no more than a few seconds, can . . . leave a trace that will last for years."[3]

In the book *The Brain & Nervous System,* it states:

. . . Our thoughts, feelings and memories exist as particular patterns of nerve messages, passing repeatedly along certain pathways in the brain. Each message would ***burn*** *a specific pathway among the billions of axons and dendrites.*[4]

In my research of numerous scientific papers, experiments and studies, one thing stands out: Stored away in the cells of your brain and body are all the things you have ever seen, heard, felt, tasted or smelled. That's why Dr. Miller was able to tell Jack after 20 years of porn, "You've destroyed your mind by fantasizing. You've dug a deep channel going in one direction." Jack had literally developed a "one-track mind."

After reading about Jack, there are some who will say, "That's a rather extreme example. I'm sure that there are men who look at pornography and don't end up like Jack."

True enough, but I think most people would be shocked at just how many "Jacks" are out there whose brains and lives have been devastated by long-term porn addiction. And I can guarantee you, with the porn floodgates wide open on the Internet, the number of "Jacks" in the world is soaring.

Your Own Private "Mobile" Porn Library and Video Store

We have already discussed the fact that once cellular-memory groups and neural pathways are formed in your brain and body, you don't necessarily require outside stimuli to access and activate them. You can call up the images, feelings and information simply by using your imagination, another tool that pornographers use to their advantage.

The makers of porn know that the erotic images stored in the male brain are so potent that they can be activated merely by a word, a woman walking by, or a passing thought. For men who are trying to overcome porn addiction, this automatic response mechanism can be a major source of frustration and discouragement.

Cellular-memory groups storing pornographic images and the neural pathways leading to them are so deep and entrenched that their influence can permeate the whole mindbody network. In a porn user's brain and body, there are so many cellular-memory groups associated with porn images that they can be activated from a thousand different kinds of outside stimuli—or, many times, for no apparent reason at all.

Porn addicts trying to overcome their addiction say that pornographic images will pop into their minds at the worst times: in church, during prayer, during a job interview, while chatting with a son or a daughter, and, worst of all, amid intimate relations with their wife.

These men are in for a lifelong struggle; the cellular-memory groups where these images are stored will always be there to beckon them back to the computer screen. A relapse is always a possibility. Pornographers know that there is a good chance they will reclaim as "customers" men who are trying to overcome porn addiction, because many give up in despair when the images keep barging back into their minds. (However, it certainly is not a hopeless situation for these men. There are ways to "re-route" your neural pathways away from these stored images and beat the pornographer at his own game. These re-routing techniques will be discussed in a later chapter.)

For other men and teens who are caught up in porn addiction but are making no effort to stop, stored porn images become a way to "look at porn in the privacy of their own minds." It's like having a mobile porn library of photos and videos to draw from at any time, night or day.

Hours better spent at productive work, with family, serving others, etc., are instead wasted in hours of private fantasy. Otherwise good, hardworking men become so distracted by their fantasies that they become "zombies." They are present in body but their minds are lost in a pornographic wasteland. They're not much good to anyone around them.

Another common problem for men addicted to porn is that they become walking "time-bombs" that can be set off at any time and without warning. Women figure that the time they have to worry most is right after a man has been looking at pornography. Thus women naturally shy away from areas near pornography bookstores or XXX movie theaters.

But what about the man who has just experienced a porn session in the privacy of his own mind, and a woman just happens to pass him at that moment? Therein lies the problem. In truth, no woman or child is entirely safe around a pornoholic.

And now with the Internet, how does a woman know if a man has just finished a porn-viewing session? It's not like he's coming out of an adult bookstore. With the Internet, any man or teenage boy inside or outside of any home, office, library or university could be operating "in the narrow tunnel at the base of the funnel" and pose a significant risk to anyone nearby.

Key Points

A reference tool for spouses, parents, clergy, counselors and others

- Many men who view pornography suffer from feelings of guilt, shame, regret and humiliation.
- Men addicted to porn lose their freedom. They often feel trapped, out-of-control and literally become slaves to their own lust.
- Pornography puts men on a emotional roller coaster—their moods radically changing without warning. This usually alienates them from their friends and loved ones and plunges them even deeper into the "self-medicating" escape of pornography.
- Pornography obsession makes a man selfish and self-centered. It damages and eventually destroys healthy intimacy in marriage, often resulting in divorce. Many men lose their family, career, reputation, good name, and eventually, their freedom. Pornography can take a good, talented, enthusiastic man and turn him into the "walking dead."

- Regular pornography viewing can make a man "blind" and "brain-damaged."
- Porn addicts can become *walking time-bombs* capable of committing serious sexual crimes and perversions.

23

Pornography Destroys Healthy Intimacy

Confusing Porn Arousal With Legitimate Sexual Intimacy

A man or woman feasting on a steady diet of pornography or cybersex through interactive chat rooms, may come to consider sexual intimacy with his or her spouse "boring" by comparison. Let's look at the case of "Jane and John."

After a night of sexual intimacy with his wife, John may think, "That porn video I watched on the Internet the other night was a lot more exciting than sex with Jane. She doesn't turn me on like she used to. I must not be that in love with her."

Or Jane may say, "It was more stimulating talking romance and sex with that guy on the Internet than making love with John. In fact, it was a lot more arousing, sensual. I must not love John that much."

In reality, the problem isn't Jane or John falling out of love with each other. The problem is that cellular-memory links in their mindbodies are totally confused.[1]

When you are in love, you naturally feel a sense of trust, tenderness and kinship with your spouse. Sexual intimacy under the influence of these shared emotions is warm, wonderful, mutually satisfying, free of anxiety and fear and, yes, stimulating and erotic.

However, when your sole motive is lust, it's a different story altogether. A sexual experience through Internet porn or cybersex chat elicits the powerful emotions of excitement, illicit arousal, escape, release, fear of being caught, shame and anger, all mixed together. This dangerous mixture can trigger—temporarily, of course—a "higher" arousal state than the normal, tender, trusting sexual experience with a spouse. But does this mean it's love? Many fine marriages end up on the scrap heap because the husband (and in some cases the wife) confuses the temporary "excitement" (stress) of pornography, cybersex chat, an adulterous affair or other illicit sexual escapade with the legitimate feelings and sensations of healthy sexual intimacy in a loving and trusting marriage.

How Can a Wife Compete With the Fantasy Women of Internet Porn?

Once a man's cellular-memories are brimming with the fantasy women and other staged images of Internet porn, he blocks out his ability to express normal sexual intimacy to his wife. She becomes monotonous, humdrum, old-hat. A wife's loving touch, her hugs, her "sweet-nothing" whispers—all of her acts of love and tenderness do not and cannot satisfy his lust. They become mere annoyances and delays for a man who is geared to "get straight to orgasm."

The porn viewer secretly wants to be stimulated and titillated by his wife akin to the way pornography stimulates and titillates him, leading to immediate orgasm. He doesn't want to waste time on hugging, talking or caressing. How can his wife possibly compete with porn's quick, slick, self-satisfaction? Simply put, the sex addict yearns for the narrow experience of porn, not the full, long-lasting love of a faithful wife.

Conversely, how can a husband compete with the perfect fantasy cyber-lover who talks with his wife for hours on end and stimulates all her emotions and passions like some exciting "hunk" from a romance novel? He can't—simple as that.

"Me–Centered" vs. "We–Centered" Sex

One of the great tragedies suffered by a man or a woman viewing pornography or engaging in cybersex, is what it does to the intimate relationship with his or her own spouse. Dr. Victor Cline states: *In my clinical experience, the major consequence of being addicted to pornography is not the probability or possibility of committing a serious sex crime (though this can and does occur), but rather its disturbance of the fragile bonds of intimate family and marital relationships. This is where the most grievous pain, damage, and sorrow occurs. There is repeatedly an interference with or even destruction of healthy love and sexual relationships with long term bonded partners.*[2]

Because pornography's core purpose is to lead every male viewer to masturbate and achieve orgasm, the following insights may prove helpful:

Pornography Turns Sexual Intimacy Into a "One-Man Show"

In *An Affair of the Mind* author Laurie Hall offers some powerful and amazingly accurate insights:

Self-absorption, self-deception, rationalizations and masturbation are common behaviors for men who use pornography. They are part of the primary nature of pornography. Much of pornography is specifically crafted to make sure this powerful conditioner kicks in. Researcher Harriet Koskoff wrote: "Pornography is primarily about masturbation, whether it is mental or actual."[3]

In a study done at the University of Manitoba and Winnipeg, researchers Neil Malamuth and Robert McIlwraith noted that Penthouse

Magazine in particular, searches for ways to increase its appeal as a stimulant for masturbatory fantasies.[4]

According to Dr. Ron Miller, Penthouse and other pornographic magazines have been successful in this search. Dr. Miller said that he never dealt with a man who was involved with pornography who wasn't also heavily involved in masturbation.[5]

So What's the Big Deal With Masturbation?

Laurie Hall continues: *Masturbation physically is a self-bent thing. Its focus is inward. It doesn't share. It doesn't know the verb "to give." It is fire that feeds itself.*[6]

So what's the big deal? Can't we grow up here? Why isn't it all right for guys to masturbate to a pretty picture if that's what they want to do? According to former U.S. Surgeon General Joycelyn Elders, masturbation could be the answer to the social problems brought on by unwed mothers and the deadly AIDS virus. After all, wouldn't it be better for guys to "relieve" themselves rather than go out and rape someone or impregnate someone or contract a sexually transmitted disease? Is it only prohibited by people who can't accept masturbation as a normal part of healthy sexuality? Not really.[7]

Dr. Victor Cline, a prominent researcher on the psychological effects of pornography, asserts that masturbation to pornography can actually *cause* the very social problems that it supposedly prevents: *In my view, pornography is one contributor to sexual illness. It can provide anti-social sexual imagery, which becomes locked into the man's mind and returns again and again to haunt and stimulate him. When he masturbates to this image,* ***without realizing it*** *he is engaging in a powerful form of learning called "masturbatory conditioning," which can lead—in time—to acting out this imagery.*[8] emphasis added)

In the fantasy world of pornography, a man is lord and master of the woman, able to use her in any way he desires. In the fantasy world of pornography, a man is able to inflict pain to cause pleasure. He becomes the final arbiter of what is good and evil.

In his heart, the porn masturbator imagines himself participating in acts that defile and use other people. In the act of orgasm or release, he rewards himself for having used his imagination. In the secret places of his heart, he begins to abandon his will to the fantasies that give him pleasure. Now he reacts rather than acts; now he becomes outer-controlled rather than inner-controlled; now he is governed the same way the animals are, by the principle of stimulus-response, rather than by self-control.[9]

The Man Who Masturbates Hangs Out a "Do Not Disturb" Sign

In *An Affair of the Mind*, Laurie Hall writes: *The word intercourse means "communication," a connection between people. When we choose to make it on our own (masturbate), we are saying we don't want to be bothered with the hard work of communication; we're not interested in connecting with anyone but ourselves. We are the center of our own universe. Being both the star and the director of our own sexual production reduces sex to a mere physical hunger. Sex becomes a one-man show rather than an opportunity to relate with another.*[10]

In *Game Free: A Guide to the Meaning of Intimacy*, Professor Thomas C. Oden wrote: *"Intimates are aware that their most significant exchanges are not merely body transactions, but as persons in encounter, of the meeting of spirit with spirit. What really happens in intimacy has to do with spirit-spirit communion or interpersonal communion, two persons experiencing their beings poignantly united."*[11]

Laurie Hall continues: *Yet when the focus is self-bent and inward, there can be no encounter with another. The masturbator is merely engaging in a bodily transaction with himself. Instead of being a way to interpersonal communion with another, sex through masturbation implodes a man, driving him further into himself. Thus, by its very nature, masturbation closes the doors to intimacy.*

When a wife approaches, she will find no handle on the door, only a quickly hung "Do Not Disturb" sign. The message is: "Sex is a solo affair. I don't need you. Your presence gets in the way of what I am trying to do here. I can make it on my own, thank you."

For some men, masturbation becomes the preferred way to "have sex." Once he has satisfied himself several times a day, a husband has nothing left to give to his wife. When she reaches for him at night, he jerks away. Why, he asks himself, should he put himself in a situation where he has to please another when he can so easily please himself?[12]

Laurie Hall concludes with this final thought: *Once a man's ability to love has been consumed on the altar of a masturbatory fire raging out of control, or a woman's emotions and passions have been used up in cybersex chat rooms, both the husband and the wife will become charter members of the Lonely Hearts Club. In that dark and companionless place, with the band playing eternal encores of "Let Me Entertain Me," everyone dances alone.*[13]

The aim of Internet pornography from the beginning has been to make sex as much a "solo affair" as possible. The porn industry doesn't want men to engage in healthy, normal sexual intimacy with their wives. Pornographers do not put banner ads up on their porn sites saying, "Check out this site, then go have a romantic evening with your wife." Rather, pornographers seek to lure men into the isolated world of fantasy and masturbation.

This is why virtually every porn site on the Internet makes reference in some way to masturbation. Using language, descriptions and images that I need not quote or describe, the pornography sites basically display big flashing signs that say, "Come and relieve yourself with us." (Ironically, there is no real relief but only a deepening of the addiction.) Again, savvy pornographers are all too aware that masturbation is the key to fostering male porn addiction and to securing "clients for life."

MAKING LOVE IS NOT ABOUT SEX

In America the term "making love" is used so loosely. In soap operas, sitcoms, movies, magazines, books, and in the minds of most Americans, when a man and a woman are having consensual sex, regardless of the context, they are "making love." What a shame that something so priceless as love could be reduced to this level. It is interesting and instructive alike to note that most cultures in the world do not conform with the American use of the term "making love." A wonderful example is the Island of Crete.

During a visit to Crete, author Robert Fulghum was chatting with a close friend. During their conversation, a translation problem came up. Fulghum's friend inquired about a concept he had found in Western literature called "making love." The term had confused him. "What is this making love?" he asked. Fulghum explained that it was a popular phrase used to describe a man and woman having sex or going to bed together, whether they are married or not. His friend smiled and explained that for Cretans, the phrase "making love" summarizes the whole process and experience of marriage and family, not just a single sex act.

In Crete, the custom of arranged marriage still exists. To them, romance and intimacy are wonderful when they happen, but they are not the sole nor the solid foundation on which to build a relationship. When two families agree that a son and a daughter are suited to each other, they are expected to *work at becoming* compatible partners. This effort is considered just as important as the work one would put forth in the pursuit and development of a lifetime vocation. For a Cretan, the whole process of becoming compatible partners is termed "making love." Time and experience, mistakes and hardships—this and more are all part of the equation whose sum is a lasting and growing relationship.

Furthermore, Cretans do not believe that love is something you "fall into," rather, love and marriage are "made." When a married couple is overheard arguing or having a spat, the neighbors simply smile and say, "Ah, they are making love."[14]

What a contrast to the way the term is used in America! Which viewpoint do you think is more accurate, healthy and responsible? Which approach to the concept of "making love" do we want our children, teenagers and young couples to embrace?

Pornography forcefully teaches with every image it portrays that "making love" is nothing more than having sex with anyone that strikes your fancy. Pornography's "lovemaking" does not require any work or sacrifice. It does not ripen, mature and mellow over time through commitment, cooperation, trials and testing. It is two (or more) people "having sex," then moving on to the next person who happens to be available.

Is it any wonder that America is plagued by divorce, teenage pregnancy, abortion, sexually transmitted diseases, and an overall exploitation and disrespect for the sacred power of creating life? Isn't it time that we reject and fight pornography's deception and lies, and embrace the wonder and beauty of what "making love" really and truly means? Maybe we need to open our eyes and our minds and learn from others in the world who have not been as tainted by pornography as we have. Perhaps the people of the tiny island of Crete could teach us a thing or two about the concept of "making love."

MARRIAGE IS NOT JUST SEX

In our age of sex therapists and sex manuals, couples experiencing intimacy problems often assume that they need to improve their techniques, work on their "stamina," or go out and buy a videotape or some exotic device. For a time, sex may even become more exciting through the use of such tools (usually for the man more than for the woman), but the deeper problem with intimacy remains. So what *is* the problem?

The problem is that couples are concentrating on an aspect of intimacy that is only 10% of the equation! Ninety percent—or more—of intimacy is not the physical act itself. True intimacy between a husband and a wife is formed over years of trust, kindness, commitment, affection, respect and having "grown" together through periods of sacrifice and trials, joys and pains, triumphs and failures. Intimacy, then, is a bonding process, brought about by years of living together, working together, loving together. This is what "welds" and "glues" a couple together so that they truly become *one* in spirit, in purpose, and in love.

True intimacy requires work and sacrifice. It cannot be gained in a few weeks or a few months—and surely not by using the latest sex manual. True intimacy is a thousand times more fulfilling and lasting than a "stand-alone sex act." And when you add true holistic intimacy to sexual intimacy, the physical aspect of a couple's relationship is enhanced a hundred-fold.

THE GOOD ART OF ORGASM

We have already discussed how orgasm is one of the most powerful peak experiences the mindbody can experience. And so, whatever process, activity or thought pattern is used to achieve orgasm becomes habitual and powerfully binding. Large cell-groups of stored images and emotions with deep neural pathways connecting them are laid down during any process leading to orgasm.

A man or woman does not need to fantasize or use pornography as the means to achieve orgasm. He or she can control and direct his or her thoughts while at the "big-picture level" of thinking, or at the top of the funnel, just as the narrowing process toward orgasm begins.

Whatever thoughts a couple is thinking as they narrow will become powerfully connected to the pleasure of orgasm and to their entire attitude toward sexuality and intimacy. During the early stages of sexual intimacy, a man and woman can direct their thoughts, and thus control and direct their emotions.

Imagine the neural pathways and cellular-memory groups that will be accessed and permanently established as they mutually ponder thoughts of tenderness, caring, consideration for the other person, love, appreciation and closeness, holding these in their minds as they maintain eye contact. What wonderful and loving messages will be communicated as they look into each other's eyes?

When thoughts and feelings of love, tenderness, respect, dignity and giving lead a man or woman to the powerful peak of orgasm, the process becomes a wonderfully welding experience of "oneness." Cellular-memory groups are established in the man's mind and body that bring him closer to his wife, not only sexually but in every other way. Likewise for his wife. And every time this kind of binding experience takes place, every time the couple reaches orgasm in this way, their relationship is deepened and strengthened.

What exactly happens to this man or woman from a "mindbody" standpoint? When sex is strictly a physical experience (as Internet porn teaches), the individuals access an extremely limited number of mindbody cellular-memory groups—most revolving around a "self-focus" on receiving pleasure and achieving orgasm. But as they begin to direct their thoughts to love, tenderness and respect, they bring into play a whole new network of cellular-memories that dramatically deepen and expand the experience.

And the difference is dramatic! It is as if they were looking through a straw before, seeing only a minuscule strand of sexual intimacy. Then suddenly they discover that they can throw away the straw and experience the whole, wonderful panoramic view of "total intimacy."

I am amazed at those women who actually buy porn magazines for their husbands or consent to watch pornographic movies or videos with them. Do they have any clue about the information that is being stored in the cells of their husbands' brain and body? These women somehow believe that supporting and/or participating with their husband in his habit will improve their marital relationship and deepen their husbands' love for them. Nothing could be further from the truth!

Typically, quite the opposite happens. The woman generally gets linked in her husband's cellular-memories with the porn images. Before long, in his mind she is merely a collection of body parts for him to "do things to."

On his way to orgasm, the husband moves toward the bottom of the funnel, narrowly focusing on the erotic images he is viewing (and/or those already stored in his cellular-memories), and he uses his wife's body to carry out his porn fantasy. All feelings of love, tenderness, appreciation, romance and caring that the woman wants her husband to feel for her are absent when pornography is present.

The woman may actually believe that the porn is deepening her intimacy with her husband. In fact what it is doing is driving him further away from her, making him more self-centered, and causing him to see her less as a human being and more as an object of lust.

This "disintegration of marital intimacy" often begins with the viewing of sexually explicit movies, certain TV sitcoms or some of the less tasteful talk shows. A woman passively watches these with her husband thinking it's no big deal. Meanwhile, his brain and body are narrowly focused on the physical activities, the sex, the body parts, setting him up for a high probability of future porn addiction. Sadly, in many cases these types of so-called entertainment also set women up for failure to enjoy true intimacy with their husbands.

Key Points

A reference tool for
spouses, parents, clergy,
counselors and others

- Contrary to the advice of some so-called sex-therapists, the arousal of pornography confuses and distorts legitimate sexual intimacy between husband and wife. Thus, when one spouse is involved with pornography, healthy intimacy in the marriage suffers greatly. When spouses use pornography together for so-called "sex-therapy," they become totally focused on physical techniques and lose sight of all the other wonderful aspects of healthy sexual intimacy in marriage.
- A spouse can't compete with the fantasy images of pornography or the fantasy lover of a cybersex chat room.
- Pornography and cybersex chat are completely *me-centered* and turn sexual intimacy into a *solo affair*, eliminating the spouse from the equation. This destroys any hope of healthy *we-centered* intimacy in the marriage.

24

Corporate America As a Victim of Internet Pornography

Internet Pornography In the Workplace

Recently I was talking with a friend of mine about my research. A computer trouble-shooter who spends his days traveling from corporation to corporation identifying and resolving computer problems, he said to me, "Mark, you would be shocked by the number of men, and a few women, who spend hours of their work day viewing Internet pornography."

He has discovered this alarming trend in several ways: In some instances he has come around the corner and passed by a cubicle or office just in time to see a sex scene quickly close on the computer screen. On other occasions he's discovered the porn viewing habits of an employee when called in to fix his computer and sees the contents listed on the worker's hard drive.

After spending several months on a special project with one of the high-tech companies in his state, he estimates that at least 50% of the male employees were viewing Internet porn at some point in their work day or work week. What might be the consequences of engaging in this practice over a number of years? Add to this the growing numbers of women and men employees engaged in cybersex chat over the Internet. Consider the following:

- An incalculable decline in productivity based on "hours wasted" sitting in front of Internet porn or cybersex chat instead of working.
- Even when employees addicted to Internet porn or cybersex are not locked onto their computer screens, they no longer are the productive people they used to be. Pornography has burned through their mindbody network, contaminating their work-related functions. They are often fantasizing about what they have seen or the cyber relationship they have started, by calling the images forth from their cellular-memories. Thus, more wasted time and inferior work and less effectual listening in the workplace due to both a lack of concentration and the extensive time spent in their own private "porn bookstore" or "fantasy romance" of the mind. Their employer has lost them.
- Men and women who fill their mindbodies with Internet porn images or engage in graphic sexual conversations in chat rooms become less honest, kind and considerate. Their overall integrity is weakened. They become moody, angry, depressed and unstable. In essence, they become a liability, a hindrance and an irritation to all those around them. Their own performance and effectiveness plummets, while negatively affecting the attitudes and performance of their fellow employees.
- Men who view Internet porn in the workplace come to see the women they work with in the same way they see the women on the computer screen—a collection of body parts, objects through which they can be sexually stimulated. These men waste time masturbating in company restrooms while fantasizing about Internet porn and the woman in the next cubicle.

- While viewing Internet porn men commonly descend to the bottom of the funnel, where their logic, judgement and values are "narrowed" right out of existence. In this confused and empty state of "mindbody," these men are at high risk of committing sexual harassment, or worse. Internet pornography can plunge them into "sexual fantasizing" which, when entertained long enough, can lead them to "copycat" what they have seen on the computer screen with the women with whom they work. This sexual behavior can range from subtle innuendos to violent rape.

Key Points

A reference tool for spouses, parents, clergy, counselors and others

- Internet porn and cybersex chat are sending shock waves through the corporate world: hours and dollars are wasted as employees sit riveted to the computer; distracted and preoccupied with fantasies and "narrowed" thinking, employee productivity and effectiveness drop; attitudes, integrity, reliability, cooperation, honesty and emotional stability begin collapsing; sexual harassment incidents and lawsuits increase.

25

PORNOGRAPHY IS RADICALLY ALTERING OUR SOCIETY

"CITIZENS OF ROME": THE MEDIA'S FOCUS ON SEX AND THE DUMBING DOWN OF AMERICA

In the darkest days of the Roman Empire, its citizens sought entertainment through the brutal savagery of the arena. It all began with the excitement and thrills of a chariot race or the clashing swords of gladiators. Little by little, the violence and blood multiplied until Roman citizens were cheering while Christians were torn to pieces by wild beasts. Rome was desensitized and "dumbed down" gradually, over time, until its people's hearts turned stone-cold.

Over the last 30 or 40 years we have experienced a similar decline here in America. So accustomed to the onslaught of sexual innuendo, sexual images, and sexual messages, in many cases we now scarcely notice them at all. They are laced throughout our television talk shows, sitcoms and commercials. The majority of Hollywood movies contain some form of nudity, sex or sexually-explicit humor—more commonly displaying all three.

But there are even more subtle places that this sexual obsession has crept into. Let me give you just one example that we are all aware of but to which we may not give a second thought.

During the years that I have been doing research and assembling this book, I have started to notice magazines at the grocery store. The grocery store is a place where families go: children, senior citizens, mothers, fathers, everyone. For many communities it's the last "central meeting place." So you would expect to find magazines that represent the average person in society's tastes and interests.

When I started paying close attention to the magazine covers and the article titles, I was amazed at the overwhelming focus on "sex" as compared to other subjects. This hit me with extra force just before Christmas when I was in our neighborhood market doing some last-minute shopping.

There I was, standing in the check-out line, Christmas music playing over the loud speaker, surrounded by my neighbors, each of us anticipating in our own way the coming Christmas morning. I was thinking about a humble stable on a night some two thousand years ago and the birth of the Christ child. And there staring me in the face were women's magazine models—breasts largely exposed and sexual titles boldly displayed. What a contrast, I thought, to the feeling and meaning of the holiday season.

I counted six different women's magazines, each prominently displaying one or more sexually graphic article titles—titles that one expects to see on the marquis of an X-rated theater or the cover of a porn magazine, but never in a neighborhood grocery store! Posed on each cover was a physically attractive female model in tight-fitting clothes. On the covers of four out of the six magazines, the model's clothing exposed a significant portion of her breasts.

Now, perhaps you're saying to yourself, "Aren't you over-reacting just a bit?" I want you to think about these magazines from a "neuro-scientific" vantage point. In other words, when people in the check-out line (especially impressionable teens and children) see these women on the covers and read the racy headlines, where do these images and there connected messages go once inside the brain and body, and what effect do they have? How do they affect the cellular memories of men, women, teenagers and small children? And are we so desensitized and "dumbed down" that we hardly notice them or simply shrug them off as "no big deal"?

Porn's Cost To Society

I once heard a man tell a story about a hard lesson he learned—only after it was too late. This fellow took special pride in his home's finely manicured lawn and its flawless landscaping. One afternoon he was in his front yard talking with his neighbor when he noticed something moving in the grass. The neighbor said, "You have mole crickets. If you don't do something quickly, your lawn will be destroyed."

The man had never heard of such a thing. He looked at his beautiful, deep green lawn, then shrugged it off as nothing to worry about.

A few weeks later he noticed brown spots starting to appear. As the weeks went by, the brown spots spread. He tried adjusting the sprinklers and used various different fertilizers and sprays, but nothing worked. Within a few months, his once immaculate lawn was in ruins.

He had an expert come out. The verdict came back: "Mole crickets!"

"But how?" he exclaimed. "I tend this lawn every day and I never saw anything but an occasional bug." The expert lifted up a section of dead sod and there, to the man's shock and amazement, the grass roots were completely severed!

"Mole crickets," he explained, "live under ground and only come out at night to eat at the roots. The blades look lush and green, but underneath the surface the crickets are eating away. You might see one or two during the day and think it's no big deal. But by the time the brown spots start appearing, it's too late; the damage is already done." The expert reached beneath a patch of brown grass and picked up a thrashing, one-inch-long insect. "This is the culprit," he said.

The man stared down at the little bug and then at his destroyed lawn. He couldn't believe it.

We enjoy freedom, peace and prosperity in this great country of ours as a result of our forefathers and mothers taking care of the roots—recognizing and destroying the lethal elements before they could do permanent damage. The grass has been green and lush, but brown spots are beginning to appear. Pornography—cyber "Mole crickets"— are eating away at the roots of freedom and decency. What are we doing to fight them? What will our children and grandchildren do when, through our neglect, procrastination and complacency, society's once-lush turf lies brown and dead?

Internet porn and sexual-oriented chat rooms are working "under the surface" in our society. You can't immediately see the damage being done. It is quietly and privately going on behind closed doors in bedrooms, dens and offices all across America. It's a seemingly little thing, really. One person on a computer here, another there. You see the signs of damage every now and then—a woman is raped, a porn-addicted father molests his daughter, a pedophile stalks a child. "But these are extremes," you think, "a few brown spots. Most of the lawn is nice and green. It's only a few mole crickets."

But under the surface, in millions of homes and offices, outside the direct view of society, a plague is eating away at the roots of freedom, decency, family values, respect, integrity and honor.

Do we even have a clue to the extent of damage that is being done? How can we accurately predict the long-term consequences for our children, grandchildren and future generations? Never before has this country experienced such an avalanche of sex and nudity on TV, in movies, magazines, ads, music and everyday conversations. Where will all this lead? How much damage will the underground mole crickets of porn inflict before we take it all seriously?

Consider the tremendous toll porn exacts on our families, our communities and our country as a whole:

- Pornography is a catalyst for "sex-related" crimes. As a direct result, every year in our communities many millions of dollars are wasted in the courts, the jails, the police forces, counseling and in therapy.
- When a porn bookstore moves into a neighborhood, the prostitution, narcotics and street crime rates sharply increase. Now that every kind of pornography is available in every home over the Internet, what will happen to these crime rates?[1]
- Pornography encourages sexual deviancy, promiscuity and irresponsibility. It encourages multiple sex partners, promotes sex outside of marriage, and scoffs at fidelity within marriage. As a result, sexually transmitted diseases are at an all-time high and continue to climb, creating an enormous drain on medical services, research and tax dollars.
- Pornography spawns an environment that is vulgar, demeaning, disrespectful, unfeeling and debased. The pornographers are succeeding at spreading their pollution to all parts of our society: in television commercials, movies and sitcoms, on radio with DJs in their commentary and in the music they play, in the movie theater, in the neighborhood bookstore, at the check-out counter at the store and corner gas station. And now with the Internet, the most vile and toxic pornographic pollution is being piped right into our homes.

The Greatest Tragedy of All

A famous couplet says, "Of all the words of tongue and pen, the saddest are these—It might have been." The great tragedy of pornography is that all who are touched by its far-reaching hand are robbed of their full potential.

The spouses and children of Internet porn and/or cybersex addicts are robbed of the full joy, beauty and peace that life offers. Yes, they can rise out of the ashes and with time and courage find a new, joyful life. But can they ever really forget the pain and darkness that the effects of pornography or cybersex brought upon them? Can they ever recover the fullness that could have been theirs during that period in their lives?

Men, women and teenagers who spend countless hours staring at pornography or engaging in cybersex chat are robbed of so much. While they sat like zombies staring at pornographic images, or carrying on romantic/sexual fantasy conversations, what marvelous contributions could they have made to their communities, their country and the world? And now with the clutter of toxic pornographic waste piled up in their minds, influencing their thoughts, their attitudes and their interpersonal relationships, will they ever attain the levels of greatness that could have been theirs?

And yes, pornography even robs those who produce it. What if pornographers were to take their drive, marketing skills, creativity, business savvy, and all the other attributes and skills they employ in their sinister craft, and dedicate their time, talents and resources to worthy and positive ventures. What an impact for good they could have!

What a tragedy. Pornography is truly a destroyer of human potential. Those who are its victims, innocent or by choice, are perhaps the saddest of all earth's creatures, for they must ask, "Were it not for pornography, what might have been?"

"Hurry Up—I Haven't Got All Second!" How Internet Pornography Robs Society of Patience and Sacrifice

Several years ago I saw a comic strip showing a man standing next to a microwave oven. He puts some left-overs in the microwave and sets the timer for 60 seconds. With his arms folded and a frustrated expression on his face, he taps his foot impatiently on the floor. Suddenly when the timer is down to 30 seconds, he screams out, "Will you hurry up? I haven't got all second!"

We live in a society of "instant gratification." We dine on fast food, we drive fast cars, we pursue careers on the "fast track," we constantly upgrade to faster computers, and we expect everything at the push of a button. Now don't get me wrong, modern technology is a wonderful thing and has brought many marvelous benefits. But, it also has made us a society that has come to want things "right now!"

We see young married couples mired in debt, in pursuit of all the luxuries it took their parents 30 years to accumulate. Debt is rampant. And the credit card companies just keep fueling the fire with their clever ads and mailing campaigns offering "easy credit." In essence what they are saying is, "Why work and sweat and save and sacrifice when you can have it all *right now*?"

People who buy into this "instant gratification" trap find themselves staggering under debt's tremendous weight. Their marriages are stressed and stretched to the breaking-point. Their lives are constantly in turmoil. Bankruptcies and foreclosures are at all-time highs as people continue to live beyond their means. One significant downturn in the American economy, and I fear that this credit "house of cards" will come tumbling down.

But however disturbing this instant material and financial gratification trend is, it pales in comparison to the "instant sexual gratification" message that is being touted and shouted all around us.

It says, "You can have it all *now*! Why wait for the commitment of marriage? Why hold back and exercise control when you can experience all the pleasure and passion of sex right now? If it feels good, then just do it. As long as you practice safe sex, that's all you have to worry about."

Pornography and cybersex blatantly promote this "you can have it all now" philosophy. Pornography and cybersex are the ultimate purveyors of instant gratification.

For decades pornographers have attempted to blanket society with their fatal message, trumpeting an attitude of "me-me-me, now-now-now." And finally they have been given the ultimate combination to spread their message of instant gratification. It is the powerful combination of pornography and the Internet. Current studies show that millions are already addicted to the Internet in general. They sit for hour upon hour, glued to their computer screen.

This is not a surprising trend. If you think about it, the Internet is an "instant gratification" tool in and of itself. At the click of a button you can instantly access information and entertainment from all across the globe. If you want it *right now*, it is there at your command. This can be a wonderful resource for learning and enjoyment. It also can be a tool of destruction when it becomes obsessive and addictive.

Combine this "push-of-a-button" Internet technology with pornography and cybersex, and what you have is the most potent provider of instant gratification on the planet! I submit that those who demonstrate impatience and lack of control when is comes to sexual impulses also demonstrate impatience and lack of control when it comes to other things in their everyday lives.

If a man, woman or teenager has developed the habit of accessing the Internet to view pornography or chat at the very moment they feel the sexual or emotional urge, they begin to lose the ability to exercise patience, self-control and self-discipline. To say that the loss of these abilities is strictly limited to their time in front of the computer screen is a significant falsehood.

When an individual develops the habit of instant gratification, it spreads to other arenas of that person's life. This is especially true when it comes to Internet pornography and cybersex chat because they literally exaggerate and accelerate the habit of instant gratification.

The viewer learns to lie to himself and deceive his family and friends in order to hide his or her porn and/or cybersex habit. Or, if family and friends already are aware of the user's habit, he will go to great lengths to hide it from the public so as not to damage his or her reputation. Can such a person lie and deceive in one area of his or her life and be totally honest and trustworthy in all others?

Some of the Effects of Porn and Instant Gratification

The viewer of pornography or the participant in cybersex chat often feels the urge to "act out" what he or she has seen or "chatted" about. The porn/cybersex addict will more often cheat on his spouse, then attempt to hide it. Can a person who breaks the sacred oath of marriage be trusted to keep other oaths and promises they make?

Furthermore, when Internet pornography or cybersex has conditioned the viewer to expect things now, whenever the impulse hits he comes to expect the same instantaneous but unrealistic response in other areas of life. If he wants a certain lane in traffic, he'll cut other drivers off or engage in "road rage" to usurp it, because Internet pornography has taught him to have *zero patience* when it comes to getting what he wants.

If a porn addict's spouse and children don't do what he says *now*, he will often lash out verbally and physically. He has been carefully tutored that he doesn't have to wait to get what he wants. And he will not wait. He has lost all remnants of patience to pornography.

The connections between the instant gratification that Internet pornography and cybersex drill into viewers' heads and the negative ways this affects them and their families, friends and work associates is a vast list indeed. With all the hatred, greed, lust, abuse and selfishness we see creeping into so much of society, we can't afford to allow the Internet pornographers to teach their "instant gratification" philosophy to our fathers, mothers husbands, wives, brothers, sisters, sons or daughters.

Internet Pornography Cultivates Crime

Studies in communities all across America have clearly shown that neighborhoods with sexually-oriented businesses (SOBs) bear higher crime rates than those neighborhoods without these types of businesses. It's is as reliable as clock-work—when an SOB moves into a neighborhood, the crime rate soars; when these businesses are shut down, the crime rate drops accordingly. These figures include sex-related crimes as well as crime in general.[2]

These harmful "secondary effects" are the reason the Supreme Court upholds zoning laws to restrict the location of sexually-oriented establishments. Unfortunately, there are no such zoning laws for the public libraries that provide access to pornography via the Internet. Our libraries are most often located near residential neighborhoods. What impact will unrestricted Internet pornography in our libraries have on our neighborhood crime rates, the safety of our women and children, and on our quality of life as a whole?

If just one porn bookstore inflicts a serious negative effect on its immediate environment, what will the prolific ambush of Internet pornography have on our families, neighborhoods and communities? Computer porn is a crime culprit that bears absolutely no resemblance to the "innocent fun" the pornographers would paint it to be.

Hang a Sign Around Your Neck: "Warning! I Look At Internet Porn"

What if it were required of each person who views Internet pornography to wear a sign reading: **Warning! I'm hooked on Internet porn**. How much easier it would be for everyone around them!

If a man proposing marriage to a woman had this sign hung around his neck, the prospective bride would at least be forewarned. She would know, for example, that this man's mindbody is jammed with a vast network of negative cellular-memories that have been established as a result of viewing pornography. This in turn would tell her that he is prone to selfishness, moodiness, anger, promiscuity, sexual dysfunction—to name but a few of his flaws. She would realize that significant portions of his brain and body have been programmed to view her as an object, a collection of body-parts to satisfy his sexual desires. At least this way, if she did consent to marriage, she would not be so confused by his bizarre behavior later on down the road. But only a fool would knowingly saddle herself with a porn/sex addict's dysfunction.

When a husband begins displaying outlandish behaviors such as moodiness, withdrawal, bizarre sexual requests, angry outbursts, chauvinistic attitudes, etc., most wives would say, "This is not the gracious man who courted me. I don't know him anymore. I'm so confused." On the other hand, the woman forewarned about her husband's pornography habit would say, "I understand this behavior. It's the pornography. . . ."

Wouldn't it be helpful if a teenage boy hooked on Internet pornography, when arriving at the house to pick up a girl for a date, held a sign saying: **I'm Hooked on Internet Porn**? This way the girl and her parents could be given proper warning and take necessary precautions. They would clearly understand this boy's mindbody has neural networks, pathways and cellular-memories that have been established as a result of pornography viewing. It's nigh inevitable that, when alone with this girl, this boy's neural pathways and cellular-memories will be activated. She will be at severe risk. Wouldn't it be helpful if she and her parents had an up-front inkling of this young man's internal mindbody structure?

Think how much easier it would be for children if, upon arriving home, their father wore a sign around his neck that said: **Avoid me – I've just been viewing pornography on the Internet at work**. This way, when he is short-tempered with his kids or gives them the silent treatment, they will understand that it's the pornography triggering their father's behavior.

Now, all this talk about hanging a sign around the neck of porn viewers is obviously tongue-in-cheek. But the point is this: When men and teenage boys (or for that matter, teenage girls and women) view pornography, it literally changes who they are; it physically and chemically alters the neural pathways and cellular-memories in their brain and body, which directly and powerfully impacts their moods, frame of mind, behavior, judgment and how they interact with others.

Most of us do not understand the enormity of the deep impact pornography has on all of society. Perhaps if every person who engaged in Internet pornography or cybersex chat had a sign hung around his neck, we would all put two and two together and exclaim, "Now I understand that person's irrational and compulsive behavior—it's the porn!"

Key Points

A reference tool for
spouses, parents, clergy,
counselors and others

- Internet pornography and sexualized media are accelerating the *dumbing down of America.*
- The distribution of pornography in a community increases not only sex-related crimes, but the crime rate overall. With pornography now available in every home, office and library with Internet access, crime rates will increase accordingly.
- With the influence of pornography dramatically expanded through the Internet, the incidence of sexually-transmitted diseases is expanding.

- Pornography obsession is destroying much of the human potential, growth and contribution in our society—*Were it not for pornography, what might have been?*
- Pornography is spawning a crippling attitude of "instant gratification" in our society.

26

Pornography Distorts and Twists Healthy Sexuality

Sex-Education Through Internet Pornography: Turning Something Beautiful Into Something Ugly

Have you ever gazed into the eyes of an innocent and beautiful new-born child? Have you ever marveled at the wonders of a tiny human being, just minutes old, seeing the world for the very first time?

I vividly remember the birth of each of my precious children. Words fail to adequately describe the sea of emotions that swept over me as I held that tiny, curled-up body, for the very first time. Wonder, amazement, joy, reverence, awe and a dozen other emotions filled me as I tried to take in the full meaning of what was happening. Each event is forever etched in my mind, yes, on my very soul.

Whenever I get so caught up in the craziness of the world that the lines of what is right and wrong begin to blur, I only need to recall the image of an innocent babe in my arms and my perspective returns. Perhaps the most remarkable thing of all is that together, my wife and I brought another human being into the world! And so it is with husbands and wives. Within them is the divine combined power to create life, a power most precious and sacred, a power greater than that of kings and presidents, greater than the power of weapons or machines.

And yet, this power is given to nearly everyone of us freely by a Higher Power. The amazing thing is that the only control on such an incredible power is our own self control. And so it is, through the sacred union of a man and a woman, life is created. Is this not a beautiful thing? Sexual intimacy between a husband and a wife should be a force that binds them together physically, emotionally and spiritually.

Why Do We View the Power To Give Life and To Take Life So Differently?

It seems to me that there are two powers that we mortals have here on earth that are above all others. One has to do with how we get into this world; the other deals with how we go out.

As for taking life, we are usually very responsible. Most innately sense how precious life is. They would never think of approaching a friend, a revolver with one bullet in the chamber, spinning the cylinder, holding the gun to the friend's head and pulling the trigger just to "see what happens." Such a person would quickly be apprehended, prosecuted and locked up. When it comes to taking a life, the seriousness of it does not have to be spelled out or debated.

But when it comes to giving life, many are not so responsible. In fact, many are near-criminal in their irresponsibility. When one abuses the power to take the life of another, it brings shock and horror. Yet the same abuse of the power to give life elicits dirty jokes, filthy song lyrics, and explicit scenes on the television, theater and Internet screens. Why is there such dramatic contrast in the way many in our society view these two powers?

And how do the pornographers portray all of this? Is there any reference in their materials to the creation of life? Are there any images of a man and a woman gazing lovingly at the precious child they in concert have brought into the world? What of the sacred bond and special intimacy between a husband and a wife?

If pornographers reserved any honor for these things, they would never display sexual images in the first place. One respected psychologist has commented on this: *Pornography is no different than viewing a veterinarian's manual filled with photographs of animals mating. Pornography's focus is on a sterile sexual act between human beings who appear to be acting solely out of carnal instinct. It is void of all of the love, respect, and honor that sets us apart from animals.*[1]

In essence, pornographers take something sacred and beautiful and twist it until it is at a level lower than common animals.

How Pornography Distorts Sex

Pornography is an inaccurate and tragically misleading form of "sex education." But because it distorts and twists sex, turning it from what most consider a God-given celebration of love into something most would consider a perversion, many experts refer to pornography as "*anti-sex education.*" When viewed, presented and discussed in an appropriate way, human intimacy is a sacred physical union shared between a husband and wife. It is a symbol of "total union." Not merely a physical union, but an all-encompassing emotional, spiritual and mental oneness. When physical intimacy is expressed as part of a complete sharing of everything—in a way that only a husband and a wife can share—it is a beautiful and sacred experience.

But when two people participate in physical intimacy hastily, guiltily, in a darkened corner of a darkened hour, then beat a hasty and guilt-ridden retreat back to their own separate worlds—a world without a joint sharing of laughter, laundry and dishes, of managing a budget, paying the bills, and planning a life together—this special power loses its luster.

Likewise, when this power is used outside the bonds of marriage, where one can give only a small part of oneself—the physical part—it almost always leads to disaster. Using sexual intimacy solely as a selfish diversion usually brings guilt, diminished self-esteem, depression, and additional abuses and self-destructive behaviors (including experimental use of drugs, alcohol and other addictions).Yet this same act enjoyed by two people committed to one another, a commitment made in a marriage union, can bring an increase in self-worth, peace of mind, love, respect, appreciation and closeness. Isn't this what we should be teaching our young people as part of sex education, in addition to the assorted health risks, protective measures, and other issues?

So What Is It That Internet Pornography Teaches Us About Sex?

For years sex education courses, in all their variety, have been a part of the school curriculum. The premise is that such instruction can safeguard our youth and influence their attitudes and behaviors with regards to sex.

If we assume that this is so, then we also have to assume that pornographic films, magazines, books and Internet images are also powerful forms of sex education and influencers of attitudes and behaviors. But what does this form of sex education teach? Pornography focuses only on the pleasures of sex and totally ignores its dark sides: the risk of sexually transmitted diseases, teenage pregnancy, rape, incest, shame, guilt, shattered marriages, and so forth.

Most pornography has a decidedly sexist flavor, primarily due to the fact that a large percentage is created by men for male consumption. Thus, Internet porn spreads an enormous amount of misinformation about human intimacy, portraying it as completely without love, self-control or responsibility. What's more, the acts portrayed are usually abusive toward women, degrading and humiliating them.

If pornography is a form of sex education—and I believe that it is—then it makes sense to label it as many professionals have: "anti-sex education," in that it presents information that is false and misleading both from a scientific and a human relationship standpoint. This is especially true of the way pornography misleads the viewer regarding the true nature of female sexual response. Is this where we want our country's men and boys to receive instruction on how to treat women?

To quote former United States Surgeon General Dr. Edward Koop:

. . . Impressionable men, many of them still in adolescence, see this material and get the impression that women like to be hurt, humiliated and forced to do things that they do not want to do. It is a false and vicious stereotype that leads to much pain and even death for victimized women.[2]

Key Points

A reference tool for
spouses, parents, clergy,
counselors and others

- Pornography is *anti-sex education.* It spreads an enormous amount of misinformation about sexual intimacy, portraying it as completely without love, self-control or responsibility. It presents information that is false and misleading both from a scientific and a human relationship standpoint. Pornography is destroying healthy sexuality.

27

MAKE YOUR CHOICE

Now you are equipped with a basic set of facts with regard to Internet pornography and cybersex, and understand the effects they have on the human brain, nervous system and body. You now comprehend the vast consequences of viewing Internet porn and engaging in cybersex.

Now it's up to you—you have some choices to make . . .

For Adults, Pornography Is About Responsible Choices, Not Censorship

There are those who believe the government should regulate everything we see, hear, touch and taste. I am not one of those people. However, I also don't believe that the constitution guarantees us the right to look at anything we choose, regardless of its source or its impact on our behavior. In this regard, I would like to quote a letter written to me by Dr. Judith Reisman, one of the world's leading authorities on pornography's effects on human behavior:

Terrence J. Murphy in "Censorship, Government and Obscenity" recounts President Abraham Lincoln's contribution to our understanding of virtue and purity:

"During the Civil War the volume of such mail (obscenity) increased greatly. Pornographers were attempting to exploit the loneliness of the Union soldiers away from home. Consequently . . . President Lincoln signed into law a bill that outlawed obscenity in the United States."[1]

The public and the 1933 and 1934 court in [the James Joyce novel] Ulysses *understood "obscene" as "tending to stir the sex impulses or to lead to sexually impure and lustful thoughts. . . ." This is, as Lincoln's postal laws said, material "of a vulgar and indecent character," signifying "lustful" as well as "sexually impure."*[2]

If pornography is an endogenously produced high, a drug which creates "a vulgar and indecent character," and "stirs the sex impulse," why would any pornography deserve the right to public access any more than would heroin? If pornography—soft, hard, Internet, comic, illustrative, pseudo child, child, etc.—stirs men, boys, women and girls to sexually abuse women and children, why prohibit it from children and not from those who are their designated abusers?

Our constitution guarantees above all, equal rights of our citizens to life, liberty and the pursuit of happiness, and to "domestic tranquility." This requires that these rights are historically of a much higher value than the right to produce and distribute a product for profit. These rights prohibit the production, use and/or distribution of a "drug" which causes a class of people to harm another class of people, i.e., pornography ***causing*** *primarily vulnerable men and boys to distrust, dislike, fear, harass, threaten and yes, to rape and murder, to sexually abuse women and children, even their own infants.*

The American Humane Association data find a 1,028% increase in child sex abuse from 1976 to 1982 and an estimated increase of 4,169% to the year 2000. The latest FBI data find that 67% of our sex abuse victims are children 0-17 years and 34% of these ***are under age 12****, while 64% of forcible sodomy victims are* ***boys under 12 years old!*** *The recent FBI announcement in October, 2000, of a 9% drop in rape neglects to mention that rape no longer includes statutory rape data or data on the rape of any* *children under age 12! The data on child rape and sodomy of boys have been thus statistically "handled" (read covered up) by the U.S. Justice bureaucracy for decades.*[3]

Now that the data are beginning to leak out we find the substantiation for what we in the child protection arena have long empirically observed. That is, we are in the midst of a sexual holocaust against all our children. This is a domestic war and anything that is aiding and abetting in such a discriminatory holocaust would violate our "domestic tranquility," and is unconstitutional, on its face.

I agree with Dr. Reisman's argument. I believe adults should have the freedom to look at anything they wish, *if* they can guarantee that doing so will not cause harm to others. Overwhelming scientific evidence clearly shows that exposure to pornography does indeed radically alter the human mindbody, and as a result can and does radically alter human attitudes and behavior. Just as those who consume alcohol and then drive are a serious threat to others, those who consume pornography and then mix in society are also a serious threat to those around them, especially women and children. Does your freedom of speech allow you to falsely yell "fire" in a crowded theater or jokingly scream "bomb" in a bustling airport? Should unrestricted pornography viewing be protected by the first amendment?

Those who cry for the "total and unbridled" exercise of freedom, without fully understanding and measuring the consequences of that exercise, play the role of blind fools and place the innocent citizen at extreme risk.

If, after reading this book, you decide to view Internet pornography or participate in cybersex, or stand by while your loved ones and others engage in it, that is your choice and you, they, and the rest of us must live with the consequences. At least you will have made your choice based on scientific facts and data rather than on the profit-motivated hype of the porn industry and its proponents.

For Children, Pornography Is Not About Choice, It's About Protection

Organizations such as the ACLU and the American Library Association propose that children ought to have the same rights of unrestricted access to Internet pornography that adults have. Are they serious? If they are, then they either do not understand the devastation pornography wreaks on a child's or teen's mindbody, or they do understand the impact and are completely—and irresponsibly—hardened and aloof to it. They are so narrowly focused on *total unrestricted freedom*, that they cannot see the forest for the trees—and our children will suffer greatly as a result. (It is interesting to note in John Harmer's book *A War We Must Win*, that the ACLU receives substantial funding from the pornography promoters and producers in Hollywood. See John Harmer, *A War We Must Win,* Bookcraft, Salt Lake City, Utah, 1999, p.21, 26-27.)

Simply put, children don't have the ability to make an informed decision with regard to Internet pornography. (Of course, neither do men and teens whose mindbody is trapped in the "narrow tunnel" of a porn-viewing session.) Having said that, let me make it perfectly clear that I believe most children from about the age of seven or eight are quite able to distinguish right from wrong. Have you ever seen a bright, sensitive child shy away from something inappropriate? Children, in most cases, innately sense when something "isn't right."

But there are many things, particularly in regards to sexuality, that they know nothing about. They have no insight on sexual matters, beyond a very limited, innocent understanding. To the contrary, children can be manipulated and coerced when it comes to pornography due to the fact that their minds are so tender, pliable and impressionable. They are forming many important cellular-memory groups for the first time.

If during these formative years pornographic images are deposited in these newly-formed cellular-memories, these potent images may lie dormant until the child's sexual drives become active at puberty. What hideous effects will these stored images have as new emotions and information related to the child's sexuality are filtered through these cellular-memories? How will these pornographic filters influence the child's behavior with members of the opposite sex, or with members of the same sex? What traumas will these filters deliver when the child grows up, gets married and is trying to form a healthy intimate relationship with his or her spouse? And how can we possibly know the extent of the structural changes pornographic images make in a child's brain and body?

There is a strong possibility that if we expose children to pornography at an early age, we may very well take away their choice to avoid it later on.

Can you imagine exposing children to a concoction of chemicals and then waiting to see, not *if* the chemicals do harm (we already know that pornographic images are harmful and stay with children for a lifetime), but *what kind* of harm they produce and how severe?

Why on earth, then, would any organization or parent with half a brain suggest that children have the right to *choose* whether or not to view pornography?

For Teenagers, Pornography Is No "Choice" At All

The same groups that say children should have access to Internet pornography also believe, of course, that teenagers ought to have the same right. And some groups who actively seek to protect children from pornography, pronounce it "okay"—and even "healthy"—for teenagers!

Again, are these people serious? Have they read the studies and scrutinized the research that shows how harmful pornography is to developing teenagers? A teenage boy's sex drive and a teenage girl's sex drive—coupled with his or her need to be loved and accepted—are incredibly powerful forces. Pornography twists, distorts and fuels these "would-be" normal and healthy impulses in ways that bring only misery and despair.

Key Points

A reference tool for spouses, parents, clergy, counselors and others

- Make your judgements and choices regarding Internet pornography based on scientific facts and data rather than on the profit-motivated hype of the porn industry and its proponents.

28

Are You Setting Yourself and Your Children Up for Porn Addiction?

Many of Us Have Been So Saturated By Nudity and Sex That We Can't Think Straight

Whether we realize it or not, most of us over the last 30 years have been so bombarded by sex in the media that we have become "desensitized" to its effects. We see so much of it all of time that we usually don't even give it a second thought. As a society, we have become rather apathetic.

A few weeks ago I had a conversation with a friend about a particular movie we had both seen. I commented that I had come away disappointed by the sexual innuendos and jokes. Initially, he challenged me, insisting that there were no such things in the movie. Then after a few moments' thought, and my giving him some specific examples, he acknowledged that I was right. "I'm so used to it that I didn't even notice," he said.

What a sad statement and a dark reflection on our media and society. He may not have "noticed," but I can assure you that every sexual joke, innuendo and scene was permanently stored in the cells of his brain and body, and that these cellular-memories impact his attitudes, his moods, his behaviors, and how he views women.

To prove my point that we are daily inundated with blatant references to sex/porn, and to help you examine all this from a brand new perspective—a clean slate, so to speak—I would like to pose the following challenge: **The 3-Week Challenge.**

The 3-Week Challenge

For the next 21 days I invite you to leave the TV turned off and to not attend any movies. Instead, listen to soothing, uplifting music, read those books that positively inspire you and are completely free of any sexual dialogue or scenes. Become fully aware of those around you and seek opportunities to help a family member, an elderly neighbor or others in need. Immerse yourself in everything good, decent and uplifting for three solid weeks. Afterwards, see if you have developed a more reverent and dignified attitude toward human intimacy and the human body.

I guarantee that after this three-week period you *will* notice the sexual innuendos, nudity, sex-talk and the like splashed throughout the TV sitcoms, in the movies and across the magazine covers. You will gain a much clearer perspective of how far down the media has brought us and how dramatically our society has deteriorated over the last 30 years.

With this fresh outlook in mind, let me offer just a few thoughts about what the media has done to demean and cheapen human sexual intimacy and the precious gift to create life.

How Parents Set Their Children Up For Internet Porn and Cybersex Chat Addictions

A hundred years from now it will not matter

what your bank account was . . .

What sort of house you lived in . . .

or the kind of clothes you wore. . . .

But the world may be different because

you were important in the life of a child.

In 1872, a 3,468-square-mile tract in the northwestern corner of Wyoming was set aside by Congress as America's first National Park. They named it "Yellowstone." The motive behind this congressional act was to protect and preserve the breathtaking beauty of the area, setting it aside to be enjoyed by future generations. Parents and grandparents wanted to make certain that their posterity would not be denied the opportunity to visit an "unspoiled" wilderness.

Since that time, Congress, environmental groups and concerned citizens have gone to great lengths to protect and preserve millions of acres of land across America. Monumental efforts have been made to save endangered species, plant more trees and reduce pollution. Mammoth governmental agencies have been formed to oversee these efforts. You can rarely pick up a newspaper or turn on the news without reading or hearing something about these environmental issues. The goal in all of this is to be responsible with our natural resources today so that we leave behind a choice legacy for future generations.

By comparison, why is so little being done to protect America's most precious resource? Everyday this delicate and beautiful resource is polluted, trampled and destroyed. Where are all of the government agencies, protection groups and outraged citizens?

As you can guess, the resource I refer to is our youngest, most innocent citizens. What are we doing to protect and preserve the minds and souls of children and teenagers? What about the minds and souls of adults who teach and train our youth? If our very actions and who we are literally come from the information and images we allow into our mindbodies, what will our children and teenagers become in the future? Unchecked, what will be the legacy we will pass on to them?

Our children, teens and young adults are bombarded from all sides by pornography and obscenity. As a result, what will the adults of the future, and the future of our country, be like?

Isn't it time we gave at least as much attention and urgency to our most valuable resource, our children, as we do our natural resources? If we do not, as surely as the rain forests are being laid waste, the minds of future generations will grow dark and cold, devoid of the capacity to appreciate beauty, lacking in creativity and purity. This all-too-chilling scenario is what the mind of a little child will become.

When polluting smoke billows out of a factory smoke stack or toxic waste is dumped into a river, the EPA (Environmental Protection Agency) steps in and takes action. After all, at stake is the air we breathe and the water we drink. Our health—even our very lives—may be in jeopardy.

But what about the pollution of the human mind? Where is the "MPA" (Mind Protection Agency) to guard us from the toxic waste of filth as it pours from our television sets and computer screens into our minds and the minds of our youth?

Just as a lack of responsibility and positive action regarding the pollution of our earth would bring eventual disaster, if we ignore the pollution of the human mind, the serious consequences will fall upon our children and their children for generations to come.

The youth of America are our legacy, our future. We owe it to them to protect and preserve the "environment" that feeds their minds with the same zeal and fervor we demonstrate in protecting the air they breathe and the water they drink.

STOP FEEDING OUR TEENAGERS SEXUAL "TWINKIES"

Several years ago in the middle of an unusually severe winter, federal agencies dropped hay from airplanes to save starving deer. Later, many of the deer were found to have died of starvation, their bellies filled with hay. The deer were fed, but they were not "nourished."

Today, federal and state agencies offer our teenagers condoms on demand and low-cost abortions. They encourage masturbation and preach slogans, that in effect, say, "Do it, but just do it safely." They offer this hay-like fodder to nourish our youth in a time of "moral winter." Through TV, movies and the Internet, teens are fed a steady diet of sex, nudity, violence, irreverence and the like. As a result, teen pregnancies, venereal disease and suicides run rampant. Our teens are dying with the empty calories of "sexual twinkies" in their souls, when what they really need is genuine moral nourishment.

ESTABLISHING THE FOOTPATH— THE FOUNDATION IS SO CRITICAL!

A number of years ago my wife and I decided to take in a movie. We went to a complex consisting of four or five separate theaters. As we were making our way to our assigned theater, I noticed a mother with two small children scurrying through one of the doors. Curious, I glanced up at the sign posted above the entrance. It read, "Friday the 13th." I was shocked! This was a well-publicized "slasher" flick, filled with murder, blood and gore. I was about to follow the woman into the theater and give her a piece of my mind, but I chose not to make a scene. (Coward!)

Back then, I instinctively felt that exposing small children to such graphic violence and blood-filled scenes would cause deep trauma and permanent scarring. But now, after having done extensive research into the inner workings of the human brain and body, I understand *why* such a movie is so harmful for children. And not just children, but all of us.

Do parents understand how critically important it is that they help implant the proper cellular-memories in their children from the time they are born? Do parents understand that—whether they are aware of it or not, or whether they are intentionally directing the process or not—they are constantly feeding the cellular-memories within their children's brains and bodies?

SETTING YOUR LITTLE BOYS AND GIRLS UP FOR INTERNET PORNOGRAPHY AND CYBERSEX ADDICTIONS

How many parents out there are unaware of the cellular-memories being formed in their children's brains and bodies based on the television programs and movies they are allowed to watch?

Next time you are parked in front of the television set alongside your children, or sitting next to them at the movie theater, pay close attention to the actors. What they are saying? What messages are they sending through their words, body language and mannerisms. Ask yourself: "Is this what I want to teach my sons and daughters about men, women, relationships, marriage and human intimacy? Is this the information I want my sons and daughters to have stored in their cellular-memories? Are these the attitudes I want them to access throughout their lives as they interact with others?"

What worries me is that in today's world we are surrounded and constantly bombarded with messages that promote sexual promiscuity, nudity, obsession with physical appearance, the promotion of women as sex objects, and three decades of an overall climate of "if it feels good, do it." What I fear is that too many of our children and teens are being raised on a constant diet of this trash.

Are we living in an era when a majority of our young men will grow up without any cellular-memories in place that promote respect as paramount in how to treat women? Will they be so smeared with raunchy images of sex, nudity, promiscuity and infidelity that these will make up the sum total of their cellular-memories? Will men and boys actually lose the ability to even see beyond the physical body parts of a woman? Will girls and women be unable to see worth in themselves beyond their outward appearance?

If this happens, heaven help us all, especially our sisters and daughters, mothers and wives.

Parents Must Sacrifice Their Trashy Sitcoms and Movies For the Good of Their Children

Many of the great triumphs in history have been achieved as a result of "self-sacrifice" and "self-control." Pilgrims have given their all for their beliefs; patriots have sacrificed their very lives in defense of their families, homes and countries; with moral conviction and integrity, men and women of principle have raised their voices in defense of what is just and right.

On a personal scale, a man might sacrifice "acting out" his lustful desires for the good of his wife and children. A young man and woman wait to engage in those physical acts that hold the power to give life until they can give their child the love and care it deserves. What is wrong with self-control? Why is it so out of fashion? What is wrong with reverencing life and love and intimacy? Why does is appear that so few are concerned with decency, respect and virtue?

Many parents act like they'll "just die" if they miss a certain movie or weekly TV program. What has happened to us? For the *good of their children*, parents must exercise self-control, intelligence and wisdom, and relinquish their sitcoms, talk shows and Hollywood movies, so many of which make light of intimate things.

Children observe such things so closely, then tend to copy—and usually exaggerate—what they see. If parents don't want their children to be vulgar, immoral or violent, they themselves should not watch, nor allow their children to watch programs or movies that are structuring their children's mindbodies to be vulgar, immoral or violent. This is like saying, "I don't want my children to get cancer," and then turning around and feeding them nothing but carcinogenic substances!

Parents, let's be a little more wise, a little more attentive when it comes to our children. Just think: soon they'll be parents, too.

WE SHOULD DEMAND MORE OF HOLLYWOOD!

Offered in the "Movies" section of our local newspaper is a listing of all of the films currently playing at the various theaters. Each is listed by title, along with a brief summary of the plot and the rating. Next to its rating are several one-word descriptions to explain the reasons why the movie was rated as it was. As I scanned these descriptions, I found a chain of words repeated over and over again for most of the movies: *sex, nudity, graphic violence, vulgarity, profanity, drug use, racial slurs* . . . Then when I checked out the advertisements for these movies, phrases such as *"The #1 Movie In America!"* and *"Come See What Everyone Is Raving About!"* prominently stood out.

We're better than this! Hollywood is better than this! To think of all the wonderfully gifted actors, writers and directors who have held our hearts in the palms of their hands. These men and women have the ability and the power to lift us to great heights, to inspire us to be and do better. Why, then, do they use their marvelous talents so often to show us the lowest, darkest and most degrading side of humanity? Why do the majority of today's movies (even many of the PG and PG-13 ones) feature *sex, nudity, graphic violence, vulgarity, profanity, drug use, racial slurs*, etc.?. *We're* better than this; *Hollywood* is better than this!

When you idly sit in front of such drivel, are you not in effect saying you support and agree with its content?

The same applies to Internet pornography. When men and women participate in such things, they are sanctioning and giving their "silent approval" to abuse, exploitation and degradation.

A man or woman cannot truthfully say, "I'm just an observer." Where pornography is concerned, there are no mere observers, only participants and non-participants. The weak "observer" argument is like someone who holds a woman's coat while looking on as other men rape her, maintaining, "I'm just an observer." Or it's like purchasing an elegant ivory piece of art while ignoring the violence and savagery that were involved in bringing it to you. How can a man or woman look at Internet pornography and ignore all those who were and are hurt by it? Knowing that porn is a stimulus or catalyst for rape, child molestation, murder, broken marriages and mangled families, how can a person say, "I look at porn, but I don't support how it is made or condone the harm it does"?

With quiet reflection and real effort, each of us knows how to discern between light and darkness, good and bad, love and hate. Isn't it time we started exercising this capacity?

DO YOU WANT CHILDREN AND TEENS TO BE MORAL OR NOT? MAKE UP YOUR MIND!

I am amazed at the mixed signals our children and teenagers are receiving. They hear, "Be responsible," "Don't do something stupid," "Don't get pregnant," "Be careful of AIDS." Then the media turn around and bombard these same children and teens with messages and images that tell them to do just the opposite. Would someone please just make up their mind?

BOYS, TEENS AND MEN NEED ROLE MODELS—NOT PORNOGRAPHY

We hear: "Men are sex machines, slaves to testosterone. . . . They can't help themselves, so they may as well give in."

NO! Boys, teens and men are *not* machines, sex slaves or dogs, and they *can* help themselves. But they need role models to show them how to use their strengths, traits and tendencies for good. The Creator gave men, teens and boys these traits and tendencies for a good and worthy purpose. Now these men or future men need someone to show them how to direct their energies, urges and desires—not how to be ruled by them. Porn brings out the worst in men by turning strength into weakness. We need to recognize and follow role models who show how to make the most of manhood. And the Hollywood bed-hopping macho-man ought not to be included among those role models.

Some argue that a "real man" is one who can hold his liquor, swear with the best of them, and eagerly go from one sexual encounter to the next. Certainly "adulthood" comes to all, if they live long enough. But "manhood" comes only to those who are worthy of it. The real man is one who has fought and triumphed in the most fierce battle of all—the battle raging within himself. When many wimp out and simply give in to carnal impulses, the real man digs in and sacrifices mindless impulse or animal lust for self-mastery.

I recall the story of a young man who traveled with his high school team to a state basketball tournament. In the hotel room his teammates decided to watch porn movies. This young man, in order to avoid the poisonous images, walked the city's streets until late into the night, only returning to the hotel room when the movies were over. **Behold a man!** At 18, more a man than many two or three times his age.

In the May 1997 issue of *U.S. News & World Report* appeared the story of another such role model: A.C. Green, an NBA basketball star, is 33 years of age and has yet to marry. Actively promoting the cause of sexual abstinence, he said: *I am still a virgin. Abstaining from extramarital sex is one of the most unpopular things a person can do, much less talk about. From a sheer numbers standpoint, it can be a lonely cause—but that doesn't mean it's not right.*

I abstain as an adult for the same reasons I did as a teen—the principle doesn't change, or the feeling of self-respect I get. My fellow ballplayers do not tell me, "You are crazy"—it's more that they think I'm being unrealistic. It's ironic, but the guys who are parents—and especially the guys who have daughters—tend to look at sex before marriage a lot more carefully now.

Now *that's* a man—informed, thoughtful, disciplined, committed to principle, placing his integrity and honor above his sexual urges.

FOOD FOR THOUGHT

How would you feel if you saw a man who you knew had just finished a porn session on his computer staring at your wife or daughter? A teenage boy emerges from a library bathroom, where he has just finished a 20-minute session of looking at porn printed off the Internet. He spies your teenage daughter and starts following her around the library, cajoling her. What would you do?

OUR GIRLS AND YOUNG WOMEN NEED GOOD ROLE MODELS

In *Just Like A Woman*, author Diane Hales states: *Girls and young women also need real-life role models—if only to counter the images of brain-dead bimbos that still monopolize the media. A recent survey of images aimed at teenagers found that women in movies or on television are far less likely than men to be seen working, using their intelligence or focusing on issues other than romance, hair, and personal appearance.*[1]

The media still largely promote and display women the same way Internet pornography does—as physical objects and collections of body parts. Isn't it time to say, "Just knock it off! Enough is enough!"

WE MUST BE CAREFUL NOT TO GO TO THE EXTREME AND CREATE "SEXUAL SHAME" IN OUR CHILDREN

While we should strive to teach our children to seek after entertainment that is decent and uplifting, and avoid pornography in all of its forms, we must be careful not to become "extremists" or "fanatics." Our focus should be on the beauty of human intimacy as opposed to constantly harping on the negatives.

Consider a message that is often communicated to children and teenagers in highly religious or moral family environments: "Sex before marriage is dirty, evil, forbidden . . . and oh, by the way, be sure to save it for someone you really care about." This is an extremely confusing message that is often transmitted to our young people.

When a child reaches puberty, he begins to feel sexual stirring, arousal and attraction for the opposite sex. If he has been taught that sex is "evil" or "dirty," and/or has observed his parents acting extremely rigid or ranting and raving about nudity, sex, pornography, etc., then this child will most likely experience "sexual shame"—the perception that "because sex is evil and dirty, I must be evil and dirty because I have these sexual feelings."

According to leading therapists and the sex/porn addicts I have interviewed, sexual shame is one of the primary catalysts leading to addiction. And sadly enough, sex/porn addiction therapists have told me that the largest percentage of their patients grew up in family environments of extreme religious and/or sexual rigidity.

The key to raising sexually healthy children and teenagers is to create an environment where human intimacy is regarded as healthy, positive, beautiful and even sacred—something to anticipate and look forward to at the appropriate time and under the right circumstances. Yes, we should teach our children about the dangers and darkness of pornography, premarital sex, self-indulgence, etc. But we should do so primarily by our own example coupled with gentle and positive teaching. We should avoid preaching lengthy sermons, interrogating our teens after dates, ranting and raving about a questionable scene on TV and any other "extreme."

For more additional insights on teaching children about sexuality, please review the last section of Chapter 34 titled, *What If My Child or Teenager Has Been Exposed To Pornography By Accident*.

Key Points

A reference tool for
spouses, parents, clergy,
counselors and others

- We must realize that, over time, the media has desensitized and "dumbed us down." What many see in the media as "no big deal," is the gateway to harder more explicit materials and porn/cybersex addiction.
- We need to encourage ourselves and others to more carefully select what we will watch on TV or on the movie screen, even taking vacations where we shut off the media and allow our mindbody to regain clarity, perspective and values.
- Adults must realize how they set themselves, their spouses and children up for addiction and abuse through the sexualized media they allow into their homes and lives. We must stop sending "mixed messages" to our teens and children.
- We must be very careful to avoid creating "sexual shame" in our children and teenagers.

29

Protecting Your Family from Internet Pornography

If after reading the facts you have made an intelligent and informed decision not to view Internet pornography or participate in cybersex chat, and you desire to protect your family and loved ones from these as well, what should you do next?

Shutting Down the "Gateway" to Internet Pornography and Cybersex

The first step is to shut down the "gateway" to Internet pornography and cybersex. Just as marijuana has been called the "gateway drug" to hard-core drug use, and beer is known as the "gateway" to hard liquor and eventual alcoholism, there are gateways that lead to Internet pornography and cybersex chat addiction.

Remember, every image we see is stored in our cellular-memories for later retrieval. The more we see a certain image or type of image, the larger grows the cellular-memory group where these images are stored. These massive cellular-memory groups become dominant, largely directing our behavior. Based on stored images and information, the following can act as "gateways" to Internet pornography and cybersex addiction:

- Music with sexually-oriented lyrics.
- Sitcoms and talk shows containing sexual jokes, innuendo or dialogue.
- Movies with suggestive humor, full or partial nudity, sex scenes and sexual dialogue.
- Sexually-oriented magazines, novels, comic books and other such publications.
- The so-called "soft-porn" magazines, calendars, movies, videos, etc.

All of the above tend to pre-program a person's mindbody to be *receptive* to Internet porn or cybersex, even on the first exposure.

Family Protection Resources

You can protect your family from inappropriate entertainment without eliminating movie and TV programs. I recommend the following resources:

1. www.FamilySafeMedia.com: information regarding the "Profanity Filter," a device that is connected to your TV/VCR/DVD and filters out all profanity.
2. www.ScreenIt.com: a free service that gives you a text-based overview of every major motion picture played in theaters. Reviews scene-by-scene sex, nudity, profanity, violence, etc. Know exactly what it is before you or your family go to see it.
3. www.CleanFlicks.com: rent movies with the sex, nudity, profanity and graphic violence edited out. This service will also edit videos you already own.

OPTIONS REGARDING THE INTERNET IN YOUR HOME

When it comes to Internet safety in the home, there are a variety of approaches:

- Simply trust your family members. "They'd never access that trash," you say. Are you sure? Say you have a satellite dish with 100 channels, five of which offer sexually-explicit entertainment. You simply hand your teenager the remote and say, "We're leaving for the weekend. Don't turn on any of those sex channels while we're gone. We trust you." What are you doing when you give a teenager unlimited Internet access? Considering his natural curiosity and the incredible addictive power of Internet porn and cybersex chat rooms, this is a highly risky approach. And remember, Internet pornographers are master manipulators; they employ dozens of techniques to expose and hook viewers who never had any intention of searching for porn in the first place.
- Don't allow the Internet into your home. An explosion of filth and garbage is there on the Internet, but there is also a world of educational material. Keeping the Internet out of your home will prevent you and your children from accessing this marvelous resource.
- Educate your spouse and your children, and surf the Internet with them. Then put the computer in a main thoroughfare in your home and directly supervise its use, vigilantly guarding what is accessed: Have you seen photos of those men in their formal red uniforms and tall hats who stand guard outside the Royal Palace in London?

Unless parents want to take on this full-time role, this latter option is not a viable one. One of the pornography addicts I interviewed spoke about how as a teen he and his friends would sneak out of bed in the middle of the night and watch pornographic movies on satellite while his parents slept. A mother related how her teenage son surreptitiously viewed Internet porn on the computer in the same room she was in while her back was turned!

Educating your family, placing the computer in a public place and surfing with them are all good ideas, but certainly not the complete solution. You can't be with them every second of the day and night. And taking into account the cunning techniques of the Internet pornographers, you never know when family members might be exposed to smut—even while you're right there with them!

A popular protection device is the use of "Internet Filtering" software or services. While filters are helpful, they have their limitations.

A WORD ABOUT INTERNET FILTERS

In my research I have spoken with hundreds of parents and spouses who have utilized Internet filtering software and services to keep pornography off of their computer screens. Some have expressed a great deal of irritation and frustration at the failings of these filters. The most common complaint is that the filters work much of the time, but pornography still gets through. The following is an overview of the two basic filtering products available and why they sometimes fail:

1. Webpage Filters or "Bad Lists"

This filtering software/service seeks to find, review and then place on a "bad list" all of the pornographic webpages on the Internet. When an Internet user attempts to access a particular webpage, intentionally or by accident, if that webpage is on the bad list, it is blocked.

This filter often fails for the simple reason that there are already over two billion webpages on the Internet and this number grows by more than seven million new webpages every day.[1] In order for a "bad list" approach to succeed, the filtering company would have to first review the Internet's existing billions of webpages and then daily review more than seven million new webpages! It's impossible for a filtering service to keep up with these staggering numbers. All pornographic webpages that the filter is unable to identify remain available to family members through intentional or unintentional surfing.

2. Word Filters

Realizing that the bad-list approach cannot succeed alone, some filtering services add a process called *word-filtering*. Word filters attempt to block websites that have sexually explicit words. Like bad lists, this approach can also fail for the following two reasons:

First, many perfectly good websites use words like "breast" in legitimate contexts such as "breast cancer" or "chicken breast." As a result, word filters are prone to block out many legitimate websites.

The second problem is far more serious. Internet pornographers have become wise to the attempts of word filters to block their sites. To get around these filters, some pornographers eliminate sexually explicit words. Thus, a family member may access a website with very ordinary, innocent sounding words, only to discover that it contains images that are pornographic. If the viewer attempts to close the site, pornographers often turn to a trick called "mouse trapping," "auto-spawning" or "looping," which automatically begins opening porn sites on the surfer's computer screen. Many adults and children have described the shock of seeing one porn site after another bursting open on their screen faster than they can close them. Finally they have to shut the computer down to cut the chain. The number of Internet porn sites that do not contain words that would show up on a word filter's list is growing rapidly.[2]

Too many families have come to realize by sad experience that Internet filters cannot fully protect them from exposure to pornography. Rather than rely on a single solution, I recommend a multiple-step process:

STEPS TO PROTECT YOUR FAMILY FROM INTERNET PORNOGRAPHY

1. Educate yourself regarding computer technology and the Internet. Too often, children know far more about computers than their parents. As a result, uneducated parents are often unaware of a child or teen's involvement with Internet porn or cybersex chat, and it's easier for kids to "pull one over" on these parents. Spend time with your children on the Internet—you'll be surprised at how much you can learn.

2. Any computer in your home with Internet access should be kept in a "high-traffic" location. Isolation and secrecy are primary components to Internet porn and cybersex involvement. Keeping the computer in a public place is a good deterrent and monitoring technique. You have a much better chance of becoming aware of any problems.

3. Educate your children regarding the advantages and dangers of the Internet. Prepare them in advance of any problems. For example:

    - Teach them never to give out their name, address or any other personal information on the Internet.

    - Teach them "why" pornography is harmful to their brain and body. Be careful not to create sexual shame or guilt. Help them understand the difference between healthy sexuality and pornography.

    - Maintain a comfortable "talking" relationship with your children regarding sexual issues. Don't lecture, preach, or create sexual guilt and shame. Keep the lines of communication open so they will be open with you in the event of a problem.

    - Role play with children about what to do if they encounter pornography on the Internet. Teach them to "crash and tell," i.e., if they accidently see a porn site to immediately turn off the monitor or computer and tell you. Teach them what to do if they see pornography on someone else's computer—at a friend's or family member's home, at school or in the library.

- Don't over-react if your child comes to you about seeing pornography. A negative response will intimidate them and stop them from coming to you in the future. Praise them for bringing the problem to you. To understand what to do when your child or teen has seen pornography by accident, please see Chapter 34 in this book.

4. Use technology to monitor, block or filter the Internet in your home. While this may not guarantee 100% protection, it's better than no protection at all. I recommend that you visit the website, www.FilterReview.com, a free service to help you find the right Internet Service Provider, filtering, blocking or monitoring system for your needs. This website is sponsored by the National Coalition for the Protection of Children & Families. This resource makes it possible for you to select the characteristics you're looking for in an Internet safety solution and provides you with options to fit that criteria. Expert reviews for each solution are also provided. For the highest level of protection against Internet pornography and other undesirable elements on the Internet, I personally recommend the following:

   - Find a service or software that allows you to create a "closed Internet environment." This allows you to select "safe" Internet sites and place them on a list. Family members can only surf to websites on this list and nowhere else. This list can be added to on a regular basis. This feature can be turned off through a password, allowing full Internet access. Only an adult should have this password, and in most two-parent households, this should be the wife alone. (National studies show that a growing percentage of women are falling prey to sexual behavior on the

Internet. If the wife feels vulnerable, she should consider a "shared password"—she has part of the password and her husband has the other. In this way, full access to the Internet is not possible unless both are present.)

- There will be times when full access to the Internet is required, taking family members outside the safety of the closed environment. This should never be done without a parent(s) present. And in most cases, even the man of the house should have his wife present. (This is automatic if she is the only one in the household with the password.) During these times of full Internet access, you should have some type of Internet *filtering* or *blocking* service in place to protect family members. And, because "safe" sites can change over time or contain links to inappropriate sites, your filtering or blocking service should also be running when safe sites are being accessed.

  Note: you may be able to find an Internet safety solution that has safe list and blocking/filtering capability combined into one package.

- Avoid randomly "surfing" the Internet—always have a specific purpose and end in mind. Once that purpose is fulfilled, turn full access off and return to the safety of the closed environment. When a family member needs full access to the Internet again, mom enters the password, stays there until the specific purpose is accomplished, and then returns the computer to the safety of the closed environment.

- In addition, some Internet safety solutions offer a *monitoring* service. This service provides a confidential report regarding each Internet site that has been accessed by each family member. This prevents family members from hiding their surfing habits by erasing the history or temporary Internet files. Just knowing that this service is in place can discourage many people from accessing inappropriate sites. And if a family member does have a problem, you will become aware of it early—before serious addiction has set in.

- I don't believe that any child or teenager should engage in Internet chat with strangers—the risks of sexual dialogue, manipulation, predators, addiction, etc. are too great. Based on the findings of my research, interviews, and work with law enforcement and therapists, there is no way I would ever allow my children or teens to participate in online chat-rooms. Although I discourage it, if you decide to allow chat-room involvement in your home, make certain you have an Internet safety solution in place that monitors chat and prevents inappropriate conversation and predatory activities. See www.FilterReview.com for solutions that offer this service.
- Pornographers love to sneak their images in through the "backdoor" of your computer—your e-mail. Whether you realize it or not, it's very easy for pornographers to obtain your e-mail address. They use e-mail as an effective means to expose the innocent and unsuspecting to hard-core porn. Their purpose is to entrap and addict as many people as possible. So, you or your children open an e-mail and suddenly "wham!" explicit images burst open on the computer screen. To combat this sinister practice, you need a safety solution that blocks e-mail assaults. Again, see www.FilterReview.com for protection options. Also, don't allow your children to access e-mail without your supervision.

While this may all seem like a lot of trouble, or even paranoid, it's the most effective way I know to protect your family. Remember, in an instant you or your loved ones can be exposed to the most depraved and explicit images, leaving a permanent record in your cellular-memories. Also keep in mind that pornographers use the most dastardly and cunning techniques to expose and entrap the innocent. You can't afford to take even the smallest chance.

5. Learn to recognize the signs of "desensitization" that could indicate your child or teen has a problem with pornography:

   - He becomes quiet, depressed, isolated from friends and family, and discontinues formerly enjoyed pursuits. He won't talk about what is bothering him and seems to dislike himself. He is increasingly argumentative, defensive and disagreeable.
   - His attitudes change: TV programs, movies, pictures, jokes, etc., that were formerly inappropriate become acceptable. He begins making comments like "you have the problem," or "you're such a prude."
   - You notice a loss of respect for women and an increased focus on, or obsession with, male/female body parts.
   - The child or teen begins acting out sexually with self and/or others.
   - Staying up late while on the computer; locking the door; quickly changing the program or turning off the monitor when someone approaches; lying about computer use; being secretive or elusive in connection with the computer—these all are signs.
   - When you try to check the Internet sites he's visited, the history and temporary Internet files have all been erased.
   - A high phone bill with strange or unfamiliar numbers is another sign.
   - Spending a lot of time in Internet chat rooms often indicates a problem.

If the signs are there and you suspect that your child or teen may have a problem, STAY CALM. Sit down with your child and express your concerns. Be very careful not to impose harsh judgement or create guilt and shame by lecturing and preaching. Ask simple questions and spend most of the time just listening. It may be that your child is simply curious and the experience with pornography has been recent and limited. A loving and objective discussion about the mindbody science behind pornography coupled with Internet safety solutions may "nip the problem in the bud."

However, the child or teen may have developed some level of addiction if one or more of the following are present:

1. He has tried to stop, but he can't control the urge to look at pornography.
2. He no longer can control the amount of time he spends on the Internet or the frequency of the episodes.
3. Looking at pornography is usually accompanied by masturbation. Pornography and masturbation have become a way to feel pleasure and/or escape stress, emotional pain, pressure, etc.
4. He finds himself obsessing over and fantasizing about pornographic images when he's not on the Internet.
5. Over time, he begins seeking out images that are progressively more explicit and "hard-core."

If after a calm discussion with your child or teen, you feel that there may be an addiction problem, you should seek specialized counseling. Please review Chapters 30-36 of this book for additional guidance.

Key Points

A reference tool for
spouses, parents, clergy,
counselors and others

- We must shut down the "gateway" to Internet pornography and cybersex addiction by controlling the media that we allow into our homes and what we see in theaters. We must sacrifice for the good of ourselves and our families.
- Take every precaution to protect yourself and your family while on the Internet. Just one exposure to pornographic images can leave a deep impression that will last a lifetime.
- Learn to recognize the "signs" of an Internet porn problem. If this problem has become an addiction, seek immediate help.

30

RECOVERING FROM PORNOGRAPHY ADDICTION—THERE *IS* HOPE

When I finished the manuscript for this book, I sent it out to leading therapists, scientists and others for review. Their feedback was very positive and encouraging—they found the book informative, revolutionary, controversial, enlightening, educational and at times even frightening. The consensus was that by the time the reader was finished, he or she would fully understand how and why pornography radically alters the human brain and body, thus deeply impacting behavior. However, among all of the reviewers one recurring commentary was offered: "There is very little in your book to help those who are already addicted to pornography or for their friends and family who want to help them. You need a chapter on pornography addiction recovery."

The wisdom of this commentary became clear to me as I discussed the information in the book with friends, family, associates and even strangers—virtually everyone I spoke with knew of someone in their own family or circle of acquaintances who had been negatively impacted by pornography addiction. I heard accounts of divorce, rape, child abuse, lost careers, ruined reputations and even criminal prosecution—all as a direct result of pornography addiction.

So, I began the arduous task of attempting to construct a chapter on "recovery." But where to begin? I'm not a psychologist or therapist, I'm a researcher and a reporter. Who would I go to for direction? For me, this was an easy decision. Who better to direct me in the construction of a recovery chapter than one of the Nation's leading pornography addiction recovery therapists, Dr. Victor Cline. In response to my request for guidance, Dr. Cline kindly offered the following comprehensive overview:

Treating Sexual and Pornographic Addictions

Sex and porn addictions require therapists with special training in these areas for patients to have a good chance of recovery. These illnesses are very difficult to treat, with relapses the norm. There are no training programs in traditional medical schools, graduate schools of psychology or social work that deal with this kind of addictive problem. And while this will undoubtedly change in the next few years, anyone now seeking professional help will need to check very carefully the background experience of any therapists that they might choose to treat them.

What you are looking for is a "sex addiction therapist" from any of the mental health healing disciplines who has a good track record in treating this problem and personal values that are reasonably congruent with the patient's values. Suggestions will be given shortly on how to find such a therapist.

In addition to having a competent, qualified sex addiction therapist, the patient will also need to attend regularly—(90% of the time) for two years or longer—weekly meetings of Sexaholic Anonymous (or other similar 12-step support group). These groups (free of charge) meet in nearly every fair sized city in America and their address and location can be found in the business pages of the phone book or by contacting Alcoholics Anonymous, who can give direction to the caller on location and time of meetings of the sexaholic group. It will be at these meetings that patients can inquire of fellow members or attendees the names of competent therapists they are individually meeting with and have found helpful and competent in receiving their own treatment. Another source of referrals is to call the National Council on Sexual Addiction & Compulsivity, who have a register of most therapists in the U.S. doing treatment in this area: 770-989-9754.

In my experience of 25 years in treating approximately 350 of these patients I find, if married, nearly universally the wives are traumatized by the husband's lies, deceptions, and-out-of-bounds sex behavior, and need treatment, too. If the wife decides to stay in the marriage for a while longer, I engage her in joint treatment with her husband. I have found that if I successfully heal the husband of his addiction but have an angry, hostile, wounded wife who can never trust or forgive her husband even though she remains in the marriage, it greatly increases the risk of relapse in the husband as he attempts unsuccessfully to placate and deal with major marital turmoil. The wife's wounding has to be addressed as well as have both parties participate in marital therapy. Thus I nearly always attempt to have the wife join with the husband in our therapy sessions. This usually predicts a successful outcome if both stay in the healing program. This program works and is successful if both parties stay with it. Sometimes the husband will find himself with years of sobriety and feel he's all "cured" and doesn't need to still attend his group meetings or therapy sessions anymore. Why waste time and money when he's doing so well? This can be very risky. And it greatly increases the chances for relapse. What I do when patients start experiencing long-term sobriety is gradually lengthen the time interval between therapy sessions. So eventually we may be meeting once every month, or six to eight weeks or longer.

The specifics of treatment by the therapist will not be presented in detail here other than to mention that we do marital therapy, put the couple in marital communication workshops (such as Marriage Enrichment), do a lot of work with relapse prevention, identify the triggers to acting out and develop strategies to protect them from the triggers, fortify them to deal with the "wave," and help them reduce and eliminate masturbation to pornography, since this increases the power of their addictive illness over them and is the royal road to acquiring new sexual addictions or paraphilias which might be acted out. We also strongly emphasize a "no secrets" rule, and how vital this is to healing.

We treat concomitantly any other addictions which they might have. All have to be treated together, otherwise the patient just shifts back and forth between addictions with no real long-term healing. We teach them the three-second rule to manage and control intrusive thoughts and imagery. We give them a lot of reading to do in the sex addiction area (like the Carnes' books, and the "white book," created by S. A. and filled with successful recovery biographies, plus monographs on many other related topics). We want them to be "world experts" on the nature of sex addiction, its genesis, its course, and helpful treatment procedures.

We also find it most important that they have hope and assured knowledge that the illness is treatable and they can get their free agency back again and have rational control over their previously driven irrational behavior. They see how this is possible as they attend S.A. and see and hear the testimonies of other people who now have long-term sobriety. These were people who were in much worse shape than they when entering treatment.

We deal with spiritual issues in therapy when this is appropriate to the unique circumstances and values of the client. We also deal with deep woundedness arising out of early life traumas which now make them vulnerable to seeking out quick-fix sexual acting out as a solution, which really doesn't work in the long-term. I also give a lot of verbal praise and genuine appreciation in response to even their smallest gains and good behavior. I never criticize or put them down when there are relapses. I just say, "This is exactly why we meet in therapy—to strengthen you and develop new strategies to deal with temptation. Now if this situation were to occur again, what might be a more powerful way to deal with it? To resist it? To remain sober? . . . etc., etc."

Male teenage patients can be quite challenging. Many deny that it is a problem and consistently lie about the details of their involvement with it. Their motivation to change may be nonexistent. They are usually brought in for treatment by an angry and/or sorrowful parent and often tend to be uncooperative and passive/aggressive in dealing with the problem. It may be helpful to consider family therapy and be therapeutically confrontive in dealing with the issues that arise. Fairly drastic limitations on home computer/Internet use may be necessary. If 17 or older, I put them into a regular S.A. group with, possibly, the father also attending to be a support to the son and be someone he can talk with about the various issues as they arise.

WHAT IF YOU OR SOMEONE YOU LOVE IS ADDICTED TO INTERNET PORN?

In chapter one I stated the following in regards to the porn addict: *Eventually he becomes powerless. He further spins out of control as the compulsion takes over his life. Even severe threats to job, family or health cannot slow down the obsession. He is caught in a cycle of the need for mood change, stimulation, escape and temporary relief, a vicious gripping cycle that both repels and draws him, repulses and arouses.*

Often the addict wants to change, in fact knows he must change or succumb to disaster. Virtually every porn/cybersex addict reaches the point where he realizes the craving is simply too powerful; he cannot stop without help. At this point, most porn or cybersex addicts enter into what Dr. Page Bailey calls the Hopeless Dialogue.

Someone you know may be trapped in the Internet porn/cybersex addiction cycle. He may be in complete denial and refuse to admit that he has a problem. He may have tried to stop himself again and again, but the result is always the same: after an hour, a day, a week, a month or even a year of maintaining self-control, he always ends up returning to the pit of porn/cybersex, and the addiction cycle starts all over again. Is there any hope of escape for such a person? The clear and resounding answer is **"YES!"** I have interviewed and personally known many who have succeeded in breaking out of the prison of Internet porn/cybersex addiction. Virtually all who did so followed a similar path. I will attempt to guide the reader through an overview of the recovery process and achieve my primary objective of offering a plan of action and **HOPE!**

I acknowledge the tremendous insights, expert tutoring and wealth of information from the following professionals: Dr. Victor Cline, Patrick Carnes for his writings in *Contrary to Love* and *Don't Call It Love*, Dr. Martha Turner, M.D., founder of the S.T.A.R. (Sexual Trauma And Recovery) program, and the miraculous work of therapists Dan Gray, Todd Olson, Scott Peterson, Mark Chamberlain and Steve Johnson through their S.T.A.R. program in Salt Lake City, Utah. Endeavoring to write this chapter without their help would have been impossible.

Key Points

A reference tool for
spouses, parents, clergy,
counselors and others

- Although it can be the most difficult of all addictions to diagnose, treat and recover from, **it can be done**. Addicts and their families should be encouraged and given a bright **hope**, that with the proper steps, they can recover and live normal, healthy lives.

31

UNDERSTANDING AND RECOGNIZING PORN ADDICTION

SAA (Sex Addicts Anonymous) offers the following definition of sexual addiction (which includes pornography addiction):

Sex Addiction can involve a wide variety of practices. Sometimes an addict has trouble with just one unwanted behavior, sometimes with many. A large number of sex addicts say their unhealthy use of sex has been a progressive process. It may have started with an addiction to masturbation, pornography (either printed or electronic), or a relationship, but over the years progressed to increasingly dangerous behaviors.

The essence of all addiction is the addicts' experience of powerlessness over a compulsive behavior, resulting in their lives becoming unmanageable. The addict is out of control and experiences tremendous shame, pain and self-loathing. The addict may wish to stop—yet repeatedly fails to do so. The unmanageability of addicts' lives can be seen in the consequences they suffer: losing relationships, difficulties with work, arrests, financial troubles, a loss of interest in things not sexual, low self-esteem and despair.

Sexual preoccupation takes up tremendous amounts of energy. As this increases for the sex addict, a pattern of behavior (or rituals) follows, which usually leads to acting out (for some it is flirting, searching the net *for pornography, or driving to the park). When the acting out happens, there is a denial of feelings, usually followed by despair and shame or a feeling of hopelessness and confusion.*[1]

TYPES OF SEXUAL ADDICTION

In *Don't Call it Love*, Patrick Carnes identifies 11 different categories or types of sexual addiction:

1. **Fantasy Sex:** Thinking/obsessing about sexual adventures; inordinate amounts of time spent losing self in fantasy about future and past; neglecting commitments because of fantasy life; dramatizing a particular role in your fantasy; creating sexualized or seductive atmospheres that you prefer to keep as fantasy and not act on; spending a large amount of time preparing for a sexual episode.
2. **Seductive Role Sex:** Having many relationships at the same time or one after another; using seduction to gain power over others; thinking that sex will give power over another; flirtatious or seductive behaviors; hustling in singles clubs, bars, or health clubs; maintaining open calendars or failing to make commitments in order to be available for sex; bringing sex or sexualized humor into conversations; having to be sexual in order to feel good about self.
3. **Anonymous Sex:** Engaging in sex with anonymous partners; cruising beaches, parks, parking lots, rest rooms and baths; having one-night stands; participating in group sex.
4. **Paying For Sex:** Paying for sexually explicit phone calls; using an escort or phone service; paying someone for sexual activity; using personal columns to find sex partners; patronizing saunas, massage parlors, or rap lounges.
5. **Trading Sex:** Making sexually-explicit videotapes and photographs; posing for sexually explicit videotapes and photographs;

exposing yourself from stage or for hire; pimping others for sexual activities; receiving money for sexual activity; receiving drugs for sexual activity; administering drugs to force sexual activity.

6. **Voyeuristic Sex:** Using sexually-explicit magazines or videotapes; having collections of pornography at home or work; patronizing adult bookstores and strip shows; using binoculars or telescopes to watch people; looking through windows of apartments and houses; sexualizing others in public places; sexualizing materials not sexually explicit.
7. **Exhibitionist Sex:** Exposing yourself in public places, such as parks, streets and school yards; exposing yourself from your home or car; being sexual or dressing and undressing in public; using choice of clothing to expose yourself; belonging to a nudist club to find sex partners.
8. **Intrusive Sex:** Making inappropriate sexual advances or gestures; touching or fondling others without permission; using sexually-explicit stories, humor or language at inappropriate times or places; using power position (e.g., as professional, clergy, or employer) to exploit or be sexual with another person; forcing sexual activity on any person, including your spouse or partner.
9. **Pain Exchange:** Receiving physical harm or pain during sexual activity to intensify sexual pleasure; causing physical harm or pain to a partner to intensify sexual pleasure; willingly giving up power or acting out the victim role in sexual activity; using sexual aids to enhance sexual experience.
10. **Object Sex:** Masturbating with objects; cross-dressing to add to sexual pleasure; using fetishes as part of sexual rituals; engaging in sexual activity with animals.
11. **Sex With Children:** Sharing inappropriate sexual information with children; exposing children to adult sexual activities; forcing sexual

activity on a child within or without the family; engaging in sex with a consenting minor; watching child pornography.[2]

Dr. Carnes comments on these various addiction types: *Engaging in behaviors that fit within a specific behavioral type does not necessarily make a person a sex addict.* ***The pattern of loss of control does.*** *. . . Note, however, that few addicts focus on one behavioral type. Most mix three to four orientations and some as many as six or seven. Addicts always have a preference for some behaviors or combinations of behaviors over others.*[3]

You may be asking, "So what's the bottom line here? How is pornography related to sex addiction" Consider Dr. Carnes' further comments on this issue: *As a culture, we have extended tolerance of the pornography industry. Playboy and Penthouse have served to desensitize us to a large and extended "cottage industry" with gross annual revenues of somewhere between seven and ten billion dollars. We spend more on pornography in one year than the annual sales of the Coca-Cola corporation.*

The debate about pornography goes far beyond this book (Don't Call it Love). *But two highly relevant facts emerged from our study of sexual addiction. First, among all addicts surveyed, 90% of the men and 77% of the women reported pornography as significant to their addiction. Second, for some, the [financial] costs were staggering.*[4]

As you can see, virtually all types of sex addiction are tied to pornography in some way. Thus, porn addiction really is "sex addiction."

LEVELS OF PORN/SEX ADDICTION

Not only does the addict engage in various types of sexual behavior as illustrated in the 11 addiction categories above, but over time the behavior escalates in its intensity and severity of consequences for the addict and others. Remember, the mindbody seeks for a higher *peak experience* each successive time; the next time he craves a "sexual fix," the addict needs harder, higher levels of material or activity to achieve the same high.

Dr. Carnes identifies three levels or ranges of addictive behavior:

Level One: Sexual behaviors that much of today's society considers acceptable, including masturbation, heterosexual relationships, homosexual relationships, pornography and prostitution.

Level Two: Sexual behaviors that are generally regarded as a "nuisance." These include: exhibitionism, voyeurism, transvestism, bestiality, indecent phone calls, and indecent liberties. The public usually finds these to be sick, pathetic or obnoxious. When prosecuted, they may involve stiff legal penalties. The risk of discovery and arrest adds to the excitement for the addict, who finds that the exhilaration of level one activities are not enough.

Level Three: Sexual behaviors that are dangerous, abusive or life-threatening, including: incest, child molestation, sexual abuse of vulnerable adults and rape.[5]

One of the typical mistakes that addicts and others make is assuming that if the addict is *only* at level one, he doesn't really have a serious problem. Nothing could be further from the truth. Even if his behavior doesn't escalate to levels two or three, he is still powerless against his addiction. And the consequences of level-one behavior alone will prove to dominate and devastate his life.

THE DANGER WITH ASSIGNING "LEVELS OF ADDICTION"

Sex addiction therapists Dan Gray, Todd Olson and their colleagues believe that preaching *levels of addiction* theory can be harmful to addicts. Because addicts come from a highly guilt/shame-based family and personal history, for a therapist to say, "That guy over there is a level-one addict, but you are a level three!" only adds to his shame, and can push him deeper into his shell of addiction. It reinforces his already impaired thinking that says he is a "bad person." He thinks, "If I'm a level three, then I must really be a scum-bag."

On the other hand, categorizing addicts by levels can lull some of them into complacency and reinforce their denial. "If I'm only a level one, then I don't need help like those other sickos." One man who was attending a group therapy session for the first time (at the insistence of his wife) commented, "Well, I just look at pornography. These other guys go to strip bars and have affairs. I really don't think I need to be here." All levels of addiction are the same in that (1) they have placed the addict in the position of being out of control, powerless to resist, and (2) their families and friends are suffering the negative consequences of their addiction—regardless of how they've chosen to "act out" or at what "level" of addiction they are presently operating.

SEX ADDICTS GENERALLY SUFFER FROM OTHER ADDICTIONS

It is interesting to note that in a survey of sex addicts conducted by Dr. Carnes and his associates, less than 17% of respondents reported porn/sex as their only addiction. Dual addictions included:

- Chemical dependency 42%
- Eating disorders 38%
- Compulsive working 28%
- Compulsive spending 26%
- Compulsive gambling .... 5%[6]

Why is this so? Why would so many sex/porn addicts also suffer from other addictions? As confusing as this paradox may seem, leading therapists have told me that sex addiction is **not just about sex!** It's about relieving emotional pain, stress, shame, etc., and escaping the harsh realities of life by any means available: pornography, sex, drugs, alcohol, food, gambling, work, etc. Society must move beyond the flawed and simplistic paradigm that says, "The addict is an immoral person who must learn self-control." Just as the rigid moralistic approach to alcoholism doesn't work with alcoholics ("Just don't drink—control yourself!"), so it is with porn/sex addicts. It's interesting to note that virtually all recovering sex addicts with dual addictions have indicated that their porn/sex addiction was the most difficult of all to control and achieve a position of "sobriety." They also tend to agree that their porn/sex addiction was more debilitating and devastating to their lives than their other addictions. So much for the foolish joke that says, "If you're going to have an addiction, this [sex] is the one to have."

WHAT ARE THE SIGNS OF PORN/SEX ADDICTION?

How do you know if you or someone you love is a porn/sex addict? Of all the addictions, sex addiction is the most complex. In this regard Dr. Patrick Carnes remarks, "Sexually compulsive people challenge, and often confound, professional understanding because of their incredible diversity. Wealth, poverty, cross-dressing, bestiality, incest, affairs, various sexual preferences—man, woman, Hispanic, black, white, young, old, legal, and illegal. How to make sense of it?"[7]

While *Self Assessment* is not the complete answer to identifying sex addiction, it at least comprises a starting point and an effective initial indicator. Consider the following from SAA's website:

A Useful Tool For Self-Assessment

Answer these 13 questions to assess whether you may have a problem with sexual addiction:

1. *Do you keep secrets about your sexual [including pornography] or romantic activities from those important to you? Do you lead a double life?*
2. *Have your needs driven you to have sex [including masturbation] in places or situations or with people you would not normally choose?*

3. *Do you find yourself looking for sexually arousing articles or scenes in newspapers, magazines, or other media?*
4. *Do you find that romantic or sexual fantasies interfere with your relationships or are preventing you from facing problems?*
5. *Do you frequently want to get away from a sex partner after having sex?*
6. *Do you frequently feel remorse, shame, or guilt after a sexual encounter?*
7. *Do you feel shame about your body or your sexuality, such that you avoid touching your body or engaging in sexual relationships? Do you fear that you have no sexual feelings, that you are asexual?*
8. *Does each new relationship continue to have the same destructive patterns which prompted you to leave the last relationship?*
9. *Is it taking more variety and frequency of sexual [including pornography] and romantic activities than previously to bring the same levels of excitement and relief?*
10. *Have you ever been arrested or are you in danger of being arrested because of your practices of voyeurism, exhibitionism, prostitution, sex with minors, indecent phone calls, etc.?*
11. *Does your pursuit of sex [including pornography] or romantic relationships interfere with your spiritual beliefs or development?*
12. *Do your sexual activities include the risk, threat, or reality of disease, pregnancy, coercion, or violence?*
13. *Has your sexual or romantic behavior ever left you feeling hopeless, alienated from others, or suicidal?*

If you answered yes to more than one of these questions, we would encourage you to seek out additional literature as a resource or to attend a Sex Addicts Anonymous meeting to further assess your needs.[8]

In addition to the above exercise, Dr. Patrick Carnes, in his profound book *Contrary to Love: Healing the Sexual Addict*, offers his **Sexual Addiction Screening Test (SAST):**

(Keep in mind as you consider the questions that "sexual behavior" and "sexual activity" include pornography and masturbation.)

1. *Were you sexually abused as a child or adolescent?*
2. *Have you subscribed or regularly purchased sexually explicit magazines like Playboy or Penthouse [or sexually explicit material on the Internet]?*
3. *Do your parents have trouble with sexual behavior?*
4. *Do you often find yourself preoccupied with sexual thoughts?*
5. *Do you feel that your sexual behavior is not normal?*
6. *Does your spouse [or significant other(s)] ever worry or complain about your sexual behavior?*
7. *Do you have trouble stopping your sexual behavior when you know it is inappropriate?*
8. *Do you ever feel bad about your sexual behavior?*
9. *Has your sexual behavior ever created problems for you or your family?*
10. *Have you ever sought help for sexual behavior you did not like?*
11. *Have you ever worried about people finding out about your sexual activities [including pornography viewing]?*
12. *Has anyone been hurt emotionally because of your sexual behavior?*
13. *Are any of your sexual activities against the law?*
14. *Have you made promises to yourself to quit some aspect of your sexual behavior?*

15. *Have you made efforts to quit a type of sexual activity and failed?*
16. *Do you have to hide some of your sexual behavior from others?*
17. *Have you attempted to stop some parts of your sexual activity?*
18. *Have you ever felt degraded by your sexual behavior?*
19. *Has sex [cybersex or pornography] been a way for you to escape your problems?*
20. *When you have sex [cybersex or view pornography] do you feel depressed afterwards?*
21. *Have you felt the need to discontinue a certain form of sexual activity?*
22. *Has your sexual activity interfered with your family life?*
23. *Have you been sexual with minors?*
24. *Do you feel controlled by your sexual desire?*
25. *Do your ever think your sexual desire is stronger than you are?*[9]

When respondents to the SAST answered *yes* to 13 or more of the questions, Dr. Carnes and his colleagues found a 96.5% incidence of addiction. Although this should not be construed as an all-inclusive method of addiction identification, it does offer the reader a place to begin.

Note: Dr. Carnes openly admits that the SAST does not effectively address the needs of women. A number of female addicts have taken the test and, while helpful, the reliability of the results was poor when compared to those of male addicts.[10] As therapists come to understand more clearly the intricacies of female sexual addiction, more effective screening methods hopefully will be developed. I am certain that a major emphasis in developing these methods will involve studies of female cybersex chat addiction and the unique characteristics of the female brain.

Dr. Carnes also found in his survey of sex addicts that they experienced many losses as a result of their additive behavior. Among these, ten were rated by addicts as the most painful. Listed in order of severity, these losses include:

- Loss of primary relationship
- Loss of children (through abortion, deaths, and loss of custody disputes)
- Loss of significant friends
- Unavailability to children (including neglect)
- Financial losses
- Guilt at having hurt others (including victims, sex partners and spouses)
- Loss of productivity and creativity
- Career losses
- Loss of integrity (including violations of personal values)
- Loss of self-esteem[11]

WHY SELF-ASSESSMENT OFTEN FAILS: THE PORN/SEX ADDICT'S WORLD OF SECRECY

Because most porn/sex addicts keep their addiction a "secret" at all costs, they initially deny that they have a problem and go to elaborate ends to hide their condition. Under these circumstances, self-assessment or assessment by family and friends is virtually impossible. Consider Dr. Carnes comments regarding this secrecy issue: *The addictive system uses secrecy as a shield, and as such it becomes a source of power. The addiction thrives on secrecy because the addict can often avoid public consequences and family confrontations. However, the sense of being alone with the secret increases the addict's despair. . . .*

Therapists often work with clients a long time without seeing the shadow of addiction. The therapist ends up feeling frustrated about spending so many hours working on the presenting auxiliary problems, marital issues for example, without ever reaching the real source of the turmoil. To the addict's family and close friends, something appears to be wrong—that faint, wavering shadow of the addiction—but often they cannot tell what that something is.

As a sexual addict, Frank told his therapy group that his addictive life was virtually undetectable because, feeling so ashamed, he worked hard to appear normal, pursuing activities in church leadership that made him seem normal and upright. Ironically, he was serving on an antipornography committee that same day he lied to a prostitute about his name and occupation so she wouldn't know who he was.[12]

An important part of treatment provided by the therapists at S.T.A.R. of Salt Lake City, is helping addicts understand the role shame plays in the addictive process. Much of the shame experienced by individuals addicted to sex/pornography originates from two core beliefs: (1) "I am basically a bad and unworthy person," and (2) "People would not accept me if they knew me as I really am (knew about my 'secret' addiction/ life)." Addicts will oftentimes experience this shame as part of a cycle. In there groundbreaking book *Facing Shame: Families In Recovery*, pages.110-112, Merle Fossum and Marilyn Mason describe this cycle in terms of the *release phase* and the *control phase*.

- **The Release Phase:** In the release phase the addict "loses" himself to the addiction. He becomes self-centered and self-indulgent. His use of pornography and/or sex represents an escape from the emotional and/or psychological stressors that plague him. In the release phase he reaches a point where he relinquishes control to his addiction and feels a relaxation of his conscious will. He enters the "acting out" part of the release phase which manifests his "addict-self" and his addictive behavior unfolds in secrecy without the knowledge of others.

  While experiencing this sense of temporary escape from fears, troubles and stress, at the same time the addict also is aware that on a fundamental level he has violated his basic values and self-respect. He has demeaned himself which in turn creates a great deal of shame. The addict then begins to rationalize and justify his behavior in order to cover the shame and reduce its intensity. He vows that he will never again fall prey to his addiction. This is the beginning of the *Control Phase.*

- **The Control Phase:** During the Release Phase, the addict's life has reached a point of unmanageability. His greatest concern now is to regain control, leave the "addict self" (secret self) and return to his "public self." He must never again allow his addiction to overcome him. This control will typically manifest itself in compulsive behaviors such as becoming a workaholic, compulsive cleaning, rigid dieting or dietary practices. Addicts may also become invasive and excessive in their efforts to help others or have a need to "save" someone in a religious sense. Just as the addict experienced a total loss of control in the Release Phase, the pendulum swings to the complete opposite as he seeks to gain total control over every aspect of his life and others lives. This type of behavior in the Control Phase is often referred to as *acting in.*

Because shame is at the center of this control-release cycle, it makes the control phase more demanding, requiring the addict to become extremely rigid in order to hide his shame and his addiction. No one must ever find out about his "secret." He becomes "super-righteous," a "super-achiever," a perfectionist that often carries control of self and others to excess. He may take on qualities of fanaticism, espousing social, political or religious beliefs in an excessive and potentially hurtful fashion. Consequently, his personality traits become more harmful and self-defeating—(there is no way he can maintain this level of intensity.) The addict becomes critical of himself and others. He may appear self-righteous and overbearing. Small things may irritate him and he may become blaming. On the other end of the control spectrum, the addict may become a pleaser and placater, avoiding conflict and trying to gain the approval of others. This is a form of "passive" control.

Regrettably, the more intensely the addict tries to control, the more he drives himself to the "breaking point" where he seeks self-medication and "release" through his addiction. Thus, the insidious cycle continues: The more self-destructively the addict releases, the deeper and more out of control grows his addiction. The more intense his addiction becomes, the more desperately he seeks control to compensate. The downward spiral of release to control and back to release continues until some catastrophe or crisis brings him to divulge his "secret" and seek help.[13]

"WHY WON'T ANYONE BELIEVE ME?"—ONE WIFE'S BATTLE WITH HER HUSBAND'S "SECRET ADDICTION"

A recent and ongoing experience of a friend illustrates the extreme difficulty and frustration of dealing with a porn/sex addict who is highly skilled at disguising and/or concealing his addiction: For privacy purposes, I will refer to my friend as "Diane" and her husband as "Dave." For many years Diane had been perplexed by Dave's behavior—highly controlling, extreme mood swings, demanding perfection of self and family, workaholic, wanting sex but giving no affection or romance, demanding demeaning and bizarre sex acts, isolated. In addition, he was spending a lot of time away from the family (especially when things "got too stressful"). He appeared to be the perfect husband and father when in public, but he was quite a different man at home.

Dave's odd behavior pointed directly to the addiction cycle. (Remember the "public-self" in the Control Phase?) Add to this the fact that he was severely abused as a child, was introduced to pornography at the age of five and was a full-blown porn addict as a teenager. He also acted out sexually as a teenager in unhealthy ways such as participating in orgies.

A couple of years ago Dave confessed to sleeping with a prostitute on a business trip to Las Vegas, but insisted that it was only a "one-time slip" and that it would never happen again. He insisted that Diane was the source of their marital problems and that if she would be a better sex partner, more effective around the home, etc., their marriage would be fine. It didn't take a rocket scientist to add up all this information and predict with near certainty that Dave had an addiction of some kind—most likely a porn/sex addiction. He may not have currently been *acting out* (which is highly unlikely, given the signs), but he was obviously *acting in* and deeply engulfed in the control phase.

Dave's "secrecy" techniques and controlling behavior were very typical of the Control Phase. He had become an "amateur psychiatrist" reading all the books and constantly "diagnosing" Diane's problems and advising her how to overcome them. Dave and Diane have been to numerous marital counselors, sessions that surprisingly, always ended up focusing all the attention, diagnosis and remedies squarely on Diane. Dave is the ultimate "actor on stage" and manipulates every counselor with whom they have visited. After all, he's a successful businessman, he gives service in the community, he is respected and admired by their friends—what more could she ask for? He's truly a wonderful man; just talk with him for a few minutes and you can tell right off how concerned he is about his wife and children. So the problem must obviously be with Diane, or so he wants everyone to believe.

The problem with porn/sexual addiction is that it's the "stealth" addiction, the "silent killer." There are no needle marks, no hangovers, no obvious physical signs. On the other hand, there are a host of emotional and behavioral signs that an experienced porn/sex addiction therapist can discern and identify. (None of the counselors Dave and Diane saw were experienced in this area.)

So how does Diane explain to these counselors about Dave's mood swings, bizarre sex requests, control, isolation, depression, etc.? How can she possibly define the "feeling" she gets that sometimes he's looking at her like she's an object rather than a person? She just ends up sounding like the proverbial nagging wife who is obsessed with picking at the little things. Her husband works hard, provides for his family and is respected in the community—why doesn't she just stop complaining and be grateful for what she has? Why can't she lower her expectations to a reasonable level? If she was more open and comfortable about sex, her marriage would improve (these are all bits of wisdom she has received from counselors).

Diane has come to believe that perhaps there is something wrong with her. Perhaps her expectations are too high. Maybe if she would perform better sexually the marriage would improve. If only she could cook better or clean more thoroughly, be more cheerful, lose a little weight or do her hair differently—be more like the woman that Dave wants—then he might change. But it seems the harder she tries, the worse he gets. Her husband's secrecy has everyone fooled (including the counselors they met with, none of whom are experienced in treating sexual addiction) and Diane doesn't know who to turn to for answers.

How this situation will turn out is uncertain. Fortunately, I am acquainted with therapists who specialize in treating various kinds of addiction, including porn/sex addiction. Without really knowing why he and his wife are going, Dave has agreed to meet with one of these therapists. The outcome of the session is unpredictable. In the presence of a skilled therapist, Dave's addiction may be unmasked; or he may become angry and storm out of the meeting; refusing to reveal his charade; or he may simply lie his way through the session. It will most likely take a crisis for Dave to end his denial and secrecy: a moment of truth with the therapist, an instance where Diane catches him viewing pornography; a time when he is arrested for sexually acting out, or the threat of divorce.

The point is, there are many spouses out there who feel like no one believes them, or understands what they are going through or who feel like they're just going insane. They may be like Diane and sense that something is wrong but are unable to uncover exactly what that something is. They may be aware that their spouse looks at porn or goes to strip bars, but discount it as "no big deal." Or their husband may be open and even arrogant about acting out sexually, yet the wife desperately holds onto the marriage anyway. Whatever the circumstances, when spouses of addicts come to understand that they themselves are usually **co-addicts**—addicted to their husband's (or wife's) addiction, obsessed with his or her obsession—this realization often unlocks the door to understanding, recovery and ultimate sanity.

Key Points

A reference tool for spouses, parents, clergy, counselors and others

- While there are many categories of sexual addiction, there is a common denominator in all of them—the majority of sex addicts report pornography as significant to their addiction.
- There are progressive levels of porn/sex addiction. However, any level of addiction places the addict in a position of being out of control and their loved ones suffer the negative consequences of the addictive behavior.
- Because porn/sex addiction is about more than sex and pornography (it's about escape, medicating pain, etc.), addicts often suffer from other addictions as well. This is why treating the *cause* and not just the outward behavior is so very important.
- Porn/sex addiction can be diagnosed. However, because most addicts keep their addiction a secret at all costs, and are usually in denial, self-assessment or assessment by family members and others can be very difficult or virtually impossible.
- The *Control Phase* and *Release Phase* of porn/sex addiction keep the addict in a downward spiral until some catastrophe or crisis brings him to divulge his secret and seek help.
- Because porn/sex addiction can be a "stealth" addiction, the addict's spouse and family can go years knowing something is wrong but being unable to discern exactly what it is.

32

Spouses of Porn/Sex Addicts are Usually Co-Addicts

Sexual co-addiction is a disease with effects that can be as devastating as sexual addiction itself. In his book *Contrary to Love,* Dr. Patrick Carnes speaks extensively about co-addiction. In one section he states:

Co-addicts also face dependency issues. Along with the addict they believe they cannot depend on others to meet their needs, so they go to great lengths to try to guarantee the relationship. Co-addicts, for example, will become super-responsible and reliable to make sure they are indispensable. They may take over more and more household chores as the addict becomes increasingly irresponsible. . . .

Co-addicts create dependency without realizing it. The woman who says "Having him around is like having another child" probably finds it easier to be close to someone who depends on her than to be intimate with an equal. And concentrating on the addict allows the co-addict to ignore his or her own problems. Thus, intimacy and dependency issues combine to keep the co-addict focused on the addict.

Dealing with the sexual addict becomes the principal life task of the co-addict. The problem takes center stage.

Because sexuality is so personal and so vital to relationships, co-addicts can be seriously damaged. Just as an alcoholic's spouse feels blamed for the alcoholism, co-addicts feel that having a spouse who is sexually out of control is a statement about themselves. Co-addicts doubt their attractiveness, their sexuality, their masculinity or their femininity. They develop performance anxiety because they believe there must be something sexually wrong with them.[1]

How Do You Know If You Are a Co-addict?

The following observations and accompanying questions have proven helpful in identifying sexual co-addiction:

1. Symptoms of sexual issues in your primary relationship may be: sleeping too much, losing sleep, eating poorly, overeating, or increasing use of chemicals.

2. Do you focus more on your partner's sexual attitudes, beliefs or needs than on your own?

3. Are you aware of trying to control your partner's sexual actions or thoughts? Are you aware of how this may be affecting you?

4. Does sex play an all-consuming role in your relationship?

5. Do you give in to the sexual demands of your partner even if they turn you off?

6. Do you use sex to try to repair the relationship when it is strained (e.g., by health issues, money matters or business setbacks, etc.)?

7. Do you feel empty after having sex?

8. Do you seldom or never experience contented intimacy, trust or commitment with your partner?

9. Do you think everything would be "OK" if only you have perfect sex?

10. Do you compare your body and feel inadequate to those of persons in magazines, films, advertising and other media?
11. Do you neglect your own wants or those of your family to comply with the sexual desires of your partner?
12. Do you withdraw emotionally or have your mind on other things while having sex?
13. Do you engage in sexual activities with your partner that you are uncomfortable with or ashamed of?
14. Do you entertain the thought, "I'm not enough of a man or woman for my partner"?
15. Do you find sex uncomfortable versus being pleasurable?
16. Do you get accused of or feel that you are "old-fashioned" or "not with the times" sexually?
17. Have you read a number of sex "how to" books for yourself or at the request of your partner so you could perform better sexually?
18. Do you believe that you have to put up with certain behaviors that are repulsive to you in order to keep your partner?
19. Do you have a constant fear that your partner will leave?
20. Do you find it difficult or impossible to express to your partner your sexual needs and desires?
21. Do you feel that your partner does not sincerely try to meet your needs?
22. Do you lie about your sexual feelings or reactions in order to please your partner (e.g., "faking orgasms")?
23. Are you embarrassed to speak of your sexual behaviors with another person or a professional counselor?[2]

If you suspect or know that your partner is a porn/sex addict and you answered "yes" to many of the above questions, you may be suffering from the disease known as *co-addiction*. Just as the sex addict lives in denial and finds it excruciatingly difficult to admit he has a "problem," so it is most often with the co-addict.

COSA (Codependents of Sex Addicts), an organization that has devised a 12-step program for co-addicts similar to that of SAA for addicts, released this telling statement concerning co-addiction: *One of the most difficult aspects of codependency is admitting our powerlessness over the addict. Our continual attempts to affect or control the sex addict render our lives unmanageable.*[3]

In their brochure *It's not your fault the one you love uses porn*, the *National Coalition for the Protection of Children & Families* (NCPCF) offers insights, guidelines and hope for those with spouses who use pornography. Much of the following information is a modification of some sections of the brochure. To learn more, please visit NCPCF's website at www.nationalcoalition.org.

Whatever You're Feeling Is OK

Once you discover that your spouse has a problem with pornography, it's normal to enter a period of denial to block the pain and devastation. After the initial shock, you probably feel some or all of these emotions: inadequate, deceived, isolated, rejected, angry, responsible, shameful, betrayed, loss of relationship, sadness, desperation, confusion, severe disappointment, fear of being alone.

As you experience these emotions, the following guidelines can help:

DON'T

- Accept blame/responsibility—it's not your fault.
- Don't criticize or accuse your spouse using "you" statements: "You're sick." "You're irresponsible and unreliable."
- Keep silent or secret: this will only enable your spouse's behavior.

- Protect him/her by accepting responsibility for their recovery and your relationship.
- Present vague suspicions or premature conclusions like: "You're a porn/sex addict, aren't you?" This only increases defensiveness and leads to more deception/secrecy on the part of the addict.
- Violate trust and confidentiality by telling family and friends about your spouse's problem.

Do

- Avoid taking responsibility for your spouse's behavior.
- Use "I" or "we" statements: "I'm confused about our sex life . . ." "We're drifting apart . . ." "I worry about you when you're late . . ."
- Talk about the signs of the problem, focusing on your spouse's behaviors and your reaction to them: "I've noticed . . . and this makes me feel . . ."
- Be honest and caring.
- Let him/her speak and vent.
- Reassure that you love him/her but want them to seek help.

Taking Action

In order to recover from addiction and co-addiction, you and your spouse must seek counseling, both as a couple and individually. A counselor can help you set guidelines or "boundaries" from which you can build a healthy relationship. These boundaries are not to punish or control, but to help you establish acceptable behavior within your relationship. These boundaries could include:

- You will only work on the relationship if your spouse is willing to do their part.

- Make sure your spouse knows the consequences of violating the boundaries.
- Stop rescuing and enabling him/her, this only perpetuates the problem. Don't cover for him/her or make excuses.
- Avoid withdrawing from the relationship as an act of revenge. It's OK to stop trusting for now, but forgiveness should be your goal.
- Don't give in to his/her sexual demands. You have the right to refuse sex, but don't use sex to manipulate.

Also Keep in Mind

- Addressing the behavior and treating the *cause* are two different things. The core cause of pornography use must be identified and treated in order to permanently change the behavior.
- You have the right to feel anger or any other emotion. Allow yourself to feel in order to heal.
- Don't shame or punish your spouse by withholding sex, embarrassing him/her in front of others, having an affair, threatening to leave and take the kids, etc.
- You are vulnerable. Don't give in to the temptation of letting him/her off the hook for the sake of staying together.
- Pornography use is often only one piece of the addiction puzzle—your spouse may be involved in other forms of compulsive sexual behavior, or other addictive behaviors.
- Obtain a medical exam for yourself. You may be at risk for a sexually transmitted disease.
- Be thoughtful and careful about what and how you communicate with your children about the problem.
- There is **HOPE!**

You May Need To Leave

You always have the option to leave the relationship. If your spouse refuses to get help, his/her porn use can quickly turn into serious addiction. If left untreated, you risk:

- Emotional abandonment or neglect.
- Physical and/or sexual abuse.
- Contracting sexually transmitted diseases, such as AIDS.
- Your children's physical safety and psychological health.
- Financial difficulty, credit problems, etc.

"Hang In There"

Don't give up. Recovery takes time. Don't expect too much too soon, from yourself or your spouse. Concentrate on your own personal and spiritual development. Nurturing yourself and taking care of you is your number one priority.

Finding a Competent Counselor and Effective Recovery Program

Whether a person is a porn/sex addict or a co-addict, their life will continue to spiral out of control unless and until they seek **help**. Just as virtually every recovering alcoholic has learned the hard way that they cannot overcome their illness "on their own," so it is with porn/sex addicts and co-addicts. But where does one find competent and effective help?

In his letter to me, Dr. Victor Cline asserted:

. . . There are no training programs in traditional medical schools, graduate schools of psychology or social work that deal with this kind of addictive problem. And while this will undoubtedly change in the next few years, anyone now seeking professional help will need to check very carefully the background experience of any therapists that they might choose to treat them.

What you are looking for is a "sex addiction therapist" from any of the mental health healing disciplines who has a good track record in treating this problem and personal values that are reasonably congruent with the patient's values. . . .

Fortunately, Dr. Cline introduced me to professional group of preeminent porn/sex addiction and co-addiction therapists, including Dan Gray, Todd Olson and their colleagues at S.T.A.R. (Sexual Trauma and Recovery). In a three-hour recorded interview, and through 18 hours of the psycho-education program I attended, they were gracious enough to walk me through an addiction recovery program. Chapter 33 contains highlights from that interview. I offer this overview that the reader might gain an understanding of how a truly competent and effective recovery program might be structured. Hopefully this will allow the reader to avoid counselors, therapists and programs that may not be effective or are not porn/sex-addiction specific. While truly great porn/sex-addiction therapists may have their own unique treatment approach, you will find that they all utilize a similar set of foundational principles, techniques and philosophies.

Key Points

A reference tool for
spouses, parents, clergy,
counselors and others

- The spouses of porn/sex addicts virtually always suffer from some level of **co-addiction** and require counseling and therapy right along with their addicted spouse.
- Discovering that a spouse is a porn/sex addict can be painful and devastating. However, following specific steps, while working with a counselor/therapist and a support group, the victimized spouse can regain a normal, healthy life.
- The spouse should set and enforce specific boundaries for their porn/sex addicted partner. If the addict consistently violates these boundaries and/or the spouse feels that their emotional/ physical health and safety are in jeopardy, they may find it necessary to leave the relationship.

33

What Should a Porn/Sex Addiction Recovery Program Look Like?

To begin with, STAR and all of the other therapists I spoke with or read about, integrated their recovery programs with a **12-Step Program** developed from AA's enormously successful 12 steps. Here is the 12-step program used by Sex Addicts Anonymous (SAA):

- We admitted we were powerless over addictive sexual behavior—that our lives had become unmanageable.
- We came to believe that a Power greater than ourselves could restore us to sanity.
- We made a decision to turn our will and our lives over to the care of God as we understood God.
- We made a searching and fearless moral inventory of ourselves.
- We admitted to God, to ourselves, and to another human being the exact nature of our wrongs.
- We were entirely ready to have God remove all these defects of character.

- We humbly asked God to remove our shortcomings.
- We made a list of all persons we had harmed and became willing to make amends to them all.
- We made direct amends to such people wherever possible, except when to do so would injure them or others.
- We continued to take personal inventory and when we were wrong promptly admitted it.
- We sought through prayer and meditation to improve our conscious contact with God as we understood God, praying only for knowledge of God's will for us and the power to carry that out.
- Having had a spiritual awakening as the result of these steps, we tried to carry this message to other sex addicts and to practice these principles in our lives.[1]

Note: During the interview the S.T.A.R. group indicated that most of their patients participate in weekly SAA group meetings **in addition to and in conjunction with** the S.T.A.R. therapy program. The spouses of addicts also participate in the SAA group meetings as "co-addicts."

* * *

(All content from this point through the end of the chapter may not be reproduced or copied in any way without the express permission of the S.T.A.R. group.)[2] Acknowledgment is given to Dr. Martha Turner, the creator of S.T.A.R.

The S.T.A.R. program is divided into **three phases**:

1. **Beginnings**
2. **Implementation of Recovery Plan**
3. **Treating the "Cause"**

(Please note that the spouses of porn/sex addicts participate in each of the following three phases of recovery right along with their husband or wife. This is very helpful to the recovery of the addict and the healing of the marriage/family. In addition to group sessions, individual therapy sessions may be carried out with the couple, with the addict alone, or with the spouse. In certain circumstances, the children may also receive individual counseling.)

PHASE I—*BEGINNINGS*

Porn/sex addiction recovery does not happen over night—it must take place in a phased approach. Because addicts hold so much shame and guilt inside, coming out of hiding and revealing their "secret" can be frightening. Because addicts often grow up in rigid, shame-based families or in families with no boundaries, creating feelings of abandonment, they often find it difficult to trust others. This creates an ideological battleground between the addict and the therapist:

Addict: "If I listen to this therapist or I start this program, I will lose my way of life—no more freedom, all kinds of restrictions and rules. Besides, I've never been able to trust anyone, why should I trust this guy? I'll have to give up my *drug of choice*—the thing I use to deal with stress and pain and panic in my life. I'll just get over this thing on my own. I don't need to involve anyone else. Besides, if anyone knew about all of this, then they'd really know what a loser and pervert I am." The addict already believes he is a bad and unworthy person, but for him to articulate his behavior in public and expose his "secret" life is worse than death.

Therapist: The therapist wants to help the addict assess the seriousness of his or her problem and cut off the process of denial by tackling such issues as: "What behaviors are you into and what is the frequency? What are the areas of your life that have become unmanageable? What are the consequences of your actions, the price you are paying for your behaviors? Do you realize that you are powerless to resist—you still keep doing stupid things regardless of the consequences? Do you realize how much you are giving up for your addiction—relationships with spouse and children, job, money, success, time, health, happiness? If you don't get some help, you're going to lose everything. You must come out of hiding and learn to trust others."

Thus is waged the battle of "secrecy, denial, distrust and isolation" vs. "openness, honesty, trust and reaching out for help."

Creating a "Safe" Environment For the Addict

In order to win this battle, the therapist must offer the addict an opportunity to "come out of the closet" and share his story with others in a safe environment, one of unconditional acceptance, empathy and understanding. This cannot happen all at once—"tell us your deepest darkest secrets right now." Rather, it begins with baby-steps: a measure of education, small break-out sessions, videos, art therapy—all low-risk, "safe" activities. Once he breaks the ice and gets to know other addicts, he is ready for more intimate, higher-risk communication and sharing. In fact, the S.T.A.R. group doesn't even require participants to disclose what their addiction is in the *Beginnings* phase, which lasts six weeks with 18 total hours of interaction, all geared to the addict's pace.

Addicts have learned to remain "out of touch" with their feelings. They have shut off their self-assessment and internal feedback mechanisms. They have issues they feel are just too painful to deal with. This "shutting off" of emotions and feelings is a self-preservation tactic. So in the *Beginnings* phase, addicts are encouraged to disclose themselves at very simple levels: "How am I feeling emotionally? How am I feeling physically, spiritually?" This lets the addict begin to get in touch with the inner-self that he has sealed off in the past. These simple exercises also prepare the addict for more intense self-disclosure in later phases.

After becoming comfortable and feeling safe in the *Beginnings* phase, many addicts make comments to the effect: *The thing I feared most was my "secret" being discovered by others and the "real" me being exposed. But instead of seeing shock, judgement and rejection on the faces of the other group members, I was supported, accepted and encouraged to share more!*

This sort of self-disclosure is a powerful and important experience for the addict to undergo early on in the recovery process. The feeling of "I'm not alone. There are others like me and I feel okay about them, so they must feel okay about me, so I must be okay!"

Addicts often express a mixture of relief and surprise their "deep, dark awful secrets" are not met with harsh judgement and abandonment—the very reactions they experienced as a child. But when they find acceptance, understanding and total support, it's a miracle and they're on the road to healing and recovery. When walking into a group session for the first time addicts find, to their amazement, that the room isn't filled with a bunch of "perverts and sleaze-bags." Many think, "Wow, these are just like the people I work with, go to church with and am neighbors with—good, decent, respected individuals!" Suddenly the addict doesn't feel so bad because he is in the presence of other "good" people who are struggling with the same problems that he is. Thus the addict's core beliefs, his impaired thinking that says, "I'm a worthless person" begins to change.

Developing a Community of Support

Instead of "I will do this on my own," which is where the addict has failed in the past, the attitude slowly shifts to "we will do this together and succeed." In the past the addict's mind-set has been "my needs will never be met if I have to depend on others." Community support through group therapy forces the addict to rely on others. Group therapy is the most successful approach because it takes the addict out of the isolated, closed-off world that feeds his addiction and brings him into a community where he can **regain** trust, companionship, honesty and reinforcement. The addict also is strengthened by **accountability**, in that the group becomes linked, cohesive and learns to check up on one another.

The two most difficult hurdles for addicts to get over are *setting boundaries* and *accountability*. In the group environment, they can finally feel "safe enough" to set boundaries (by replacing old addictive habits with healthy alternatives they can pursue with structure and purpose), and to be accountable. This is a far cry from the old addiction cycle that said, "I'm not accountable to anyone and I don't have any boundaries."

During phase one (*Beginnings*) the addict is guided through the process of creating a *recovery plan*. In phase two, this recovery plan is implemented.

The above description of phase one is greatly abbreviated and simplified. To give the reader an idea of just how complex, specialized and involved porn/sex addiction therapy and recovery are, consider the full overview of the S.T.A.R. group's phase one or *Beginnings* program:

- Discussion of Addiction
  - Definition
  - Cycle
  - Behaviors
- Set-ups for Addiction
- Eleven Behavioral Types
- Defining Bottom Line Behavior
- Life Impact/Unmanageability
- Family Genogram
- Family Sculpture
- Family Roles
- Systems, Shame, Dysfunction and Obsession
- Shame Cycle
- Understanding Powerlessness
- Triggers
- Sexual Co-dependency
- What is Co-Addiction?

- Nine Characteristics of Co-Addiction
- The Withdrawal Experience
- Definitions and Types of Abuse
- Boundaries:
  - Definition
  - Visualization
  - Creation: Both External and Internal
- Affirmations
- Guided Imagery
- Using the Tools of Recovery
- Development of a Model for Recovery:
  - Pitfalls: Avoiding the Extremes
  - Maintenance and Support
- Creation of Treatment Plans

PHASE II—*IMPLEMENTATION OF RECOVERY PLAN*

In phase two the addict learns to extinguish the addictive behavior by implementing his or her own unique recovery plan created in phase one. While phase three will uncover and seek to cure the "causes" of the addictive behavior, phase two helps the addict get control of his or her life so that the addiction and shame cycles cease spiraling downward. Phase two teaches the addict how to replace addiction rituals with healthy rituals that create "life-balance"—spiritually, physically, emotionally, socially, etc. Phase two provides the addict with a daily plan that he or she can follow to "deal with everyday life" without turning to the medication of addiction. The addict learns daily, healthy rituals and activities that establish sobriety. In fact, the S.T.A.R. group doesn't permit an addict to enter phase three unless and until he has been sober for at least 30 days. When the emotional trauma and shame contributing to addiction are uncovered in phase three, it can be an extremely painful experience. The addict is rediscovering and allowing himself to experience emotions and feelings that he has been suppressing, masking and medicating for many years. When these are suddenly uncovered, if the addict has not yet learned to control his addictive behavior and achieved sobriety, he will immediately turn to "self-medication" to relieve the stress and pain.

Recognizing the "Triggers" of Addictive Behavior

One of the focal points of phase two is to help the addict identify, recognize and avoid the "triggers" that lead to acting out their addictive behaviors. Triggers are the *early warning signs* that the addict is heading down the path to acting out. In the initial stages of recovery therapy, most sex/porn addicts describe the *wave* or *trance* they felt as they plunged headlong into acting out their addiction, an overwhelming feeling, an uncontrollable influence that suddenly comes over them out of nowhere and guides them down into the bottom of the funnel. When logic, reason and presence of mind return, the addict finds that once again he or she has acted out—"It suddenly hit me and before I knew what was happening I had spent three hours looking at Internet porn," or "I was coming out of the strip bar having spent the entire afternoon inside" or "I was getting dressed after another one-night stand."

What the addict learns in phase two is that this *wave* or *trance* doesn't "suddenly come over them out of nowhere for no reason." This is an *illusion*. The reality is they had been gradually sliding down the funnel toward acting out for some time—hours, days, weeks or even months beforehand. When the wave or trance finally hits them, it's not "all of a sudden," but the result of a succession of circumstances, events and decisions. The wave or trance is part of the *preoccupation phase* of addiction. The addict must learn the *triggers* that plunge him into this phase.

The following is a list of triggers that can lead an addict down the funnel to acting out.

Triggers

I. Sensory Triggers

A. Visual Triggers

1. The human body or parts of it
2. Someone who reminds us of a person we have been addicted to in real life, porn images or fantasies
3. Magazine covers in grocery stores, newspapers, catalogues, billboards, TV, movies, and other media featuring men or women in sexual and non-sexual settings
4. Articles of clothing like underwear, bathing suits or even outerwear
5. A "Raincheck" kind of look from another person

B. Sound Triggers

1. Music—songs that spawn addictive feelings or have played in the background of pornographic Internet sites, videos, etc.
2. Voice—a certain tone or quality in someone's voice

C. Touch Triggers

1. Hugs
2. Handshakes
3. Touch on an area of the shoulder

D. Scent Triggers

1. Cologne or aftershave associated with someone we have been addicted to
2. A cologne or aftershave we wore when we were addicted or when we acted out.

II. Situations

A. Disappointed expectations

B. Receiving a compliment from a man or woman—whichever sex we are addicted to

C. Someone acting in a loving way towards us (compassion, kindness, thoughtfulness)

D. Emotional intimacy

E. Being criticized—especially when this is perceived as unfair

F. "I have done something I regret"—committing a mistake or violating one's values

G. Being with parents or siblings

H. Being shamed

I. Being in a victimizing situation

J. B.L.A.H.S.T. (feeling Bored, Lonely, Angry, Hungry, Stressed or Tired)

III. Emotional Triggers

A. Shame over one's past life history

B. Feeling lonely or unloved

C. Feeling abandoned

D. Inner-child associations

E. Feeling inadequate about everything one does

F. Not being perfect

G. Roots of co-dependency

H. Needing to make a good impression

I. Anger and rage

J. Feeling good ("I don't deserve to feel this good.")

K. Stress

L. Not dealing directly with feelings—a feeling that's not identified and not dealt with honestly and appropriately

M. Feelings which cause shame because we are "not allowed to have those feelings"

IV. Other Possible Triggers

A. Dreams

B. Fantasies

C. Places—parent's home, homes of people to whom we have been addicted, certain parts of town, driving past strip bars, adult bookstores, being in office or den where computer is located, etc.

D. Activities

- Cruising
- Looking—"girl-watching/guy-watching"
- "Rainchecks"

After years of acting out, addictive behavior becomes automatic or robotic. Remember, the mindbody seeks efficiency and habit so it can free its resources to focus on achieving new and higher "peak experiences." If a trigger for an addict is *stress*, and the mindbody has learned that the most efficient way to deal with stress is to immediately enter the *preoccupation phase* and start down the funnel, then the next thing the addict knows, he is acting out his addiction—automatically, without even thinking! It's like taking the same route home from work everyday. Sometimes your mind is preoccupied and suddenly there you are, pulling into your driveway and thinking, "I don't even remember driving home. Where did the time go?"

In phase two the addict learns to recognize his or her triggers and then to *consciously* **interrupt the mindbody's automatic response**. New cellular-memories and pathways must be created and accessed until they become efficient and automatic, replacing the old addictive cellular-memory pathways. In phase two this is referred to as *awareness and interruption techniques* or *consciousness and manageability*. In the past, unaware of the triggers leading up to acting out, the addict perceived that the wave or trance hit him without warning and he had no choice but to give in. By learning new techniques, the addict regains his or her **choice-point**—that point at which he or she can decide whether or not to start down the funnel to acting out.

Setting Limits and Boundaries

Once an addict identifies his triggers, he must then learn to recognize when these triggers are present. This is accomplished when he learns to pay attention, to be conscious of his own mindbody physiology—emotions, feelings, sensations, etc. Without summoning this awareness, triggers are activated and the addict's physiology changes enough to start him sliding down the funnel, where he loses all logic, reason and sense of values and the mindbody goes into automatic response or "survival mode," which consists of the acting out of the porn/sex addiction.

So, the addict must learn to manage his physiology and **set limits** and **boundaries** for himself. Another way to say this would be "the addict learns to create a safe haven." He learns to pay attention to the simplest, seemingly unimportant life-management decisions that have long been feeding his addiction. For example, "I'll just skip lunch and keep working," "I'll start on that project tomorrow," "I'll just stop at the bookstore to look around," "I'll just surf the cable channels to see what's on," "Wow, can you believe how short her skirt is?" (These are only examples. The previous page contains over 40 triggers. There are actually many hundreds of possible triggers that lead an addict back into the path of acting out.) All of these are examples of things that in the past have *triggered* the addict into entering the *preoccupation phase* and eventually heading down the funnel to acting out his addiction.

The addict soon learns what his limits are and how to create for himself a safe haven. When he gets the idea to skip lunch and keep working, for instance, he can stop, notice the trigger, and say "If I skip lunch, I might exceed my physical limits, become hungry, fatigued, irritable and this will start me down the road to seeking relief and self-medication through my addiction. I'm going to eat lunch right now." Likewise, if he feels the urge to "stop by at the bookstore and just look around," the addict takes notice of this thought and says, "I know if I go into the bookstore I'll eventually end up in the sex manual isle, and this will start me down the road to acting out my addiction." And so he drives right on past.

The S.T.A.R. group therapists are quick to point out that triggers are often in and of themselves addictive behaviors and part of the ritual leading to acting out. For example, isolation is an addictive behavior, too much stress is an addictive behavior, increased arguments with a spouse, procrastinating a major project deadline, driving down a certain street, walking past a certain house—all of these can be addictive behaviors that in turn lead to the acting out of the sexual addiction itself. These behaviors can become daily **rituals** that the addict has adopted over many years. Obviously, addicts cannot be expected to suddenly stop acting on these triggers or acting out these rituals after years of addiction, simply because they become aware of them or simply have a desire to stop. Addicts need **tools** they can use to become aware of their physiology, avoid triggers, set limits, etc.

The following is a list of some of the tools that the S.T.A.R. group teaches recovering porn/sex addicts to use in their daily lives. These tools can become **daily healthy rituals** that replace destructive daily addictive rituals:

Using the Tools

For those who struggle with sexual addiction/sexual co-dependency, the incorporation of the following tools will enable consistent, long-term recovery. Remember, there are no shortcuts! The more tools you use on a consistent (daily) basis, the further you will progress in your own recovery.

Therapy Meetings

- *Attend regularly*
- *Join a home group*
- *Get involved; service*

Phone Calls

Work the 12 Steps

- *AWOL (a way of life)*
- *Attend 12-step meetings*
- *Use "A Gentle Path Through the 12 Steps" by Carnes*

Get a Sponsor

Define Your Bottom Lines

Abstain From Acting Out

Personal Reflection

- *Daily readings, a feelings journal, a self-care checklist*

Spirituality

- *Prayer, meditation, nature, yoga, tai chi, etc.*

Interests/Hobbies

- *Music, reading, gardening, etc.*

Exercise

- *Walk, hike, bike, swim, etc.*

Relationships

- *Avoid toxic people*
- *Be selective*
- *Develop safe, non-sexual relationships*

Rest and Relaxation

- *Proper and adequate rest/sleep*
- *"Gentleness" breaks*

Nutrition

- *Three balanced meals*
- *No junk food*

Consistent Therapy

Become Aware of Other Compulsive Behaviors or Addictions

The addict may incorporate any or all of these tools to help set and honor limits and boundaries, become aware of and avoid triggers, and break out of the addiction cycle. In essence, the implementation of these tools will bring the addict to the wonderful attainment of the state known as **sobriety**.

What To Do In Case of an Emergency

As has been pointed out, an addict must not wait until the *wave* or *trance* hits him or her to begin to implement tools and techniques. Once this state is reached, will power is not enough and the addict will usually give in and act out his addiction. This is why it is so critical to recognize the signs and triggers early. This is why the consistent practice of healthy daily rituals is so important.

However, in the recovery process, the addict will be faced with times when he has exceeded his limits and has failed to heed the warning signs, thus finding himself faced with the over-powering *wave* beginning to wash over him. For these "emergency situations" the addict can learn and practice specific techniques to interrupt or alter his physiology and, hopefully, lead the mindbody to access new cellular-memory groups and pathways as opposed to automatically heading down the old addiction super highway. These techniques are different for each addict and vary according to circumstances and situations. Here are a few examples:

Deep breathing exercises: Change the mindbody's physiology in times of stress, panic, fear, lust, etc. Restore peace, calm and clear thinking.

The three-second rule: Establish a practice of not allowing an addictive behavior to continue for more than three seconds. Immediately turn off such actions as fantasizing, scoping out an attractive woman, channel surfing, listening to certain kinds of "trigger" music, etc.

Changing the meaning: Remember, to the mindbody, *meaning is everything*. If in a time of crisis the addict can change the meaning of the addictive behavior, perhaps he can avoid acting out. This is often referred to by therapists as "contaminating the fantasy."

- Rather than gazing at a woman's body parts, look her in the eye and say to yourself, "This is a human being, not an object. This is someone's daughter, sister, mother."
- Speed up the video to the end. Rather than focusing on the sexual acting out, watch yourself confessing to your wife, saying goodbye to your children as you are hauled away to prison, seeing your name spattered across the front page as a "pervert" for all of the community to see, etc.—visualize the possible consequences before proceeding.
- Visualize yourself sitting at the computer screen drooling for hours at pictures you've seen hundreds of times before.
- Visualize the face of your therapist and your 12-step group as you tell them about your slip up.
- Change the meaning of pain, stress, loneliness and other "trigger" emotions. Learn to let the emotion "pass through you" and realize

that it is not earth-shattering, it will not destroy you, you can survive this. Learn to develop healthy pain and stress management skills so that these no longer act as triggers to push you toward your porn/sex addiction for relief.

- Acknowledge the trigger and then let it go: “That’s a very attractive woman, isn’t it great to be a man?” “I wonder what’s for dinner tonight. . . .” Rather than commencing some giant battle of will power and blowing the woman up into some fantasy sex goddess, let the image and experience “move through you”—change its meaning.
- Addiction is about limits, restrictions and bondage. Recovery and sobriety are about abundance and freedom. Some addicts feel that recovery will saddle them with too many rules and restrictions. This meaning must be changed. The addict must recognize that healthy sexual behavior is liberating and expansive, whereas addictive sex means bondage because the addict can never get enough of a fix.

Two important features of these techniques (and many others like them) are:

1. The addict creates the parameters of his chosen techniques, i.e., when he speeds up the video to the end of his acting out, he identifies the consequences rather having them stereotyped and forced on him by a third party, which would only add to his feelings of shame.
2. The addict doesn’t wait to use these techniques until there is a crisis. Rather, he practices them in group “what-if” sessions, daily personal rituals, meditation, etc. The mindbody is establishing new programming and pathways in practice so that the techniques are more easily accessed in times of crisis.

Withdrawal

As an addict begins feeling relief from his addictive behaviors, he also will begin feeling pain, anxiety, stress, loneliness—all emotions that were previously buried or, upon surfacing, were immediately medicated using the sexual addiction. The addict must learn that he "can feel pain and get through it"; he can and will survive life's challenges without turning back to his addiction. An addict typically carries the illusion that he has to find an escape, that he isn't strong enough to withstand the pain of withdrawal. This is impaired thinking. Instead the addict must change the **meaning** of the addiction.

Dan Gray commented to me that he has "never yet had a recovering addict explode into a thousand pieces in my office because the addict couldn't have sexual release."

With the proper tools and education, an addict learns to "lean into the pain" and get through it in healthy, positive ways. He learns the truth that "Not only can I feel pain and survive, but I can become a stronger person in the process." Rather than always focusing on avoiding pain, stress and anxiety, an addict in recovery actually begins to feel more of it. But the *meaning* of these feelings gradually is changing—"This is making me stronger, tempering my metal. I'm passing through a refining fire and therefore it has a positive purpose in my life."

This mindbody-altering process is illustrated powerfully in Victor Frankl's book *Man's Search For Meaning*, which shares the story of his incarceration in a Nazi concentration camp and how radically different the prisoners fared according to the *meaning* they gave their sufferings.

PHASE III—*TREATING THE "CAUSE" OF ADDICTION*

Phase three takes place in an open-ended group setting. The same group meets once every week for at least one year, and in some cases for many years. (This is in addition to weekly SA or COSA 12-step meetings.) This phase is where the most difficult and in-depth work is done with recovering addicts and their co-dependent spouses. This is where the "cause" of the addiction is uncovered and treated as opposed to temporarily treating the symptoms of "acting out," which is the focus of phase two.

Thirty days of sobriety is required by the S.T.A.R. group before a recovering addict can enter phase three. This allows the psychological and physiological arousal/stimulation of the addiction to subside. It also prevents the preoccupation with the addiction from getting in the way of dealing with the deeper emotional issues, childhood traumas, family history, etc. There is greater accountability to the group in phase three. Members of the group "check in" each week, not only physically, spiritually and emotionally, but also sexually.

For example, each group member reports in as to whether he or she had any *slips* during the past week and thus violated their sobriety. A slip may constitute any number of things and is specific to each addict's recovery plan. In other words, what is a slip for one may be irrelevant to another.

In phase three the definition of *sobriety* is raised to a more advanced level. Over time, each addict redefines what sobriety means to him or her. An addict may start out in phase two with the commitment "I will not have sex with myself (masturbation) or anyone else other than my spouse." Later in phase three he may raise this to "I will not allow myself to recall or fantasize sexually for more than three seconds (the three-second rule). If I do, it is a slip from my sobriety."

In addition, each recovering addict reports to the group regarding what he is doing to enhance the meaning in his life as well as how he is doing with self-care, limits and boundaries, healthy daily rituals, hobbies, service, etc.

A great deal of trauma work is performed in phase three, especially in helping the addict discover and heal his wounded "inner-child." *Family of Origin* work is also mapped out as the recovering addict learns that sexual addiction is a "systemic problem" and is rarely if ever isolated to one individual in a family. All of this work is done in the nurturing and trusting community of the group setting, using techniques such as imaging, psychodrama, role playing, break-out sessions and others. The group becomes a microcosm of real life. Each member is able to offer feedback and learn from the life experiences of the other members, including other addicts and their spouses.

The beauty of phase three is that once the chains (causes) of addiction are loosened and freedom obtained, recovering addicts begin to discover who they *really* are—their gifts, talents, interests and healthy passions. Their lives gain new *meaning* and they blossom in miraculous ways. Suddenly they are retaining employment and gaining promotions, they are finishing their education, marriages are rescued and loving relationships are formed with spouses and children. The addict finds himself reaching out to others in love and service. A whole new world, a whole new life *meaning* emerges for the addict and his or her family—like walking out of a perpetual night of darkness into the resplendent light of a new day.

An Important Note About Flexibility In Recovery Programs

Dan Gray, one of the founders of the S.T.A.R. program in Salt Lake City, brought a very important point to my attention. He observed, "In my opinion, a porn/sex recovery program that is centered around rigid rules and lists of 'must-dos' (attending SAA meetings, continuing psychotherapy for years, etc.) is too much of a blanket approach. I think it's more powerful to act in the role of a consultant and guide the addict as they decide the level of treatment and involvement they need, with sobriety and life fulfillment as the ultimate touchstone. Then, if they're not achieving those, (sobriety and life fulfillment) they can be directed to a more intense and/or longer recovery program."

Key Points

A reference tool for
spouses, parents, clergy,
counselors and others

- Just as AA's 12-Step program has helped countless alcoholics live normal and productive lives, SAA's 12-Step program is helping porn/sex addicts attain sobriety.
- In addition to SAA, a qualified therapy program can be invaluable to the recovery process. In Phase I, in a community of support, the addict begins learning to set boundaries and be accountable. The addict is guided through the process of creating their own recovery plan. In Phase II, the addict learns to extinguish the addictive behavior by implementing the recovery plan they created in Phase I. They regain control of their life so that the addiction and shame cycles cease spiraling them downward. The addict learns to recognize the *triggers* of their addiction early and the application of various tools to avoid "acting out." The goal of Phase II is to help the addict achieve sobriety and the ability to deal with life's stresses in healthy ways.
- In Phase III, the most difficult and important work begins—treating the *cause* of the addiction. Only through Phase III can the addict be healed and achieve life-long sobriety.

34

What If My Child Or Teenager Has Been Exposed To Pornography By Accident?

Recently I received a call from a mother whose eleven-year-old son had been exposed to pornography while innocently surfing on the Internet. She was upset, and rightly so. Although she had many questions, they all revolved around two main issues:

1. Will this exposure cause long-term damage or leave permanent scarring on my son?
2. Does he need counseling or therapy?

When I took these questions to the therapists at the S.T.A.R. group, their response was as follows:

A. The real question and key is "What meaning do the images seen have in the child's mindbody?" Talk with the child calmly, gently and directly about the experience. Find out what impact it had on him and how he felt about it. "What did you see, and how do you feel about it?"

B. Help the child place the exposure in context: "What does this mean and how should I react to it?" In many cases it is the *reaction of the parents* that can take a "minor incident" as it pertains to *meaning* in the child's mindbody, and blow it all out of proportion so that it becomes a serious problem. The parent must stay **neutral** when assessing the child's experience.

C. **WARNING!** Do not shame the child, become angry or make a big deal out of the exposure. Doing so can link the exposure with highly emotional cellular-memories in the child's mindbody and turn the exposure into a traumatic experience where before there was none. Linking shame and guilt to the sexual images can actually start the child down the path to addiction.

D. Do make this as an opportunity to have a positive discussion with the child (at his level and without preaching or sermonizing) about human sexuality, pornography, etc. Be sure that he understands that human intimacy is a sacred and a beautiful act that pornography distorts into something dirty or ugly. Be careful not to present sex as *dirty*, *sinful*, *shameful* or *forbidden*. This approach with children and teens creates sexual shame and is one of the primary contributors to porn/sex addiction in later life.

E. Don't send mixed messages. Imagine how confusing it is for a child when he is told, "Sex is sinful and dirty, and, by the way, be sure to *save it for someone you really love*." And if that isn't confusing enough, imagine when this child reaches puberty and senses the onset of sexual urges. He might automatically assume, "If sex is bad then my feeling this way is bad, and that means I must be a bad person." **Meaning is everything!**

The above guidelines apply to children or teens who have experienced one exposure or those who may just be starting to experiment with regular viewing. If after calmly and gently assessing the situation you determine that the child or teen has a problem, don't hesitate to schedule a counseling session with a **qualified therapist**. This is especially critical if the child or teen is developing an addiction. The earlier the addiction is treated, the easier it will be for the him to pull out of the addiction cycle and have a chance for a sexually and emotionally healthy, normal life.

For more information regarding teenagers and the challenges of pornography and sexuality, visit the outstanding website, www.sexandyoungamerica.com, or call 513-521-6227.

Key Points

A reference tool for
spouses, parents, clergy,
counselors and others

- If a child or teen has accidently been exposed to pornography, a parent should remain calm, objective, and listen intently. Avoid reacting, preaching, lecturing and especially inflicting guilt and shame on the child. Be careful not to present sex as dirty, sinful, shameful or forbidden—distinguish between pornography and healthy sexuality. Seek counseling and therapy for the child or teen only if needed.

35

HELP FOR RELIGIOUS LEADERS

With pornography addiction approaching epidemic proportions, growing numbers of individuals are approaching their religious leaders for help. Very few of these leaders are trained therapists or counselors. Consequently, many are feeling inadequate and overwhelmed. The following guidelines should prove helpful. I wish to acknowledge the wonderful work and advice of Dan Gray and Todd Olson and their Sexual Trauma and Recovery (S.T.A.R.) Program. I also want to thank the National Coalition for the Protection of Children & Families (NCPCF) for their excellent brochure titled *caught in the PORN trap—For Clergy & Lay Leaders, Advising Victims & Their Loved Ones*. To obtain this brochure, visit NCPCF's website at www.nationalcoalition.org.

WHAT TO DO WHEN SOMEONE DISCLOSES PORNOGRAPHY USE

1. **Listen:** First, listen to the individual to discover how he/she feels about their pornography use and to ascertain the seriousness of the problem. Do they see their situation as "no big deal?" Is their porn use creating problems in their marriage? Are they unable to control

their urge to look at porn, the amount of time they spend with it and the frequency? Is the content of the material becoming progressively more explicit and hard-core? Why are they telling you about their problem and why now?

As you ask questions, listen objectively and let them do most of the talking. Be very careful not to display shock or disgust. Don't preach, lecture or quote scriptures regarding the evils of sexual sin. Remember, porn addiction is virtually always *shame-based.* With rare exception, the addict already feels dirty, evil and unworthy. Taking a *rigid religious* approach will only alienate the individual, increase their guilt and shame, and push them deeper into their addiction. You're there to listen and assess their situation. Treatment and recovery will come later.

2. **Assess The Seriousness of the Problem:** The following are samples of the types of questions you can ask to better understand the extent of the individual's problem. These questions are not intended to be diagnostic, but only to give you an idea of the scope and seriousness of the problem.

   - How long have you been viewing pornography?
   - At what age did you start?
   - How often do you look at pornography and for how long?
   - When was the last time you looked at pornography?
   - What does looking at pornography do for you?
   - Does your pornography viewing include masturbation?
   - How do you feel after viewing pornography?
   - How do you obtain pornographic materials, i.e., adult bookstores, videos, cable TV, Internet, etc.?
   - Have you tried to stop looking at pornography? How many times? What happened?

- Do others know about your pornography use?
- If so, what do they think about it?
- If they don't know, why not?
- What do you think would happen if others found out, like your spouse or other family members? (Remember, an addict's greatest fear is that his/her secret life or "dark side" will be discovered.)
- Are there other behaviors you are involved in of a sexual nature (such as phone sex, cybersex chat, voyeurism, strip bars, prostitutes, affairs, anonymous sex, child pornography, sexual assault, etc.)

In some cases, you may find the pornography use is of recent origin and limited. Through understanding, support and education, you may be able to help the individual discontinue their use of pornography. However, if the individual's involvement with pornography is progressive—they can't control when and how long they view it, they need harder and more explicit material each time, they keep vowing to stop but can't, their sexual "acting-out" is moving beyond just looking at pornography—then their behavior has become compulsive and they probably have a porn/sex addiction. This requires outside help including a 12-Step Recovery Program, a qualified therapist, and even inpatient care in severe cases. It also requires that you confront the individual about the seriousness of their compulsion or addiction.

3. **Confront With Love:** You have a responsibility to confront the pornography user—do so with understanding and love. Remember, pornography is a *drug*. Porn addiction is as real and powerful as alcoholism or cocaine use. (Many experts agree that it's the most powerfully addicting drug in history.) You should approach pornography addiction just as you would any other addiction. Keep in mind that porn addiction is not about the pornography, any more

than alcoholism is about the alcohol. Pornography use is only a symptom—it's used to escape and medicate much deeper problems. Simply labeling the individual as a "sinner" or "dirty" or a "pervert" is inappropriate and counter-productive. If you've taken the time to truly listen and understand the person's situation, heart, concerns, pain and fear, your confrontation will communicate both truth and grace. A confrontation should communicate the following:

"I care about you as a person. I believe that what you are doing is dangerous, negatively impacting your marriage and family, eroding your emotional health and your relationship with God. For your sake and your family, this behavior has to stop. I will support you and guide you to receive counseling, therapy and begin your pathway to recovery. I will help you determine how to confess this behavior to significant people in your life (such as your spouse). I will pray with you and for you. I will be available to talk when you're feeling vulnerable, down or out of control. And, with your permission, I will hold you accountable to decisions and commitments you make regarding this behavior."

4. **Refer the Individual to Professionals:** Make yourself aware of 12-Step programs and qualified porn/sex addiction counselors and therapists in your community. Give the individual the appropriate contact information. Follow-up and make sure that contact has been made and an appointment set. Ask the individual for permission to stay in communication with his/her counselor or therapist as they progress in their recovery program. If you require information regarding counselors/ therapists and programs in your area, contact your local AA or SAA organization. You may also contact the *National Council on Sexual Addiction & Compulsivity* at 770-989-9754. They have a register of most porn/sex addiction therapists in the U.S. In addition, visit NCPCF's website at www.nationalcoalition.org for more information regarding their outreach program and referral service.

HELPING THE PORN ADDICT'S LOVED ONES

Pornography/sex addiction usually takes a severe toll on the addict's family, especially the spouse. Often the spouse discovers their partner's addiction by accident. Or, the spouse has confronted the addict about abnormal behaviors, like sexual withdrawal, which leads to the addict's disclosure. In the crisis of discovery/disclosure, the spouse may seek help from their church or pastor. This "victim" will usually come to you with intense and varied feelings of betrayal and devastation. How can you best help this individual?

1. **Listen:** Depending on how the discovery or disclosure occurred, the spouse will usually show one or more of the following responses:
   - Shame and embarrassment
   - Shock and disbelief
   - Betrayed and deceived
   - Anger: "How could they? The person I love the most has hurt me the worst."
   - Feeling *responsible* for the addict's actions, or being judged by the addict as being "not woman (or man) enough."
   - Fear: "What will happen to our marriage?" "What else is he/she doing?" "What if others find out about this?"
   - Blame: the spouse may have been told that he/she is the reason for the addict's behavior.
   - Confusion: "I thought I knew my husband/wife." "How could this have been going on behind my back?" "What else don't I know about him/her?"
   - Violated: a spouse expects their partner to be faithful. Porn use is viewed as *infidelity*.
   - Diminish: wanting to escape the reality and pain of the situation, the spouse may down-play their partner's problem.

"It's just a phase." "All men like to look." "He told me he's going to stop."

2. **Respond:** The spouse needs to hear from you that their partner's pornography use is **not his/her fault**. Making comments like, "Perhaps if you were more attentive sexually, your spouse wouldn't need to look at pornography," or placing the blame in any way upon the victimized spouse, is inappropriate. Stress that the porn-using spouse is the only one responsible for their choices. Pornography use is a sign of much deeper issues. Even if one is unhappy in their marriage, that doesn't excuse their porn use.
3. **Assess the Situation:** Being married to a porn user/addict can be a very difficult situation. Pornography often causes the user to be withdrawn, depressed, angry and emotionally distant. The user may be asking their spouse to engage in sexual behaviors that are uncomfortable for her. The spouse may be aware of other sexual acting-out behaviors such as phone sex, strip bars, prostitutes or affairs. The porn user/addict may be spending a lot of time away from home, or when in the home, he/she stays isolated and aloof, leaving their spouse with all of the responsibilities of a family and household. In some cases, there may even be sexual and/or physical abuse. All of these things and more take their emotional and physical toll on the victimized spouse. A gentle, sensitive and understanding approach to questioning will help you assess the details and the seriousness of the situation.
4. **What is the Spouse's Response to the Situation:** Find out how the victimized spouse is feeling, reacting and behaving as a result of the situation. Are they depressed? Having sleeping or eating problems, sudden weight loss/gains, hopeless or suicidal thoughts? Is he/she having anxiety-racing thoughts, heart palpitations, or having significant trouble concentrating? Is he or she having trouble with work, taking care of the children, or functioning normally? If daily activities seem impossible to accomplish and are inhibited by depression and/or anxiety, strongly encourage him/her

to see a doctor and personal counselor. The tendency in these situations is to focus on the porn user/addict's problem and behaviors. However, this is a time of crisis for the spouse who is a victim and needs help, support and advocacy.

5. **Offer Assistance**: Communicate how you can assist the spouse in their situation. Discuss the possibility of helping them confront the porn user/addict. Indicate that you can offer support and accountability from the church in stressing the importance of the user/addict stopping their destructive behaviors. Help the spouse identify "safe" people with whom to confide and receive on-going support. The porn user/addict's fear of disclosure to outsiders should be respected, however, in order to heal, spouses should not be bound to keep the "secret" from all parties. They need an outlet, too.
6. **Refer the Spouse to Professionals:** Remember that in virtually every case, the spouse of a porn/sex addict suffers from *co-addiction*, and needs counseling to deal with the crisis, and begin the healing and recovery process. The spouse also needs direction in how best to help their porn using partner by setting boundaries and discontinuing "enabling behaviors." Become aware of therapists and recovery/support groups for spouses (co-addicts) in your area such as *COSA* and others. It's extremely important for victims to be with others experiencing similar issues in their lives. This lessens feelings of isolation and hopelessness, and provides a close community of support. Encourage the spouse to insist that their user/addict partner seek separate help and therapy. They should also seek counseling as a couple.
7. **Stay in Contact and Follow Up:** Before the spouse leaves, set another appointment to see how they're coping and to confirm they have contacted your referrals. In addition to in-person meetings, you should also maintain regular contact by telephone. After the initial crisis phase, the spouse needs to know that others (you) understand that the injury takes time and effort to heal. The spouse

may need to make difficult decisions regarding boundaries, safety, staying in the relationship, etc. Deep depression often hits weeks after the initial discovery or disclosure, when shock wears off and the implications sink in. For this reason, you should continue contact and support beyond the initial crisis phase.

8. **Safety Issues and Boundaries:** Depending on the circumstances, you may need to help the spouse set boundaries for their safety and well-being and that of their children. For example:
   - Insist that no pornographic material be allowed in the home. Implement Internet safety solutions that prevent the user/addict from gaining unprotected access to the Internet.
   - Consider a period of sexual abstinence until the victim spouse is comfortable and convinced that the user/addict is seriously seeking help and discontinuing behaviors. In some cases, therapists may recommend an extended period of abstinence as part of the healing and recovery process.
   - If the user/addict admits to sexually acting-out with others, consider testing for sexually- transmitted diseases.
   - If the user/addict's behaviors are compulsive and violent, the spouse may be in danger of domestic violence or sexual assault. Victims need to know that they are not required— by God or their spouse—to endure this behavior. The police should be contacted if there is any threat of, or actual, violence. It may be necessary to help the victim find a "place to go" for safety.

As a religious leader, you may feel awkward, overwhelmed or helpless in dealing with issues of sexual addiction or abuse. In addition to the resources you might find in your community, I highly recommend NCPCF's *Victim Assistance HelpLine*. This wonderful resource is available for addicts, their spouses, concerned friends, neighbors or family, and religious leaders and counselors. Services include:

- Crisis counseling

- Assessment of caller's needs
- Referral to counselors in the caller's community
- Accurate educational information regarding the impact of pornography and its messages
- Resources and educational materials on sexual addiction and pornography
- Consultation with pastors or mental health professionals on how to help their clients and parishioners.

The *HelpLine* is staffed by mental health professionals or those under their supervision. All services are confidential within ethical and legal constraints.

Available Monday through Friday during normal business hours, the *Victim Assistance HelpLine* number is **1-800-583-2964**.

In addition, if you are counseling teenagers regarding the challenges of pornography and sexuality, I highly recommend the website: www.sexinyoungamerica.com, or call 513-521-6227.

Key Points

A reference tool for spouses, parents, clergy, counselors and others

- When someone discloses pornography use, listen calmly and objectively and avoid *religious rigidity*. Be careful not to create guilt and shame in your response. Once trust and confidence have been established, assess the details and seriousness of the situation by asking questions. Confront with love and understanding remembering that pornography is a *drug* as real and powerful as alcohol or cocaine. If it appears that the porn use has progressed to an addiction, refer the individual to a qualified therapist and 12-Step program in your community.
- Don't forget about the spouse of the porn user/addict. Listen with love and understanding and make certain he/she understands that it's **not their fault**. Assess the situation and how the spouse is responding to it. If mental or physical health issues arise, it may be necessary to refer the spouse to a medical doctor and/or counselor. Stay in contact beyond the initial crisis. Help the spouse set boundaries. Determine if the spouse and/or children are at risk. And remember that most spouses of porn/sex addicts suffer from *co-addiction* and should be referred to a recovery program and support group.

36

Real-Life Stories of Recovery and Hope

One consistent theme that plagues pornography/sex addicts and their co-addicted spouses, is the feeling of utter hopelessness and despair. These individuals often feel like they're on the perpetual "roller-coaster ride from hell" and can't get off.

In conducting research for this chapter on recovery, I had the opportunity to interview a number of recovering porn/sex addicts. Each one had been through—and in most cases was continuing in—some type of formal recovery program. While each had his own unique story to tell, there were four elements that were consistent in every case:

- Even though my years of study and interviews had proven this again and again, I was still surprised to find recovering addicts to be extremely intelligent, personable and successful in many aspects of their professional and family lives. To put it simply, *I was very impressed.* As a businessman, these were the type of men I would hire and enjoy working with. As a person, these were individuals I would welcome as friends.
- Each of the addicts had experienced something significant in his family and personal history that led him to seek the *self-medication*

of pornography/sex addiction. Before entering therapy, not one of them realized and/or fully understood what this catalyst was or that it even existed.

- Each had reached a point where he felt powerless to resist. Each described a life out of control and dominated by his addiction cycle. Each experienced an event or set of circumstances that brought them to admit that they had a problem and seek outside help. **They each had felt for years that there was no way out, no hope to ever have a normal life.** Each had embraced activities they considered to be shameful and perverted. Some had engaged in behaviors that were dangerous and/or illegal. Each went to great lengths to *keep their addiction a secret*— living in fear that others might discover what "evil," "bad," or "perverted" people they were.

- The most remarkable thing about each of the interviews was the incredible **HOPE** that I felt. Through consistent participation in and dedication to a prescribed therapy program and participation within his 12-step group, each man had gained **control** over his life. They spoke of the wondrous freedom and joy of being able to live a "normal" life. Each admitted without hesitation that his addiction still lurked somewhere in the background, and probably always would. But, what he had once thought to be a hopeless dream—a life free of acting out—was now a reality! Each felt he had individual worth, that he was a "good person" and that he finally "had his life back." And perhaps most wonderful of all, he had discovered the tools and learned the skills to stay that way, free and sober.

I would like to share highlights from just two of the remarkable interviews I had with recovering pornography/sex addicts. I have changed the names to allow the individuals to retain their privacy.

Steve's Story

Steve grew up in a rigid home teeming with physical and emotional abuse. He remembers as a child and teenager feeling like he wasn't good enough and could never measure up to what others (especially his father) thought he should be. At age 12 or 13, Steve reached puberty and learned about sex (both fact and fiction), primarily from his male cousins. They introduced him to masturbation and he was immediately "hooked." He said, "The first several times I felt awful. But then I thought, 'This feels too good and there's too much pain in my life.' So I ended up in it for the long haul. I had found my 'drug,' a way to numb the pain in my life."

Steve was not sexually active as a teenager and did not become involved with pornography until shortly after he was married. "The first time I saw an adult video," he related, "my jaw dropped. Afterward I couldn't get it out of my mind. I thought about it and obsessed over it everyday for weeks and months. Then came more videos and more obsessing."

Because Steve is a highly creative and artistic person, he finds it very easy to daydream and fantasize at an intensely detailed level. He said, "I could remember every video in vivid detail and play them back in my mind as if I were actually watching them on the TV screen." In fact, because of his vivid imagination, he didn't even need a porn magazine or video to act out his addiction. Once he'd witnessed the initial images, he could create his own porn movies in his mind— inserting people that he knew and changing the script and the setting at will. He literally created his own mobile "video-porn archive" that he could access and escape to at any time.

With pornography feeding his fantasies, Steve's masturbation sessions became even more frequent and intense. He found himself escaping into his fantasy world and, as a result, his work, his family, his health and his spirituality began suffering severely. "The only reason I entered therapy is that I got to the point where I was in so much emotional pain that I couldn't look in any other direction," he said. "I got to the point where I didn't care who found out about my secret. I had lost touch with reality. My thinking was so impaired that I thought 'If I have to give up fantasy and masturbation, what can possibly take their place?' It didn't even occur to me that perhaps joy or service or love or hobbies or family could fill the void."

"The initial stages of therapy was the most awful period of my life. I had to vocalize to others about this miserable fear I had that no one know about my addiction, not even my wife. My wife was terrified when she found out about it and had a very hard time. I had to start trusting others when I had never trusted anyone in my life. I had to stop living in fear and start living with hope. It wasn't until I started uncovering all of the root problems from my childhood that I was able to truly address my addiction."

In therapy and group sessions, Steve acquired the tools and skills to control and eventually stop his fantasizing and replace masturbation with healthy alternatives. He learned to recognize the "triggers" that were causing him to self-medicate and found ways to stop them from firing. And most importantly, he uncovered and resolved the childhood issues and traumas that had pushed him into his addiction in the first place.

Steve told how the last three years in which he has been in recovery have been the best years of his life. He has never met so many high-caliber, wonderful people, people who have just as many deep-rooted hang-ups as he does. He has felt a real sense of brotherhood, of belonging, and has come to accept that he is a normal, good and valuable person. "Now instead of everyday being filled with despair and hopelessness," he reports, "it is filled with normal challenges. And I haven't faced anything that I can't stand back, take a deep breath and then deal with in a healthy way. I've gained the skills to deal with life in a way that is 180 degrees from where I was. Taking the bitter with the sweet is part of life, but the bitter isn't going to be all of the time and it doesn't have to dominate my life. I have learned to feel it and then let it pass through me."

Steve's Advice To Anyone Caught In Addiction: "For any of us who have walked the darkest road or down the darkest holes, there is a lifeline. This lifeline is to look beyond fear and hopelessness and realize that these emotions are a *shroud*—something that is nearly physically placed in front of you. And if you can walk through that shroud, there is light on the other side, and people waiting, people who can relate exactly with everything that you've gone through—with what your life has been like and with what your pain and addictions are.

It as if you're wearing a hood over your face and your hands are bound so that you can't remove the hood, and you live in the darkness of addiction. What you're doing in therapy is learning from others, a step at a time, how to unbind your hands and then lift the hood from your face. And know that you will find your old mind-set and habits slapping your hands away and your self-talk saying things like, 'What are you doing? You can't lift that hood off! You're a loser. Don't be an idiot. You're so stupid.' And there all around you are loving supportive people saying, 'You know what, it's a hood, that's all it is and it's covering your face. Let us teach you how to untie just one hand at first, and then the other. You can do it. We have done it. You'll be okay."

Richard's Story

Richard comes from a family with a long history of addiction and abuse. His mother's parents died from alcoholism. His father experienced severe physical abuse as a child. You can imagine the sad legacy of dysfunction that was passed on to Richard as a result. His father was a heavy smoker, a workaholic, and a perfectionist in the extreme. From his time as a small child through his teenage years, Richard remembers his father always kept *Playboy* magazines on the coffee table for all to freely view. Richard knows that the combination of inheriting the "seeds" of addiction from his family of origin and the accessability of pornography set him up for his own porn/sex addiction as a teenager.

The first stages of Richard's addiction involved voyeurism where, in sixth grade and junior high, he and his friends peeked through windows and secretly took pictures of women and girls they found attractive, including their own sisters. Over time, this evolved to pornographic materials of various kinds, including hard-core magazines and videos—when they could get them. This was his way of escaping from the stress and abuse of home life.

Interestingly enough, Richard was not sexually active as a teenager. His sole interest was the "visual." Then, as often is the case, he acquired "companion addictions" to his voyeurism/porn addiction. He began using marijuana, other illicit drugs, and alcohol. He found with alcohol that though he couldn't stop, he didn't get sick, no matter how much he drank. But then remembering the awful death of his grandparents, he gave up drinking altogether.

After high school Richard became very active in a Christian faith. It was at this point, he says, "that I began to 'white-knuckle' my porn addiction and control it through sheer will power." This method worked, until one day as Richard was making sales calls for an employer, he dialed a wrong number and **by pure accident** encountered a phone-sex line. For the next month he became a phone-sex junkie, amassing a phone bill of over $1,200. His boss confronted him, referred him to counseling with his clergy, and he managed to quell the behavior. From that time until he was married five years later, he had no other problems. He said, "It wasn't because I didn't have the opportunity or the desire, it was because I feared what would happen if my mother or my minister found out."

But after Richard got married and discovered "physical sex" for the first time, he said it was like a switch was turned on. He'd finally discovered the "drug" he had been missing all of his life. Sex (with his wife, himself or others—it didn't matter) became the medicine that allowed him to escape from the worries and pressures of life. From that point forward, Richard went to great lengths to lie, hide and steal in order to act out his addiction.

Richard's addiction was a progressive one. It began with watching adult movies in hotel rooms. Then he got brave enough to start calling escort services, which eventually went to picking up prostitutes and driving them to secret places to have sex. His life became a cycle of pornography, strip bars and prostitutes. Eventually, the addiction progressed to having affairs.

He lied to these women, convincing them that he was leaving his wife and family.

Richard noted that the progression of his addiction didn't take long: "Once I started watching the porno movies, it didn't take long at all to progress to the prostitutes and the affairs. From the 'visual' to the 'physical' was very quick. I just needed that little nudge to get me there. And when I discovered Internet porn, it became a huge trigger for me. All I had to do was access porn on the Internet and it would put me into a major tailspin of sexually acting out. The 'visual' input of porn images stoked the fire of my addiction and created an immediate and desperate need to seek physical gratification."

For the first six or seven years his wife knew nothing about his addiction. Richard said, "I became a master liar. Every time someone would get close to finding out or would start asking questions, I would blow up and turn the tables so it appeared they were being unfair or falsely accusing me. I lived every day in fear that 'this would be the day' someone would discover my secret. But it was also an exciting day because I knew that I would have time to go do something sexual with someone. I would put myself to sleep with those thoughts and wake up every morning, obsessing and planning my next sexual encounter."

Thinking back to the peak of his years of addiction, Richard described his life as follows: "I had the ideal position in a company that I helped create. I had what most would consider the ideal position in my church. My wife and I were looked upon as the consummate couple and ideal family. We were building our own home and our fourth child was on the way. And I was at the pinnacle of my sexual addiction—life was great."

The idea that "life was great" violated what I knew about the despair of addiction. I asked Richard how it was that he escaped the shame/guilt part of the addiction cycle. His response was fascinating. He said, "I learned early on to shut off the guilt and shame. The pain was so unbearable that I learned to turn it off, to detach myself emotionally. I did experience tremendous guilt and shame after acting out, but I would immediately shut it off and bury it deep. I was in complete and total denial. It wouldn't have mattered if my whole family was lined up in front of the strip-club door. I simply had to get in there."

I wondered how on earth a person in so much denial and secrecy—feeling like his life was going so well—could ever get into therapy. But like every other sex/porn addict I have interviewed or read about, Richard's fantasy and charade eventually went into melt-down. In order to support his porn and prostitute habit, he had been embezzling money from his company. He was caught and his secret life was exposed. Reflecting on that time in his life he said, "I went from being at the top of the hill—really living a lie at the top of the hill—to drowning." He lost his job, his house, his standing in his church, and feared that he would lose his family because, "I was sure that once they knew my secret, there was no way they would want to live with a monster like me."

Richard's children and wife stuck by him as he went through some very painful and trying times. He and his wife met with a myriad of traditional clinicians, marriage counselors and others who treated symptoms and didn't understand that he was carrying around an addiction. Finally he was lead to a real porn/sex addiction therapist and a 12-step SAA program, where his addiction was properly diagnosed and where now he reports, "I came to understand my addiction, what feeds it, how to control it and move forward. I finally understood my family of origin, childhood issues and the fact that porn and sex were my drug, my cocaine, the thing I needed to get me through the day."

Richard made it clear that once he learned the tools and skills to control his urge to look at pornography, all of the other aspects of his sexual addiction came under control. "Once I shut off the visual input, the rest took care of itself," he said.

When I asked Richard, "How would you say your life is different today than it was during your addiction years?" he responded, "It's funny that you should ask because my wife and I were just discussing that the other day. Our fears today are so different from those we had when I was in the addiction cycle. We feel that today we are dealing with 'normal' issues in our lives. There are no lies to uncover. There is nothing that causes me to look over my shoulder everyday. Today, our issues are dealing with our teenage children, their being on the phone too long, wondering whether or not I'm making enough money to support my family—these are the kind of issues we deal with, and we do it openly and honestly and we don't wonder if 'my addiction cycle' is creating our problems."

"We feel today that our lives are as **normal** as any other family's lives are normal. When I began therapy we dealt with issues like: was I having a relapse, were we going to make it, did I pick up any sexually-transmitted diseases, paying money back to people I had stolen from, rebuilding honesty and trust—my addiction was the center and focus of our lives. It's even a little scary now because I never really had to deal with 'reality' during the 15 years that I lived a lie. But now we have a healthy family environment and have healthy relationships, which is one of the greatest gifts someone can ever receive."

In addition, through his own recovery and honesty, Richard has created a network of recovery in his own extended family. Since his own recovery, two drug-addicted brothers have entered therapy and saved their own marriages and families.

Richard's Advice To Anyone Caught In Addiction: "We go through the years believing that our addiction is the 'normal' way to deal with the stress and problems of life. We avoid really dealing with the core issues, the cause. No matter which addiction therapy program you choose, two things are critical for recovery: humility and patience. Without these, it doesn't matter how many therapy sessions or group meetings you attend. If you don't humble yourself and admit that your belief that you have to self-medicate to get through the day, that you don't have a problem, that you're no good, that you can keep it all a secret, that you're not hurting anyone but yourself—that these are all lies—then it will be very difficult if not impossible to step out of the addiction cycle. You have to admit, 'I'm not being honest with myself and I have to do whatever it takes to get better.'

And then you have to realize that it's not going to happen over night. And even though you have an illness, even though the memories still cause pain for you and your loved ones, **it's okay**. The reality of today is that yesterday is behind you and there really is a tomorrow. That tomorrow can be and truly is a place you want to be."

Contact Information For the S.T.A.R. Group of Salt Lake City

You can contact the S.T.A.R. Group for any of the following needs:

- For information regarding porn/sex addiction treatment programs for individuals and couples.

1. For reference materials such as books, cassette tapes and videos on porn/sex addiction treatment and recovery as well as various treatment alternatives.
2. Training programs for therapists, counselors and other professionals.

Mailing address: 151 E. 5600 So.
Suite 204
Salt Lake City, Utah 84107

Phone: (801) 262-2400

37

Final Thoughts

Life and Time Are So Very Precious

"Dost thou love life? Then do not squander time, for that is the stuff that life is made of."

—Benjamin Franklin

Why are the finest wines so costly and treasured? Time—they take such enormous amounts of time to mature. Time is the only thing of which we all have exactly the same amount—rich or poor, young or old. No matter who we are, we each can spend only 24 hours a day.

But how many days do each of us have left on this planet? How will we use each precious hour? Just remember, when we say "Yes" to one thing we automatically say "No" to another. We cannot do everything during our brief earthly sojourn. So, we must choose. And hopefully we will choose wisely, for as the song says, *Time flies on wings of lightning, we cannot call it back. It comes then passes forward along its onward track. And if we are not mindful, the chance will fade away. For life is quick in passing, 'tis as a single day.*[1]

EACH OF US IS BORN "GOOD"

I reject the notion that we are by our very nature, destined to be slaves to instinct and appetite, scarcely better than dogs or pigs; and that there is nothing we can do about it. I believe each of us is born with a built-in goodness, with a "light" or conscience inside of us; a built-in lens or pair of glasses through which we see the world and those around us.

Starting out, this lens is inherently one of virtue, decency, kindness, optimism, joy and acceptance of all people. As toddlers we see and treat others according to our view through this bright new lens. Just look at children's smiles, the sparkle in their eyes. They are so full of life, so quick to forgive, accept and love. They are filled with enthusiasm. Hate, despair, prejudice, vulgarity, promiscuity, pessimism and the like do not come to them naturally—these are *learned* behaviors.

Pornography darkens and distorts this lens or light within us. By way of the influence of pornography we see others (especially the male view of women and girls) through the spyglass of selfishness, lust and callousness. In fact, the pornography lens is really not a lens at all, but a mirror in which we see others according to our own selfish needs. Everything viewed through the pornography lens is slanted toward "my desires," "my needs," "my pleasure," "me, me, me." Pornography is the ultimate negative radio station with the call letters *WIIFM—What's In It For Me?*

LIFE IS A "STEWARDSHIP"

Each of us has been given innate talents and gifts. This stewardship is ours to use in making the world a better place. How does participation in Internet porn and cybersex chat fit in with this stewardship?

What Do You Want To Be Remembered For?

Imagine you are attending your own funeral. As the speaker begins to offer your eulogy, you hear the words, "He spent thousands of hours during his lifetime gawking at naked women," or "She was a real 'free thinker'—a pioneer among female sex video viewers," or "She was really hot in those cybersex chat rooms," or "His wife and children can think back with embarrassment on the porn magazines he hid around the house," or "He was an inconsiderate, unloving man with little respect for women—thanks to his favorite hobby, Internet pornography."

Take a Moment of Silence To Notice How You "Feel" About This

Each of us possesses, from birth, the gift of discernment. It is our conscience, an inner voice that helps us to distinguish right from wrong. We just have to close out the noise of the world and listen to this inner voice. You have this gift. You just have to learn how to tap into and follow it.

This inner voice can best be heard during quiet, peaceful, meditative times. It isn't a loud voice, rather it whispers.

Try this exercise: Sit quietly in a private place where you will not be disturbed. Have some soothing music playing in the background. Now imagine in your mind's eye the "perfect world," a world filled with peace, virtue, kindness, gentleness. In this world everyone is more concerned about the needs of their neighbors than they are for their own wants and desires. Everyone is serving and giving to those around them.

There are no jails in this world, because there is no crime. There are no lawyers or judges, because everyone works out their differences in peace and consideration. Men and women are given equal respect and there is no discrimination. All are treated with respect and enjoy equality, regardless of race, religion, possessions, station or profession.

Now, while you have this image resting gently in your mind, picture everyday actual life. See how this world's inhabitants interact with each other. See the smiles of the children. Feel the joy and happiness. Just bask in that feeling for a few moments.

Now think of PORNOGRAPHY, with its focus on body parts, its sex scenes, its raucous bump-and-grind assault. What did this do to the image you had of the perfect world? How did the introduction of porn into the scene alter your feelings? Were you able to imagine the two existing side by side, or was one or the other forced from your mind?

The noise and darkness created by pornography does not harmonize with the goodness and light that exist within each of us. Pornography does not fit in the "perfect world" most intelligent, decent people would envision.

LIVE "IN THE MOMENT"

It is my hope that your journey through the pages of this book have brought you to a clearer understanding of the power and potential of your own magnificent *mindbody*. Within you are trillions of cells, intelligent and waiting, waiting to carry out your instructions, your intentions, all based on the *meaning* that life has for you. I hope that you have come to realize that every image, sound, sensation, every piece of information you allow into your mindbody every moment of every day, is stored in your cellular-memories and becomes a permanent part of *who you are*. The sum-total of these memories determines who you will become, so "guard well the entrance gates" to your mindbody.

After years of research, interviews and observation, I have come to the conclusion that one of the greatest tragedies of pornography is that it robs the viewer of his presence of mind and awareness of all the beauty, potential and power within and around him. He sacrifices *moments* that could be filled with true peace and joy, for the "robotic" pursuit of momentary sensation. He severs the vital link between his mind and his heart.

In his startling book *Wherever You Go, There You Are* Jon Kabat-Zin eloquently speaks of living in the fullness and joy of the moment: *Like it or not, this moment is all we really have to work with. Yet we all too easily conduct our lives as if forgetting momentarily that we are* here, *where we already are, and that we are* in *what we are already in. In every moment, we find ourselves at the crossroad of here and now. But when the cloud of forgetfulness over where we are now sets in, in that very moment we get lost. "Now what?" becomes a real problem.*

By lost, I mean that we momentarily lose touch with ourselves and with the full extent of our possibilities. Instead, we fall into a robotlike way of seeing and thinking and doing. In those moments, we break contact with what is deepest in ourselves and affords us perhaps our greatest opportunities for creativity, learning, and growing. If we are not careful, those clouded moments can stretch out and become most of our lives. . . . our lives unfold only in moments. If we are not fully present for many of those moments, we may not only miss what is most valuable in our lives, but also fail to realize the richness and depth of our possibilities for growth and transformation.[2]

May each of us make the commitment to refuse and rebuff the robotlike world of pornography that would steal from us the precious gift of "being fully present" and living *in* every moment of our lives.

Suggested Reading

Protecting Children and Families From Illegal Pornography and Online Predators:

A variety of booklets, manuals, brochures, videos and fact-sheets. Order online at www.enough.org

Books by Judith A. Reisman, PhD:

Kinsey, Sex and Fraud

The book that shook that foundations of the sexual rights movement built on the fraudulent science of Alfred Kinsey. An amazing book considering American Sex Education is based largely on his research and scientific authority.

Soft Porn Plays Hardball

Its Tragic Effects On Women, Children, and The Family. Must reading for understanding the power of sexual images and their negative and destructive impact on men, women, children, and ultimately families.

Sexually Explicit Media: Changes In the Structure of the Human Brain & American Law & Public Policy

A scientific paper created in fulfillment of a grant commissioned by the Ontario Human Rights Commission, Ontario, Canada. An in-depth look at pornography's effect on the human brain, body and behavior.

To order, call 1-800-837-0544.

Books by Patrick Carnes, PhD:

Out of the Shadows: Understanding Sexual Addiction

The first work ever published on sexual addiction. *Out of the Shadows* is extensively used by therapists and counselors and remains the premier text in the porn/sex addiction recovery field.

Don't Call It Love: Recovery From Sexual Addiction

This clear, helpful, well-organized guide . . . points the way toward healing twisted relationships and reclaiming healthy sexuality. This landmark book also helps us better understand all addictions, their causes, and the difficult path to recovery.

Hope and Recovery: A Twelve Step Guide for Healing from Compulsive Sexual Behavior

By applying the Twelve Steps of AA to sexual addiction, a powerful recovery plan has emerged. Written by recovering sexual addicts and filled with a mixture of sensible advice and healing insights, this book has become an integral part of compulsive sexual behavior recovery.

To order, call 1-800-328-0098.

Books by John Bradshaw:

At the core-cause of virtually all addiction is some level of *toxic shame* in the life and family of the addict. John's wonderful books help us understand this shame and the healing process.

Healing the Shame That Binds You

Homecoming: Reclaiming and Championing Your Inner Child

Bradshaw on: The Family: A New Way of Creating Solid-Self Esteem

John Bradshaw's books are available at most major bookstores or at www.amazon.com.

The videotape and audiotape for Bradshaw's first book, *Bradshaw on: the Family*, as well as other tapes are available for purchase from: John Bradshaw, 5003 Mandell, Houston, Texas, 77006, (713) 529-9437

Other Recommendations:

Pornography's Effects on Adults and Children
By Dr. Victor B. Cline

This 17-page treatise is one of the most widely quoted works in the porn/sex addiction therapy field. It contains a clear and concise overview of pornography addiction and its impact on individuals, families and society.

To order contact Morality In Media, (212) 870-3222

A War We Must Win: A Frontline Account of the Battle Against the Pornography Conspiracy; Protecting Your Hearts and Homes Against the Subtle Invasion
By John Harmer

As Ronald Reagan's lieutenant governor in California, John Harmer worked to promote effective laws to maintain an orderly society and fought the war against obscenity. In this monumental book, John describes both the threat to the moral values necessary for a law-abiding people and what citizens must do to combat it.

Order at www.deseretbook.com

Molecules of Emotion: The Science Behind Mind-Body Medicine
By Candace B. Pert, PhD

This is the book that opened up a whole new world for me. I highly recommend it to anyone with a desire to understand the complex and fascinating links between the brain and the body, and the intricate system that comprises the single organism called the "mindbody."

You will find this book at most major bookstores or you can order it online at www.amazon.com

Meaning & Medicine: Lessons from a Doctor's Tales of Breakthrough and Healing
By Larry Dossey, M.D.

This is a revolutionary new look at medicine and the mind-body connection to healing by a frank and unconventional physician-writer— a book that taps the power of hope and healing that lies within each of us.

This book can be ordered online at www.amazon.com

The Mozart Effect: Tapping the Power of Music to Heal the Body, Strengthen the Mind, and Unlock the Creative Spirit
By Don Campbell

After reading this book, you may never hear music the same way again. Don shows how music transcends mere entertainment to bring about healing and wholeness. He reveals how music is one of the most transformative forces in human experience—how it literally has life-and-death potency.

This book can be ordered online at www.amazon.com

Caught in the Net: How to Recognize the Signs of Internet Addiction—and a Winning Strategy for Recovery
By Dr. Kimberly S. Young

Think that computer addiction is a joke? Think again. This groundbreaking book is the first to explore on-line addiction in a serious way and to consider the effects on individuals and their families. *Caught in the Net* is an important book for anyone who spends their mornings and evenings connected to the Net. Not limited to pornography and cybersex chat, this book explores Internet addictions as a whole.

This book can be ordered online at www.amazon.com

An Affair Of The Mind: One Woman's Courageous Battle to Salvage Her Family From the Devastation of Pornography
By Laurie Hall

In this amazing book, Laurie relives the nightmare that nearly destroyed her family, warning others of porn's seductive, addictive nature. She opens her heart and bares her soul, imparting keen insights and comfort. She learned of her husband's secret addiction to pornography after more than 18 years of marriage. Since then, she has courageously held her family together, raised their two children, and supported countless others through similar situations. Through research, tenacity, and faith, Laurie has found a way to reach out to her husband, and together they have begun to slowly rebuild their marriage.

I highly recommend this book to anyone who is addicted to pornography or knows someone who is.

This book can be ordered online at www.amazon.com

CHAPTER NOTES

Introduction: What Makes Men and Women Do Such Stupid Things?

1. Dr. Judith Reisman, *Soft Porn Plays Hardball*, Huntington House Publishers, Lafayette, Louisiana, 1991, p.10
2. First quarter 2001 Global Internet Trends report from Nielsen/Net Ratings, as reported by CyberAtlas, *The Big Picture Geographics*, www.cyberatlas.internet.com/big_picture/geographics/article/0,,5911_782281,00.html
3. Nielsen Net Ratings: *Sixty percent of Americans are online*, as reported in *Techpc@work*, www.nua.ie/surveys/index.cgi
4. Statistics from Cyveillance, a Washington D.C. artificial-intelligence-search-and-analysis development company, specific stats can be viewed at their website at www.cyveillance.com/newsroom/pressr/000710.asp>
5. Based on an interview with Chris Johnson, CEO of *SurfPartner Corporation*, 6/30/01. For more information regarding SurfPartner, see their website at www.surfpartner.com
6. Richard C. Morais, using Private Media Group statistics in his *Forbes Magazine* article, "*Porn Goes Public*," 6/14/99

Chapter 1: Internet Porn and Cybersex Chat Are "Drugs," and Pornographers Are "Drug Dealers"

1. David Mura, *A Male Grief: Notes on Pornography and Addiction* (1987), as quoted by Dr. Judith Reisman, *Soft Porn Plays Hardball*, Huntington House Publishers, Lafayette, Louisiana, 1991, p.17
2. From the teachings of Dr. Page Bailey, *The Page Bailey Institute International*—Behaviorally related programs and tutorial services, Portland, OR offices: 503-775-7668, Phoenix, AZ offices: 602-867-9594, 2001

3. Dr. Judith Reisman, *Soft Porn Plays Hardball*, Huntington House Publishers, Lafayette, Louisiana, 1991, p.18-19
4. Dr. Victor Cline, *Pornography's Effects on Adults and Children*, Morality in Media, New York, p.4
5. Dr. Judith Reisman, *Soft Porn Plays Hardball*, Huntington House Publishers, Lafayette, Louisiana, 1991, p.20
6. From numerous interviews with Internet pornography and cybersex addicts. Also from conversations with Dr. Victor Cline, Willie Draughon, and C.Y. Robi

Chapter 2: The "Undernet"—A Pornographer's Marketing Dream Come True

1. Based on an interview with Chris Johnson, CEO of *SurfPartner Corporation*, 6/30/01. For more information regarding SurfPartner, see their website at www.surfpartner.com
2. Statistics from Cyveillance, a Washington D.C. artificial-intelligence-search-and-analysis development company, specific stats can be viewed at their website at www.cyveillance.com/newsroom/pressr/000710.asp>
3. Modified from *Enough is Enough, Take Action Manual*, third edition, Enough is Enough, 1995-1996, all rights reserved, p. 20, www.enough.org
4. Timothy Egan, *Wall Street Meets Pornography*, New York Times Website, www.nytimes.com/2000/10/23/technology/23PORN.html, 10/23/00
5. Ibid.
6. Richard C. Morais, using Private Media Group statistics in his *Forbes Magazine* article, "*Porn Goes Public*," 6/14/99
7. Timothy Egan, *Wall Street Meets Pornography*, New York Times Website, www.nytimes.com/2000/10/23/technology/23PORN.html, 10/23/00

Chapter 3: What's the Big Deal? Internet Pornography Doesn't Really Hurt Anyone . . .

1. See "Focus on the Family" transcript of Dr. James Dobson interviewing Ted Bundy at the Florida State Prison on 1/23/89.
2. Ibid.
3. Ibid.
4. Ibid.

5. Ibid.
6. Ibid.
7. Franklin Mark Osanka and Sara Lee Johnson, *Sourcebook on Pornography* Lexington Books, Lexington, Massachusetts, 1989, p.18-19
8. Dr. Judith Reisman, *Soft Porn Plays Hardball*, Huntington House Publishers, Lafayette, Louisiana, 1991, p.9
9. Ibid.
10. C.E. Koop, *Report of the Surgeon General's Workshop on Pornography and Public Health*, American Psychologist, 42 (10), p.944
11. Dr. Judith Reisman, *Soft Porn Plays Hardball*, Huntington House Publishers, Lafayette, Louisiana, 1991, p.10
12. Roy Pinchot, *The Human Body: The Brain,* Torstar Books, New York, 1984, p.98-99
13. Ibid.
14. Dr. Judith Reisman, *Soft Porn Plays Hardball*, Huntington House Publishers, Lafayette, Louisiana, 1991, p.18-20

Chapter 4: It's Not About the 1st Amendment, It's About Money

1. Richard C. Morais, using Private Media Group statistics in his *Forbes Magazine* article, "*Porn Goes Public*," 6/14/99
2. Ibid.

Chapter 5: The Internet—A Law Unto Itself

1. Willie Draughon, Assistant Chief of Criminal Investigations, Utah State Attorney General's Office
2. Lisa M. Bowman, *ZDNet News*, www.zdnet.com/zdnn/stories/news/0,4586,2411499,00.html 12/17/99)
3. For more information on this event, contact the non-profit organization Enough is Enough, 1-800-2ENOUGH, www.enough.org
4. Ibid.
5. Penthouse website, 07/97, www.penthouse.com, as quoted by Enough is Enough brochure titled *Safe Journeys on the Information Superhighway*, available at www.enough.org
6. *Enough is Enough* newsletter, Vol.6, No.2, December, 1998
7. Ibid.

Chapter 6: Pornography Is Not Protected By the First Amendment

1. *Random House Webster's College Dictionary*, 1992 edition
2. Dr. Victor Cline, *Pornography's Effects on Adults and Children*, Morality in Media, New York
3. John Harmer, *A War We Must Win,* Bookcraft, Salt Lake City, Utah, 1999, p.54

Chapter 7: Pornography and Cybersex Are Drugs As Real As Cocaine

1. Dr. Judith Reisman, *Soft Porn Plays Hardball*, Huntington House Publishers, Lafayette, Louisiana, 1991, p.16-17
2. Ibid. p.19
3. Dr. Kimberly Young, *Caught in the Net*, John Wiley & Sons, New York, 1998, p.112-116
4. Dr. Victor Cline, *Pornography's Effects on Adults and Children*, Morality in Media, New York, p.3-4
5. Ibid., p.3
6. Ibid.
7. Ibid.
8. Ibid.
9. "The Pornography Industry Today," *The World & I,* December 1992, p.511, 516
10. Dr. Victor Cline, *Pornography's Effects on Adults and Children*, Morality in Media, New York, p.4
11. Ibid.
12. Ibid.
13. Ibid.
14. Ibid.
15. Ibid.

Chapter 8: How Internet Pornographers Use Mind-Body Science To Attract and Addict Their Customers

1. Dr. Judith A. Reisman, *Sexually Explicit Media: Changes In the Structure of the Human Brain & American Law & Public Policy (Jan. 18, 1993),*

The Institute of Media Education © May, 1996, published in R.S.V.P. America, Crestwood, KY

2. Daniel Goleman and Richard Davidson, *Consciousness: Brain, States of Awareness, and Mysticism*, Harper and Rowe, New York, 1979, p.10

3. Dr. Judith A. Reisman, *Sexually Explicit Media: Changes In the Structure of the Human Brain & American Law & Public Policy (Jan. 18, 1993),* The Institute of Media Education © May, 1996, published in R.S.V.P. America, Crestwood, KY, Part 1, p.1&2

4. Neuroscientist, Dr. Gary Lynch, University of California, Irvine, *The Brain: Learning and Memory*, The Anneberg/CPB Collection, WNET, 1984

5. Ibid.

6. Steve Parker and Dr. Alan Maryon-Davis, *The Brain & Nervous System*, Franklin Watts, New York, 1990, p.13

7. Daniel Goleman and Richard Davidson, *Consciousness: Brain, States of Awareness, and Mysticism*, Harper and Rowe, New York, 1979, p.12

8. Ibid.

9. Dr. Candace B. Pert, *Molecules of Emotion, The Science Behind Mind-Body Medicine*, Touchstone/Simon & Schuster, 1999

10. Alberta Steinman Gilinski, Ph.D., *Mind & Brain-Principles of Neuropsychology*, Praeger Special Studies, Praeger International

11. From the teachings of Dr. Page Bailey, *The Page Bailey Institute International*—Behaviorally related programs and tutorial services, Portland, OR offices: 503-775-7668, Phoenix, AZ offices: 602-867-9594, 2001

12. Alberta Steinman Gilinski, Ph.D., *Mind & Brain-Principles of Neuropsychology*, Praeger Special Studies, Praeger International

13. Dr. Candace B. Pert, *Molecules of Emotion, The Science Behind Mind-Body Medicine*, Touchstone/Simon & Schuster, 1999

14. Ibid. p.306

15. Alberta Steinman Gilinski, Ph.D., *Mind & Brain-Principles of Neuropsychology*, Praeger Special Studies, Praeger International

16. Daniel Goleman and Richard Davidson, *Consciousness: Brain, States of Awareness, and Mysticism*, Harper and Rowe, New York, 1979, p.12

17. F.I.M. Craik and R.S. Lockhart, "Levels of Processing: A Framework for Memory Research", *Journal of Experimental Psychology* (General) 104:268-94

18. Peter Russell, *The Brain Book*, Penguin Books, USA, Inc., 1979, p.106 & 154

19. Steve Parker and Dr. Alan Maryon-Davis, *The Brain & Nervous System*, Franklin Watts, New York, 1990, p.20
20. D.A. Norman and D.E. Rumelhart, *Explorations in Cognition,* Freeman, San Francisco, 1975, p.374
21. Steve Parker and Dr. Alan Maryon-Davis, *The Brain & Nervous System*, Franklin Watts, New York, 1990, p.38
22. Alberta Steinman Gilinski, Ph.D., *Mind & Brain-Principles of Neuropsychology*, Praeger Special Studies, Praeger International
23. Peter Russell, *The Brain Book*, Penguin Books, USA, Inc., 1979, p.105
24. Dr. Judith A. Reisman, *Sexually Explicit Media: Changes In the Structure of the Human Brain & American Law & Public Policy (Jan. 18, 1993),* The Institute of Media Education © May, 1996, published in R.S.V.P. America, Crestwood, KY, Part 1, p.17

Chapter 9: How Imagination, Memory and Advertising "Hook" Internet Porn Viewers

1. Alberta Steinman Gilinski, Ph.D., *Mind & Brain-Principles of Neuropsychology*, Praeger Special Studies, Praeger Internationa, p.172
2. Ibid. p.366 & 378
3. Peter Russell, *The Brain Book*, Penguin Books, USA, Inc., 1979, P.106 & 157
4. Ibid., Chapter 2
5. Dr. Judith Reisman, *Soft Porn Plays Hardball*, Huntington House Publishers, Lafayette, Louisiana, 1991, Chapter 2
6. "Preserving the Presence of the Past," *American Psychologist,* February, 1983, p.161
7. Dr. Victor Cline, *Pornography's Effects on Adults and Children*, Morality in Media, New York, p.7
8. Dolf Zillman and Jennings Bryant, "Symposium on Media Violence and Pornography," Media Action Group, Toronto, Canada, 1984
9. Dr. Judith Reisman, *Soft Porn Plays Hardball*, Huntington House Publishers, Lafayette, Louisiana, 1991, p.11
10. Dr. Judith A. Reisman, *Sexually Explicit Media: Changes In the Structure of the Human Brain & American Law & Public Policy (Jan. 18, 1993),* The Institute of Media Education © May, 1996, published in R.S.V.P. America, Crestwood, KY, p.ii, 21-24

11. John Harmer, *A War We Must Win,* Bookcraft, Salt Lake City, Utah, 1999, p.118

12. Dr. Kimberly Young, *Caught in the Net*, John Wiley & Sons, New York, 1998

Chapter 10: Just Once *Will* Hurt: Why Internet Pornography/Cybersex Is So Highly Addictive

1. Dr. Candace B. Pert, *Molecules of Emotion, The Science Behind Mind-Body Medicine* (Touchstone/Simon & Schuster, 1999) p.140-143

2. From the teachings of Dr. Page Bailey, *The Page Bailey Institute International*—Behaviorally related programs and tutorial services, Portland, OR offices: 503-775-7668, Phoenix, AZ offices: 602-867-9594, 2001

3. Ibid.

4. Ibid.

5. Ibid.

6. Ibid.

7. Ibid.

Chapter 11: The Male and the Female Brain: How Men and Women Are Wired Differently

1. Steven Pinker, *How the Mind Works*, W. W. Norton & Company, New York, 1997, P.470

2. Richard C. Morais, using Private Media Group statistics in his *Forbes Magazine* article, "*Porn Goes Public*," 6/14/99

3. Steven Pinker, *How the Mind Works*, W. W. Norton & Company, New York, 1997, p.472

4. Ibid., p.470

5. Helen Fisher, *The First Sex,* Random House, 1999, p.8

6. Anne Moir & David Jessel, *Brain Sex: The Real Difference Between Men & Women*, Carol Publishing Group, New York, 1991, p.43

7. Ibid., p.46

8. Dr. Judith Reisman, *Soft Porn Plays Hardball*, Huntington House Publishers, Lafayette, Louisiana, 1991, p.21

9. Anne Moir & David Jessel, *Brain Sex: The Real Difference Between Men & Women*, Carol Publishing Group, New York, 1991, p.44

10. Ibid., p.170
11. Helen Fisher, *The First Sex,* Random House, 1999, p.11
12. Ibid., p.11-12
13. Anne Moir & David Jessel, *Brain Sex: The Real Difference Between Men & Women*, Carol Publishing Group, New York, 1991, p.47
14. From the teachings of Dr. Page Bailey, *The Page Bailey Institute International*—Behaviorally related programs and tutorial services, Portland, OR offices: 503-775-7668, Phoenix, AZ offices: 602-867-9594, 2001
15. Anne Moir & David Jessel, *Brain Sex: The Real Difference Between Men & Women*, Carol Publishing Group, New York, 1991, p.47, and Helen Fisher, *The First Sex,* Random House, 1999, p.15
16. Ibid., *(Brain Sex)* p.48
17. Ibid.
18. Ibid., p.170
19. Helen Fisher, *The First Sex,* Random House, 1999, p.5
20. Ibid.
21. Diane Hales, *Just Like a Woman*, Bantam Books, 1999, p.244
22. Ibid.
23. Anne Moir & David Jessel, *Brain Sex: The Real Difference Between Men & Women*, Carol Publishing Group, New York, 1991, p.96
24. Ibid., p.95
25. Helen Fisher, *The First Sex,* Random House, 1999, p.62
26. Anne Moir & David Jessel, *Brain Sex: The Real Difference Between Men & Women*, Carol Publishing Group, New York, 1991, p.81
27. Ibid., p.103
28. Ibid.

Chapter 12: How Male and Female Brain Differences Affect the Way Each Views Human Intimacy

1. Anne Moir & David Jessel, *Brain Sex: The Real Difference Between Men & Women*, Carol Publishing Group, New York, 1991, p.106
2. Helen Fisher, *The First Sex,* Random House, 1999, p.198
3. Ibid.
4. Diane Hales, *Just Like a Woman*, Bantam Books, 1999, p.311
5. Ibid.
6. Ibid.

7. Anne Moir & David Jessel, *Brain Sex: The Real Difference Between Men & Women*, Carol Publishing Group, New York, 1991, p.110
8. Helen Fisher, *The First Sex,* Random House, 1999, p.203
9. Ibid.
10. David Jessel, *Brain Sex: The Real Difference Between Men & Women*, Carol Publishing Group, New York, 1991, p.107
11. Diane Hales, *Just Like a Woman*, Bantam Books, 1999, p.141

Chapter 13: The Funnel of Sexual Arousal and The "Narrowing Process"

1. From the teachings of Dr. Page Bailey, *The Page Bailey Institute International* — Behaviorally related programs and tutorial services, Portland, OR offices: 503-775-7668, Phoenix, AZ offices: 602-867-9594, 2001
2. Ibid.
3. Anne Moir & David Jessel, *Brain Sex: The Real Difference Between Men & Women*, Carol Publishing Group, New York, 1991, p.108
4. Helen Fisher, *The First Sex,* Random House, 1999, p.201

Chapter 14: How Internet Pornographers Target the Male Brain

1. Anne Moir & David Jessel, *Brain Sex: The Real Difference Between Men & Women*, Carol Publishing Group, New York, 1991, p.81
2. Dr. Judith Reisman, *Soft Porn Plays Hardball*, Huntington House Publishers, Lafayette, Louisiana, 1991, p.18-19

Chapter 15: How Internet Pornography Makes Men Stupid

1. *Deseret News*, Salt Lake City, Utah, 12/21/99
2. Dr. Victor Cline, *Pornography's Effects on Adults and Children*, Morality in Media, New York, p.9
3. Ibid.
4. Ibid.
5. Dr. Judith A. Reisman, *Sexually Explicit Media: Changes In the Structure of the Human Brain & American Law & Public Policy (Jan. 18, 1993),* The Institute of Media Education © May, 1996, Published in R.S.V.P. America, Crestwood, KY, p.25
6. Ibid., p.21-24

7. Dr. Judith Reisman, *Soft Porn Plays Hardball*, Huntington House Publishers, Lafayette, Louisiana, 1991, p.139
8. Ibid., p.151
9. Ibid.

Chapter 16: How Internet Pornographers Target the Female Brain

1. John Harmer, *A War We Must Win,* Bookcraft, Salt Lake City, Utah, 1999, p.56
2. Diane Hales, *Just Like a Woman*, Bantam Books, 1999, p.312
3. Dr. Kimberly Young, *Caught in the Net*, John Wiley & Sons, New York, 1998, p.112
4. *Sexual Addiction FAQ, Women*, Netaddiction.com, 1998, The Center For Online Addiction
5. Posted on MSNBC's website, December, 1999
6. Kimberly S. Young, James O'Mara, and Jennifer Buchanan, *Cybersex and Infidelity Online: Implications for Evaluation and Treatment*, Abstract

Chapter 17: How Cybersex Chat Rooms and Internet Pornography Make Women Stupid

1. Dr. Kimberly Young, *Caught in the Net*, John Wiley & Sons, New York, 1998, p.142
2. Ibid., p.122
3. Ibid., p.108-109

Chapter 18: The Victims of Pornography

1. Bruce R. Wright, *The Wright Exit Strategy: Wealth—How to Create It, Keep It and Use It,* SAMMI Press, 1997, 1-800-997-2664)

Chapter 19: Pornography Destroys Women's Rights

1. C. Everett Koop, M.D., *American Medical News*, 10/10/86, p.7
2. Neil Malamuth, *Rape Proclivity Among Males*, Journal of Social Issues, 1981, P.138-157

3. Dr. Judith Reisman, *Soft Porn Plays Hardball*, Huntington House Publishers, Lafayette, Louisiana, 1991, p.14
4. Ibid.
5. Ibid.
6. Ibid.
7. Dr. Judith A. Reisman, *Sexually Explicit Media: Changes In the Structure of the Human Brain & American Law & Public Policy (Jan. 18, 1993),* The Institute of Media Education © May, 1996, published in R.S.V.P. America, Crestwood, KY, p.19

Chapter 20: Pornography Triggers Child Abuse

1. Alberta Steinman Gilinski, Ph.D., *Mind & Brain-Principles of Neuropsychology*, Praeger Special Studies, Praeger Internationa, p.350
2. "Assault by Film," *Washington Post*, 4/13/79, p. D-4
3. Donna Rice Hughes, *Kids Online: Protecting Your Children in Cyberspace,* published by Fleming H. Revell, a division of Baker Book House Company, Grand Rapids, MI, 1998, p.88
4. Ibid.
5. Dr. Judith Reisman, *Soft Porn Plays Hardball*, Huntington House Publishers, Lafayette, Louisiana, 1991, p.12
6. A Trojan Horse in the Local Library–A new ACLU attack on community standards, Enough is Enough, www.enough.org
7. Dr. Judith A. Reisman, *Sexually Explicit Media: Changes In the Structure of the Human Brain & American Law & Public Policy (Jan. 18, 1993),* The Institute of Media Education © May, 1996, published in R.S.V.P. America, Crestwood, KY, p.12-13
8. B. Trebilcock, *Child Molesters on the Internet: Are they in your home?"* Redbook
9. Ibid.
10. Ibid.
11. A. Olsen, Police Chief, Warwick, RI, Associated Press, 1994
12. Detroit Free Press, FreeP/Tech website, *Children and the Internet by the Numbers*, 7/20/99, www.freep.com/tech/qkidnos20nf.htm
13. M. Brick, head of the Florida Department of Law Enforcement, Associated Press, 1994

14. Enough is Enough website, Sharks: *Recent News Stories of Sexual Violence Against Children that was fueled by Pornography*, 2/20/98, www.enough.org

15. David Finkelhor, *Answers To Important Questions About the Scope & Nature of Child Sexual Abuse,* July 1993, p.8, as quoted by Enough is Enough website, Sharks: *Alarming Facts About Child Molestation*, 2/20/98, www.enough.org

16. Dr. William Marshall, *A report on the Use of Pornography by Sexual Offenders,* Ottawa, Canada, 1983, as quoted by Enough is Enough website, Sharks: *Alarming Facts About Child Molestation*, 2/20/98, www.enough.org

17. Tom Minnery, *Pornography—A Human Tragedy,* Tyndale House, Wheaton, IL, as quoted by Enough is Enough website, Sharks: *Alarming Facts About Child Molestation*, 2/20/98, www.enough.org

18. Adult Video News Magazine, as quoted by Enough is Enough website, Sharks: *Alarming Facts About Child Molestation*, 2/20/98, www.enough.org *National Victim Center, 1992*, as quoted by Enough is Enough website, Sharks: *Alarming Facts About Child Molestation*, 2/20/98, www.enough.org

19. *The National Resource Center on Child Sexual Abuse*, as quoted by Enough is Enough website, Sharks: *Alarming Facts About Child Molestation*, 2/20/98, www.enough.org

20. Ibid.

21. *Associated Press*, 6/94, as quoted by Enough is Enough website, Sharks: *Recent News Stories of Sexual Violence Against Children that was fueled by Pornography*, 2/20/98, www.enough.org

22. *Dallas Morning News*, 12/93, as quoted by Enough is Enough website, Sharks: *Recent News Stories of Sexual Violence Against Children that was fueled by Pornography*, 2/20/98, www.enough.org

23. *Associated Press*, 12/93, as quoted by Enough is Enough website, Sharks: *Recent News Stories of Sexual Violence Against Children that was fueled by Pornography*, 2/20/98, www.enough.org

Chapter 21: Internet Porn is Destroying Our Teens—Our Future

1. Terry Lawson, *Knight Ridder Newspapers*, Deseret News, 3/6/99

2. Tom Minnery, *Pornography: A human Tragedy*, Tynsdale House, Wheaton, IL, as quoted by Enough is Enough website, Sharks: *Alarming Facts About Child Molestation*, 2/20/98, www.enough.org

3. *Facts in Brief*, The Allan Buttmacher Institute, 1994, as quoted by Enough is Enough website, Sharks: *Alarming Facts About Child Molestation*, 2/20/98, www.enough.org

4. K.E. Davis and G.N. Braucht, *Exposure to Pornography, Character and Sexual Deviance*, Technical Reports of the Commission on Obscenity and Pornography, 1970

5. Dr. Judith Reisman, *Soft Porn Plays Hardball*, Huntington House Publishers, Lafayette, Louisiana, 1991, p.11

6. Ibid.

7. Dr. Judith Reisman, *Soft Porn Plays Hardball*, Huntington House Publishers, Lafayette, Louisiana, 1991,

8. Donna Rice Hughes, *Kids Online: Protecting Your Children in Cyberspace,* Published by Fleming H. Revell a division of Baker Book House Company, Grand Rapids, MI, 1998, p.87

9. Dr. Judith A. Reisman, *Sexually Explicit Media: Changes In the Structure of the Human Brain & American Law & Public Policy (Jan. 18, 1993),* The Institute of Media Education © May, 1996, Published in R.S.V.P. America, Crestwood, KY, p.10

10. Ibid.

Chapter 22: Men Are Porn Victims

1. Laurie Hall, *An Affair of the Mind*, A Focus on the Family Book, Tynsdale House, Wheaton, Illinois, 1996, p.98-99

2. Ibid., p.100

3. Dr. Judith A. Reisman, *Sexually Explicit Media: Changes In the Structure of the Human Brain & American Law & Public Policy (Jan. 18, 1993),* The Institute of Media Education © May, 1996, Published in R.S.V.P. America, Crestwood, KY, Introduction

4. Steve Parker and Dr. Alan Maryon-Davis, *The Brain & Nervous System* (Franklin Watts, New York, 1990) p.38

Chapter 23: Pornography Destroys Healthy Intimacy

1. The concept of "Jane and John" was taken from Dr. Judith Reisman, *Soft Porn Plays Hardball*, Huntington House Publishers, Lafayette, Louisiana, 1991, p. 22

2. Dr. Victor Cline, *Pornography's Effects on Adults and Children,* Morality in Media, New York, p. 5
3. Laurie Hall, *An Affair of the Mind,* A Focus on the Family Book, Tynsdale House, Wheaton, Illinois, 1996, p. 103
4. Ibid.
5. Ibid.
6. Ibid., p. 101
7. Ibid.
8. Ibid., p. 103-104
9. Ibid., p. 104
10. Ibid., p. 105
11. Ibid., p. 106
12. Ibid.
13. Ibid., p. 111
14. Robert Fulghum, *Maybe (Maybe Not),* Villard Books, New York, 1993

Chapter 25: Pornography is Radically Altering Our Society

1. National Law Center for Children and Families (1997), *NLC summary of "SOB land use" studies,* as quoted in *Just Harmless Fun?* Bruce Watson and Shyla Rae Welch, © Enough is Enough, 2000, see www.enough.org, for full text.
2. Ibid.

Chapter 26: Pornography Distorts and Twists Healthy Sexuality

1. Concepts gleaned from Jeffrey R. Holland, *Of Souls, Symbols, and Sacraments*, Deseret Book, Salt Lake City, Utah, 2000
2. C. Everett Koop, M.D., *American Medical News*, 10/10/86, p.7

Chapter 27: Make Your Choice

1. Dr. Judith A. Reisman, *Kinsey: Crimes & Consequences,* Second Edition, © 1998, 2000, by The Institute of Media Education, P.O. Box 1136, Crestwood, Kentucky, 40014, 1-800-837-0544, p. 238
2. Ibid.

3. Dr. Judith A. Reisman, *The Kinsey Effect, The FBI Uniform Crime Report Minimizes Child Abuse: For, 67% of Reported Sex Abuse Victims Are Children & 64% of Forcible Sodomy Victims Are Boys Under 12* (see full text), 0 January, 2001, The Institute of Media Education, P.O. Box 1136, Crestwood, Kentucky, 40014, 1-800-837-0544.

Chapter 28: Are You Setting Yourself and Your Children Up for Porn Addiction?

1. Diane Hales *Just Like a Woman,* Bantam Books, 1999, p. 147

Chapter 29: Protecting Your Family From Internet Pornography

1. Statistics from Cyveillance, a Washington D.C. artificial-intelligence-search-and-analysis development company, specific stats can be viewed at their website at www.cyveillance.com/newsroom/pressr/000710.asp
2. Ibid.

Chapter 31: Understanding and Recognizing Porn Addiction

1. © Sex Addicts Anonymous, 2001. For more information, visit the official SAA website at www.saa-recovery.org.
2. Patrick Carnes, Ph.D., *Don't Call It Love: Recovery From Sexual Addiction*, A Bantam Book, New York, 1992, p. 43-44.
3. Ibid., p.44
4. Ibid., p. 57
5. Patrick Carnes, Ph.D., *Contrary to Love: Healing the Sexual Addict*, Hazelden Educational Materials, Center City, Minnesota, 55012-0176, 1994, p. 79 & 82.
6. Patrick Carnes, Ph.D., *Don't Call It Love: Recovery From Sexual Addiction*, A Bantam Book, New York, 1992, p. 35
7. Patrick Carnes, Ph.D., *Contrary to Love: Healing the Sexual Addict*, Hazelden Educational Materials, Center City, Minnesota, 55012-0176, 1994, p. 12
8. © Sex Addicts Anonymous, 2001. For more information, visit the official SAA website at www.saa-recovery.org.

9. © 1989 by Patrick Carnes, Patrick Carnes, Ph.D., *Contrary to Love: Healing the Sexual Addict*, Hazelden Educational Materials, Center City, Minnesota, 55012-0176, 1994, p. 218-219.

10. Ibid., p.221

11. Patrick Carnes, Ph.D., *Don't Call It Love: Recovery From Sexual Addiction*, A Bantam Book, New York, 1992, p. 83.

12. Patrick Carnes, Ph.D., *Contrary to Love: Healing the Sexual Addict*, Hazelden Educational Materials, Center City, Minnesota, 55012-0176, 1994, p. 20-21.

13. S.T.A.R. Program

Chapter 32: Spouses or Porn / Sex Addicts are Usually Co-Addicts

1. Patrick Carnes, Ph.D., *Contrary to Love: Healing the Sexual Addict*, Hazelden Educational Materials, Center City, Minnesota, 55012-0176, 1994, p. 136-137.

2. S.T.A.R. Program

3. © 1983, Twin Cities COSA, as quoted by Patrick Carnes, Ph.D., *Contrary to Love: Healing the Sexual Addict*, Hazelden Educational Materials, Center City, Minnesota, 55012-0176, 1994, p. 133.

Chapter 33: What Should a Porn/Sex Addiction Recovery Program Look Like?

1. © Sex Addicts Anonymous, 2001. For more information, visit the official SAA website at www.saa-recovery.org.

2. S.T.A.R. Program

Chapter 37: Final Thoughts

1. R. B. Baird, *Improve the Shining Moment*, Hymns of the Church of Jesus Christ of Latter-day Saints, Deseret Book, Salt Lake City, Utah, 1979

2. Jon Kabat-Zin, *Wherever You Go There You Are: Mindfulness Meditation In Everyday Life*, Hyperion, New York, New York, 1994, p. xiii, 4